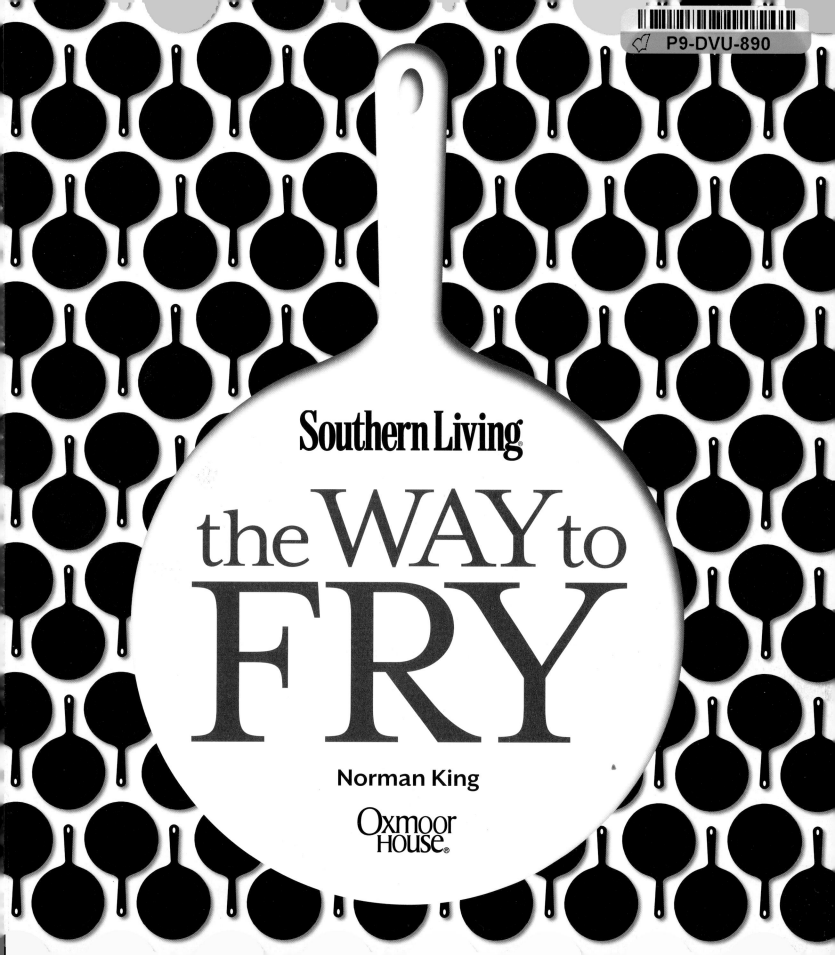

Southern Living®

# the WAY to FRY

Norman King

**Oxmoor House®**

ISBN-10: 0-8487-3818-7
ISBN-13: 978-08487-3818-1
Library of Congress Control Number:
    2012953754

Printed in the United States of America
First Printing 2013

## Oxmoor House

Editorial Director: Leah McLaughlin
Creative Director: Felicity Keane
Senior Brand Manager: Daniel Fagan
Senior Editor: Rebecca Brennan
Managing Editor: Rebecca Benton

## Southern Living The Way to Fry

Editor: Susan Hernandez Ray
Art Director: Claire Cormany
Project Editor: Emily Chappell
Director, Test Kitchen:
    Elizabeth Tyler Austin
Assistant Directors, Test Kitchen:
    Julie Christopher, Julie Gunter
Recipe Developers and Testers:
    Wendy Ball, R.D.; Victoria E. Cox;
    Tamara Goldis; Stefanie Maloney;
    Callie Nash; Karen Rankin;
    Leah Van Deren

Recipe Editor: Alyson Moreland Haynes
Food Stylists: Margaret Monroe Dickey,
    Catherine Crowell Steele
Photography Director: Jim Bathie
Senior Photographer: Helene Dujardin
Senior Photo Stylist: Kay E. Clarke
Photo Stylist: Mindi Shapiro Levine
Assistant Photo Stylist:
    Mary Louise Menendez
Senior Production Manager:
    Greg A. Amason

### Contributors

Designer: Ellen S. Padgett
Recipe Developers and Testers:
    Erica Hopper, Tonya Johnson,
    Kyra Moncrief, Kathleen Royal Phillips
Copy Editors: Julie Bosche,
    Dolores Hydock
Proofreader: Donna Baldone
Indexer: Mary Ann Laurens
Interns: Morgan Bolling, Susan Kemp,
    Sara Lyon, Staley McIlwain,
    Emily Robinson, Maria Sanders,
    Katie Strasser
Food Stylist: Ana Kelly
Photographers: Beau Gustafson,
    Beth Hontzas, Sarah Lion,
    Becky Stayner
Photo Stylists: Anna Pollock,
    Leslie Simpson
Stylist: Stephanie Granada

### Southern Living®

Editor: M. Lindsay Bierman
Creative Director: Robert Perino
Managing Editor: Candace Higginbotham
Art Director: Chris Hoke
Executive Editors: Rachel Hardage Barrett,
    Hunter Lewis, Jessica S. Thuston
Food Director: Shannon Sliter Satterwhite

Test Kitchen Director:
    Rebecca Kracke Gordon
Senior Writer: Donna Florio
Senior Food Editor: Mary Allen Perry
Recipe Editor: JoAnn Weatherly
Assistant Recipe Editor: Ashley Arthur
Test Kitchen Specialist/Food Styling:
    Vanessa McNeil Rocchio
Test Kitchen Professionals: Norman King,
    Pam Lolley, Angela Sellers
Senior Photographers: Ralph Lee Anderson,
    Gary Clark, Art Meripol
Photographers: Robbie Caponetto,
    Laurey W. Glenn
Photo Research Coordinator:
    Ginny P. Allen
Senior Photo Stylist: Buffy Hargett
Editorial Assistant: Pat York

### Time Home Entertainment Inc.

Publisher: Jim Childs
VP, Strategy & Business Development:
    Steven Sandonato
Executive Director, Marketing Services:
    Carol Pittard
Executive Director, Retail & Special Sales:
    Tom Mifsud
Director, Bookazine Development &
    Marketing: Laura Adam
Executive Publishing Director: Joy Butts
Associate Publishing Director:
    Megan Pearlman
Finance Director: Glenn Buonocore
Associate General Counsel: Helen Wan

# Contents

# Welcome

The term *frying* is often greeted with fear, adoration, intrigue, disgust, or a mixture of all four. Well, in the South, frying is part of our culinary history. However, many Southerners have grown wiser about the dietary issues of our present world and realized that some facets of our culinary heritage are not compatible with our current reality. The world has become more efficient and most of us simply do not need the number of calories and fat found in classic recipes that were designed for a time involving heavy manual labor. With this revelation, we now realize our recipe catalogue may be a bit outdated.

But for Southerners, changing the way we cook and eat isn't so simple. To us, our food is more than calories and fat grams. Southern food is integral to our culture, Southern food is our history, and most important, Southern food is love. And what is needed more than a drastic change in our cooking methods is a new balance between the past and the present. This adjustment requires knowledge—knowledge of how to prepare and enjoy a real meal that provides true nourishment and acknowledges our need to connect to our treasured past.

In this book you'll get an honest and clear look at the frying process from all angles. You'll learn how to fry chicken like your grandmother did, keeping classic flavors alive and well, *and* how to make a lighter, oven-fried version you can proudly serve to your family and guests. I've also added some tips on how the modern Southern cook can arrange meals out of traditional favorites to create lighter and more nutritionally balanced menus. They're under the label "Make It a Meal," and you can find them sprinkled throughout the book. Be sure and flip through to find "Norm's Notes"—they'll give you solutions to problems I encountered while testing the recipes. Plus, check out the chapter "Just for Fun." It's a little naughty, a little nice, but all in the spirit of good fun. Overall, I hope this book guides you to some wonderful recipes, and helps you discover that frying really is all it's cracked up to be.

*Norman King*

> *Southern food is integral to our culture, Southern food is our history, and most important, Southern food is love.*

# The Art of Frying

# The Basics Behind the Crunch

*Discover why frying has become part of the South's favorite foods.*

**Here's Why We Fry**

We'll fry almost anything in the South. Pickles? Sure. Pie? Of course. Although this may sound unnecessary and slightly gluttonous to our now health-obsessed national psyche, there was a time when foods high in fat and calories were a necessity. The Southern standard of eating seasonal, local, and high-calorie foods comes from a culture centered on farming. As farmers toiled for hours in the field, they needed a lot of calories to make it through the day. With fats being such a concentrated source of energy, it made sense to add them to a diet designed for fueling manual labor. Salt, sugar, and starch were also a necessary part of the equation to enhance flavor and texture.

**Necessity, Not Indulgence**

The availability of foods grown locally and the need for high-quality sustaining sources of energy inspired Southerners to create recipes designed to provide the strength needed to produce a full day's work. That's why hardtack, beaten biscuits, fatback sandwiches, and big, hearty, bacon-layered breakfasts exist. In our traditional culinary lexicon, lard and butter are not bad words, they're fuel. For example, have you ever wondered why someone would fry a tomato? Because when it comes to providing energy, it takes a whole lot of tomatoes to generate a day of farming. However, if you slice them, cover them in batter, shallow-fry them, and add a heavy pinch of salt, you've increased the caloric value by three times. So with a whole lotta farming giving a whole lotta local produce, Southerners created many of the foods we treasure out of necessity, not indulgence.

**Let's Balance, Not Blame**

Fried foods play the role of villain far too often, but that doesn't have to be the case. Frying at the proper temperature and maintaining that temperature result in minimal oil absorption. And, eating fried foods in moderation is key. As an example: A drumstick and wing dipped in a seasoned flour and fried have about 225 calories and 14 grams of fat. However, four (2¼-inch) commercially prepared chocolate chip cookies have 275 calories and 15 grams of fat. If you added oven-roasted potatoes and sautéed greens to the fried chicken, you would have a complete balanced meal. That is not so with the cookies.

What's needed is balance, not blame. Balance can lead us down the road to making choices more in line with our needs. Sometimes we just want fried shrimp and hush puppies, and that's fine. Just like a slice of red velvet cake is fine, or ribs, or brisket. They all taste great, but don't make them the anchor of the plate at every meal. Remember, moderation is key.

Foods are energy providers and the building blocks of life. They're not just a clinical assortment of calories, vitamins, phytochemicals, starch and protein molecules, and water. Foods at their finest can nourish, heal, and lighten our bad moods. A connector of people, a love shared, an event celebrated—food is all of these things and more. While I always focus on good eating habits, I lovingly recall sitting on my Grandma Sue's counter and watching her fry chicken in a cast-iron skillet older than my father. Nowadays, it's me who's cooking and Grandma Sue who's sitting at the counter. To me, that's what it's all about: the warm feeling that comes from sharing

*To me, that's what it's all about: the warm feeling that comes from sharing good food and fun times with those you love.*

good food and fun times with those you love. Okay, and maybe a small helping of nutritional caution on the side.

## Frying Defined

Golden, crispy, delicious. Frying is a unique cooking method. The process of submerging food, whether partially or fully, in hot oil or fat for a period of time, then removing it and allowing it to drain and rest, creates a moist, juicy, and tender interior with a crisp and crunchy exterior. Most foods suitable for frying will contain a fair amount of water. When food is submerged in oil or a food surface comes in contact with hot oil or fat, the water in the food evaporates, creating steam. The food cooks inside, while at the same time, the exterior is on its way to a crispy finish. The goal of frying is not to allow the food to become greasy and oversaturated with oil or fat, but to produce a delightful treat with wonderful aroma, taste, and texture. And that's achieved by maintaining the oil at the proper temperature when frying.

# Tools to Get the Job Done

**For Stovetop Deep-Frying:**

- Enameled cast-iron Dutch oven (5- to 7-qt.) with lid (non-glass lid for safety in case of grease fire)
- Oil/candy thermometer
- Tongs
- Metal slotted spoon or "spider"
- Fine wire-mesh small strainer (for skimming)
- Wire rack set in a 15- x 10-inch jelly-roll pan
- Paper towels (for draining)
- Kitchen timer
- Proper ventilation
- Kitchen towels

**For Stovetop Shallow-Frying:**

- 12-inch cast-iron skillet with lid (non-glass lid for safety in case of grease fire)
- Oil/candy thermometer
- Tongs
- Metal slotted spoon or "spider"
- Fine wire-mesh small strainer ( for skimming)
- Wire rack set in a 15- x 10-inch jelly-roll pan
- Paper towels (for draining)
- Kitchen timer
- Proper ventilation
- Kitchen towels

**For Electric Deep-Frying:**

- Electric deep-fat fryer
- Tongs
- Metal slotted spoon or "spider"
- Fine wire-mesh small strainer (for skimming)
- A wire rack set in a 15- x 10-inch jelly-roll pan
- Paper towels (for draining)
- Kitchen timer
- Proper ventilation
- Kitchen towels

When using an electric deep-fat fryer, make sure you have enough space above the unit for the lid to open and steam to escape without the lid coming in contact with kitchen cabinets. Also, you'll need enough space on both sides of the fryer to place equipment and items to be fried on one side and a drain rack on the other.

**Cleaning Your Cast-Iron Skillet:**

When cared for properly, cast iron develops a shiny patina called "seasoning" that makes it nearly nonstick. Here are my secrets for perfectly preserved pans:

- Clean with a sponge under running water while the cast iron is still warm but cool enough to handle with ease. Kosher salt is also a good scrubbing agent for baked-on stains. The most important tip is to never use soap!

- Before cooking, apply vegetable oil to the cooking surface, and preheat the pan on low heat, increasing the temperature slowly.

- Reseason if food particles start to stick, rust appears, or you experience a metallic taste.

1. Electric fryer
2. Frying pan
3. Enameled cast-iron Dutch oven
4. Oil/candy thermometer
5. Tongs
6. Metal slotted spoon
7. Fine wire-mesh strainer
8. Wire rack and a 15- x 10-inch jelly-roll pan
9. Paper towels
10. Kitchen timer
11. Kitchen towel

# Oils to Know

Here is a list of a few of our favorite oils for frying:

**1. Grapeseed Oil:** A little pricey, especially when needed for deep frying, but well worth the money. Its high smoke point and neutral flavor make it ideal for both deep and shallow frying.

**2. Peanut Oil:** A true Southern icon. Great for deep frying due to its high smoke point. This is our favorite oil for deep frying turkeys.

**3. Vegetable Oil (Soybean Oil):** The all-around work horse. A high smoke point, neutral flavor, and wide availability make this oil hard to beat in any application.

**4. Canola Oil:** Best used in shallow frying where temperatures tend to be lower than for deep frying. It's a good idea to discard this oil after one use because it tends to pick up and transfer flavors to foods more than other oils.

**5. Olive Oil:** Save your pricey extra-virgin style for salads and go with a blended version for frying. Olive oil is best suited for shallow frying at temperatures below 375°.

**6. Bacon Grease:** We know it's not really oil but adding a tablespoon or so to your frying oil will impart a smoky pork flavor to just about anything. We love to add it to oil when frying catfish, chicken, pork chops, and French fries.

# Dredge, Batter, and Coat

**Dredging** is lightly coating food to be fried in flour, cornmeal, breadcrumbs, or another starchy crumbed item. Dredging aids fried food in browning and helps develop a crisp crust. Dredging is often essential when making fried foods.

**Batter** is used to protect moist foods that are to be fried. Batters tend to be high in water content and contain flour, a liquid, and seasonings to protect foods and give texture and flavor to the exterior. Sometimes leavening agents are used in a batter to produce an airy, crispy crust.

**Coating** often involves dredging a product in flour and shaking off the excess, and dipping into a batter or other wet mixture (beaten eggs, milk) to help the adherence of a coating, which is usually some crumbled, dried, grain-based product, like breadcrumbs, crushed crackers, or crushed cookies. A coating gives fried foods added crunch and enhanced flavor.

Dredging | Battering | Coating

# A Pause for Caution

The most common mistake made when frying often involves controlling the heat. Proper pan and oil selection can help with controlling the oil temperature, but the knobs on the stove work best. You will rarely need to have your stove at high heat for frying. In most cases, it is best to fry over a medium heat and let the oil slowly rise to the desired frying temperature. This method tends to cut down on your risk of the oil getting too hot, causing the food to burn, or—even worse—starting a grease fire. We don't want to scare you, but it is important to be cautious when frying to prevent burned food, injury due to oil splatters, and fires.

# Grease Fires: Too Hot to Handle

Follow these steps:

1. Stay calm.

2. Turn off heat source if knobs on stove allow.

3. Cover pot or skillet with a non-glass lid, damp kitchen towel, baking sheet, or jelly-roll pan large enough to completely cover the opening of the pot or skillet. (Once the fire is out, turn off the heat source if you could not reach it due to an exposed flame.)

4. Do not touch the pot or skillet until it has cooled completely.

5. If you fail to put out the fire by smothering, call 911 immediately. Try using a class B or BC fire extinguisher to put out the fire. They are non-toxic and easy to clean up once the fire is out.

6. Never, and I mean never, throw water, flour, or sugar onto a grease fire. They are highly combustible in this type of fire.

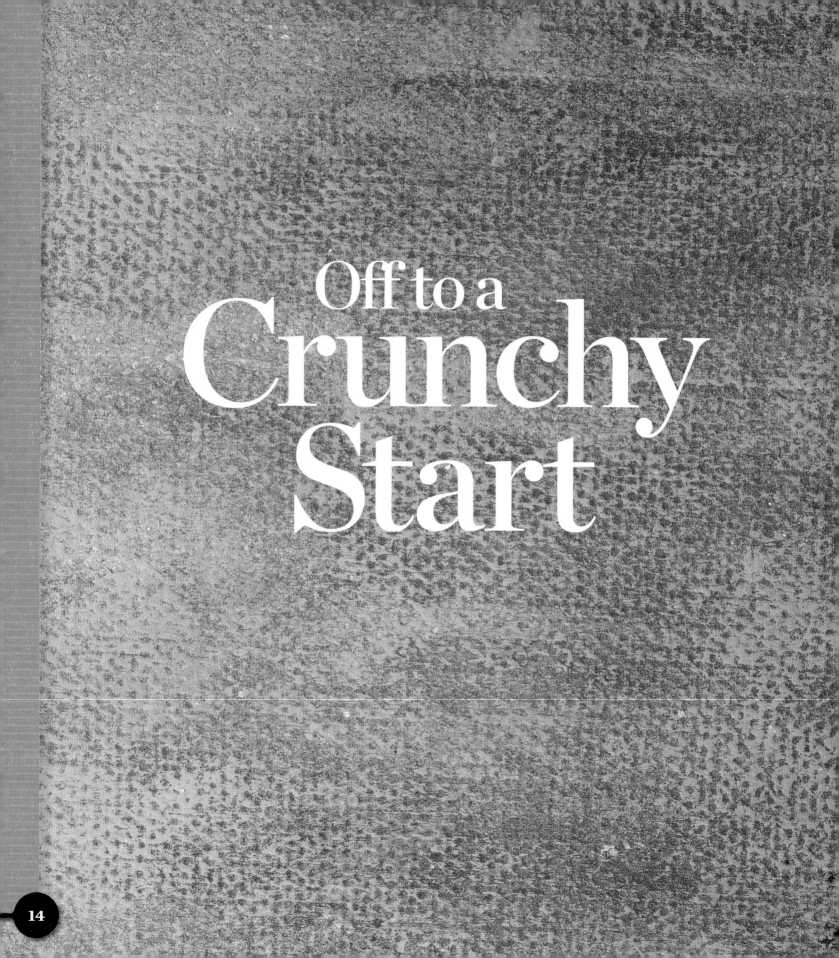

# Off to a Crunchy Start

Okra Rellenos, *page 29*

# Warm Goat Cheese Salad

*Look for goat cheese that's semifirm and creamy on the inside when preparing this recipe.*

**Makes:** 6 servings    **Hands-on Time:** 36 min.    **Total Time:** 2 hr., 36 min.

⅓  **cup olive oil**
⅓  **cup lemon juice**
1  **Tbsp. thinly sliced green onions**
1  **Tbsp. honey**
1  **tsp. Dijon mustard**
½  **cup Italian-seasoned breadcrumbs**
1½  **Tbsp. grated Parmesan cheese**
1½  **Tbsp. sesame seeds**
3  **(4-oz.) goat cheese logs**
1  **large egg, lightly beaten**
3  **Tbsp. butter**
1½  **(5-oz.) packages sweet baby greens**
12  **pitted ripe olives, sliced**

**1.** Whisk together first 5 ingredients.

**2.** Combine breadcrumbs, Parmesan cheese, and sesame seeds.

**3.** Cut each goat cheese log into 4 slices. Dip in egg, and dredge in breadcrumb mixture. Cover and chill 2 hours.

**4.** Melt butter in a medium skillet over medium-high heat. Fry goat cheese, in 2 batches, 1 to 2 minutes on each side or until browned; drain on paper towels.

**5.** Toss salad greens with olive oil mixture. Top with olives and warm goat cheese rounds.

## NORM'S NOTE
### Chill Your Cheese

You will get the best results when frying foods with a delicate texture, like goat cheese, if you chill the cheese before you prepare it. Chill it for a few hours so that you will have clean and firm slices. That way the cheese will maintain a neat, round shape when you fry it.

# Fried Green Tomato Sliders

**Makes:** 12 servings    **Hands-on Time:** 20 min.    **Total Time:** 30 min.

1½  cups shredded red cabbage
1½  cups shredded napa cabbage
 1  cup matchstick carrots
 ⅓  cup thinly sliced red onion
 3  Tbsp. olive oil
 2  Tbsp. fresh lime juice
 ½  cup chopped fresh cilantro, divided
    Salt and pepper to taste
 ½  cup mayonnaise
 2  to 3 tsp. Asian Sriracha hot chili sauce
12  slider buns or dinner rolls, warmed and split
12  cooked bacon slices
12  fried green tomatoes

**1.** Stir together first 6 ingredients and ¼ cup cilantro in a medium bowl. Season with salt and pepper to taste. Let stand 10 minutes.

**2.** Stir together mayonnaise, sriracha, and remaining ¼ cup cilantro. Spread buns with mayonnaise mixture. Top bottom halves of buns with bacon, tomatoes, and cabbage mixture. Cover with top halves of buns, mayonnaise mixture sides down.

Off to a
Crunchy Start

# Off to a Crunchy Start

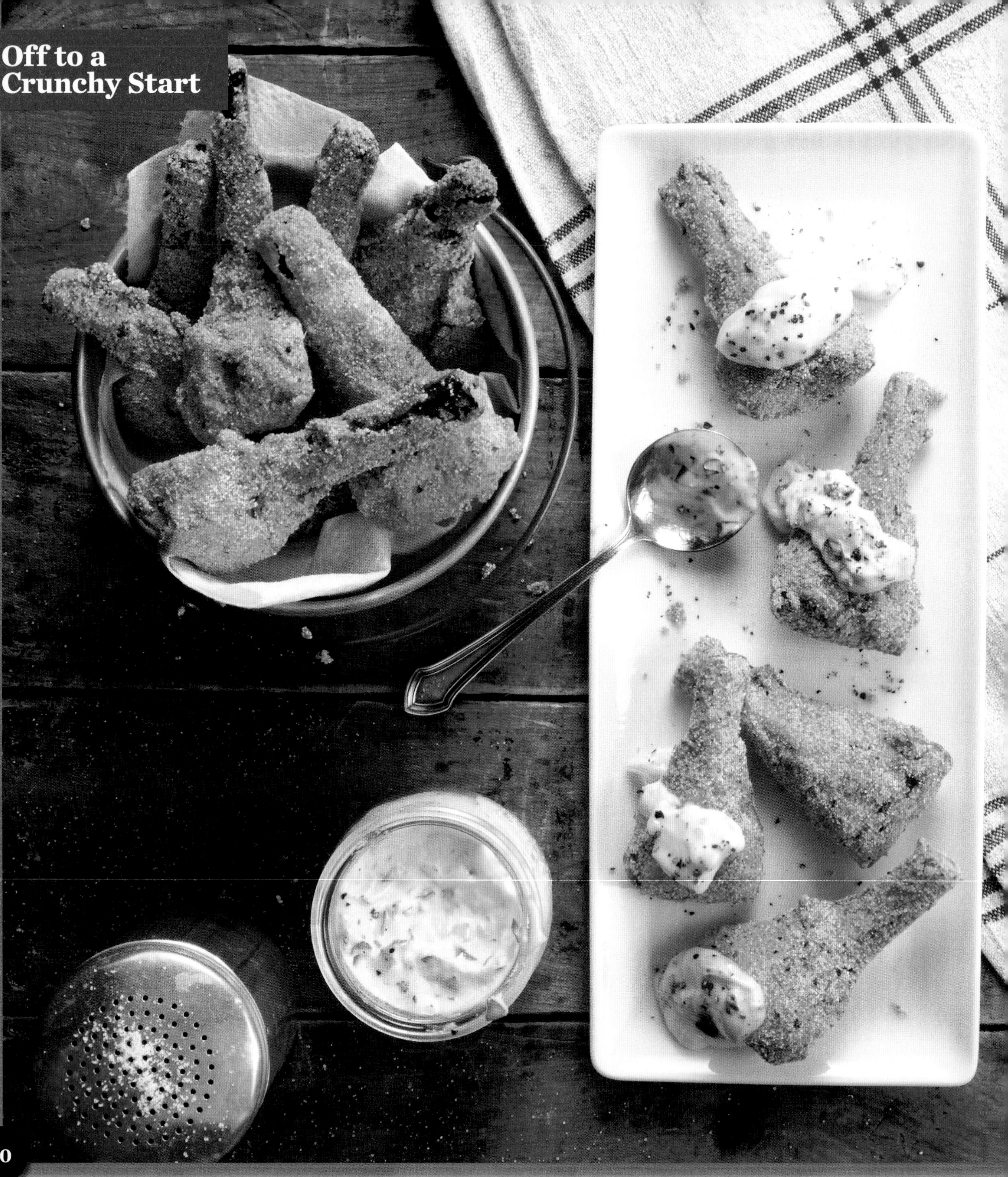

# Cornmeal-Fried Artichokes

*This is based on the Italian fritto misto, or mixed fry, that includes small pieces of battered and fried meats, fish, and vegetables, especially artichokes. Keep fried artichokes warm between batches on a rack in a jelly-roll pan in a 225° oven for up to 30 minutes.*

**Makes:** 3 to 4 servings    **Hands-on Time:** 30 min.    **Total Time:** 35 min., including desired mayo mixture

- 4 **fresh artichokes (about ¾ lb. each)**
  **Canola oil**
- 1½ **cups plain yellow cornmeal**
- 2 **tsp. kosher salt**
- 1½ **tsp. freshly ground pepper**
- ¾ **cup buttermilk**
- 1 **large egg**
- ¾ **cup all-purpose flour**
  **Desired Mayo Mixtures:**
  **Chipotle-Lime Mayo**
  **Pepperoncini Mayo**
  **Garlic-Lemon Mayo**
  **Herb-Shallot Mayo**
  **Garnish: freshly ground pepper**

**1.** Cut 3 inches from top of each artichoke, using a serrated knife. Discard top portion. Remove and discard leaves from bottom portions of artichokes. Trim green skin from sides and stems, using a paring knife, being careful to leave stem ends intact. Cut each artichoke lengthwise into fourths. Remove and discard chokes.

**2.** Pour oil to depth of 3 inches into a Dutch oven; heat over medium-high heat to 350°. Combine cornmeal, salt, and pepper in a shallow bowl. Whisk together buttermilk and egg in another bowl.

**3.** Toss artichokes in flour. Dip in egg mixture, and dredge in cornmeal mixture, shaking off excess.

**4.** Fry artichokes, in batches, in hot oil 5 minutes or until tender and golden brown. Drain on a wire rack over paper towels. Serve with Mayo Mixtures. Sprinkle with ground pepper.

## Chipotle-Lime Mayo

**Makes:** about ¾ cup
**Hands-on Time:** 5 min.
**Total Time:** 5 min.

- ⅔ **cup mayonnaise**
- 1 **Tbsp. minced canned chipotle pepper in adobo sauce**
- 1 **tsp. lime zest**
- 2 **tsp. lime juice**
  **Salt and pepper to taste**

Stir together mayonnaise, minced chipotle pepper, lime zest, and lime juice. Season with salt and pepper to taste.

## Pepperoncini Mayo

**Makes:** about ¾ cup
**Hands-on Time:** 5 min.
**Total Time:** 5 min.

- ⅔ **cup mayonnaise**
- 3 **Tbsp. chopped pepperoncini peppers**
- 1 **tsp. lemon zest**
  **Salt and pepper to taste**

Stir together mayonnaise, pepperoncini peppers, and lemon zest. Season with salt and pepper to taste.

## Garlic-Lemon Mayo

**Makes:** about ¾ cup
**Hands-on Time:** 5 min.
**Total Time:** 5 min.

- ⅔ **cup mayonnaise**
- 1 **garlic clove, pressed**
- 2 **tsp. lemon zest**
- 1 **Tbsp. lemon juice**
- ⅛ **tsp. ground red pepper**
  **Salt to taste**

Stir together mayonnaise, pressed garlic clove, lemon zest, lemon juice, and ground red pepper. Season with salt to taste.

## Herb-Shallot Mayo

**Makes:** about ¾ cup
**Hands-on Time:** 5 min.
**Total Time:** 5 min.

- ⅔ **cup mayonnaise**
- 2 **Tbsp. finely chopped fresh flat-leaf parsley**
- 1 **Tbsp. Dijon mustard**
- 1 **shallot, minced**
  **Salt and pepper to taste**

Stir together mayonnaise, parsley, Dijon mustard, and minced shallot. Season with salt and pepper to taste.

# Macaroni-and-Pimiento Cheese Bites

*Southern cooks have a secret—pimiento cheese is just as delicious as an appetizer as it is on a sandwich or cracker. By giving the pimiento cheese bites a quick fry, they gain a crisp crust that pairs perfectly with the slightly melted cheese on the inside of the popper.*

**Makes:** 5½ dozen    **Hands-on Time:** 50 min.    **Total Time:** 8 hr., 50 min.

1    (8-oz.) package elbow macaroni
3    Tbsp. butter
¼    cup all-purpose flour
2    cups milk
1    tsp. salt
¼    tsp. ground red pepper
⅛    tsp. garlic powder
1    (8-oz.) block sharp Cheddar cheese, shredded
1    (4-oz.) jar diced pimiento, drained
¾    cup fine, dry breadcrumbs
¾    cup freshly grated Parmesan cheese
2    large eggs, lightly beaten
½    cup milk
     Vegetable oil

**1.** Prepare pasta according to package directions.

**2.** Meanwhile, melt butter in a large skillet over medium heat. Gradually whisk in flour until smooth; cook, whisking constantly, 1 minute. Gradually whisk in 2 cups milk and next 3 ingredients; cook, whisking constantly, 3 to 5 minutes or until thickened. Stir in Cheddar cheese and pimiento until melted and smooth. Remove from heat, and stir in pasta.

**3.** Line a 13- x 9-inch pan with plastic wrap, allowing several inches to extend over edges of pan. Pour mixture into prepared pan. Cool slightly; cover and chill 8 hours. Remove macaroni mixture from pan, and cut into 1-inch squares.

**4.** Stir together breadcrumbs and Parmesan cheese in a shallow dish or pie plate. Whisk together eggs and ½ cup milk in another shallow dish or pie plate; dip macaroni bites in egg mixture, and dredge in breadcrumb mixture.

**5.** Pour oil to depth of 1 inch into a large skillet; heat to 350°. Fry bites, in batches, 2 minutes on each side or until golden.

### Golden Baked Macaroni and Pimiento Cheese:

Prepare recipe as directed through Step 2. Pour macaroni mixture into a lightly greased 13- x 9-inch baking dish; do not chill. Omit eggs and ½ cup milk. Stir together breadcrumbs and Parmesan cheese; sprinkle over mixture. Omit oil. Bake at 350° for 15 to 20 minutes or until golden and bubbly.

# Off to a Crunchy Start

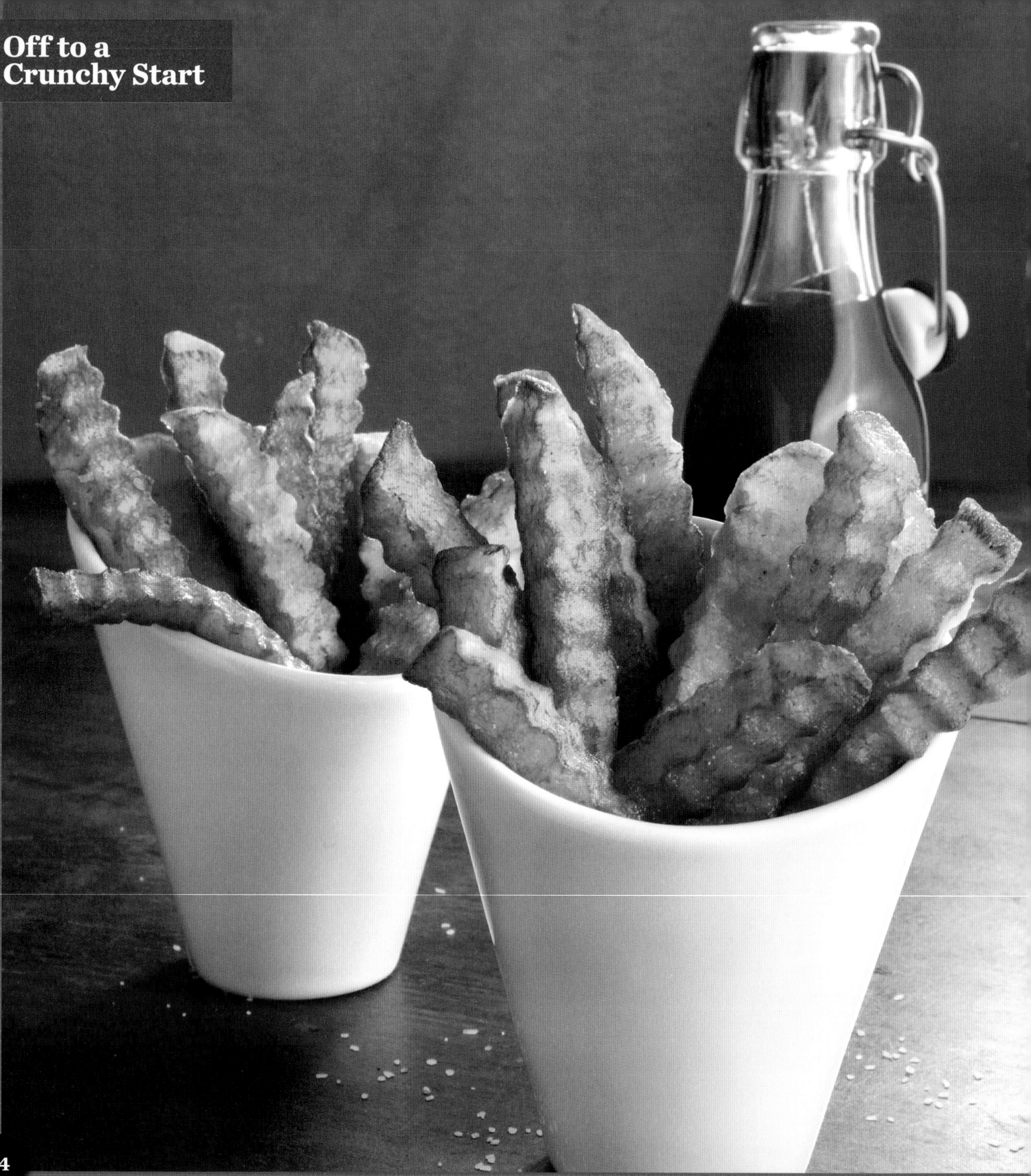

# Crinkle-Cut Fries

*Skip the freezer section and make a homemade version of this kid-favorite American classic.*

**Makes:** 6 to 8 servings
**Hands-on Time:** 50 min.
**Total Time:** 50 min.

- 4 lb. russet or Idaho potatoes, peeled
  Vegetable oil
  Salt to taste
  Ketchup

**1.** Cut potatoes into ½-inch-wide strips with a waffle cutter.

**2.** Pour vegetable oil to depth of 4 inches into a Dutch oven, and heat to 325°. Fry potato strips, in batches, until lightly golden, but not brown, 4 to 5 minutes per batch. Drain strips on paper towels.

**3.** Heat oil to 375°. Fry strips, in small batches, until golden brown and crisp, 1 to 2 minutes per batch. Drain on clean paper towels. Sprinkle with salt, and serve immediately with ketchup.

**Note:** We tested with Wesson vegetable oil.

# Rice Croquettes

*Serve these crisp rice bites with your favorite rémoulade sauce.*

**Makes:** about 1½ dozen
**Hands-on Time:** 25 min.
**Total Time:** 55 min.

- 1⅓ cups extra-long-grain enriched white rice
- ½ tsp. salt
- 1½ cups panko (Japanese breadcrumbs), divided
- 3 large eggs
- 1 cup shredded Parmesan cheese
- 2 Tbsp. chopped fresh basil
- 1 tsp. minced garlic
- ½ tsp. freshly ground pepper
  Vegetable oil

**1.** Bring 2⅔ cups water to a boil over medium-high heat; add rice and salt. Cover, reduce heat to low, and simmer 20 minutes or until liquid is absorbed and rice is tender. Let cool 10 minutes.

**2.** Stir together rice, ½ cup breadcrumbs, and next 5 ingredients.

**3.** Shape rice mixture into 18 (¼-cup) balls. Dredge in remaining 1 cup breadcrumbs.

**4.** Pour oil to depth of 3 inches into a Dutch oven. Heat oil to 350° over medium-high heat. Fry rice balls, in batches, 2 to 2½ minutes on each side or until golden brown. Drain.

## HOW TO:
### Fry Sweet Potato Chips

1. Thin slices are essential for transforming sweet potatoes into crispy chips. A mandoline is the perfect tool for the job.

2. Take the time to let the oil reach the correct temperature at the start of each batch. This will result in crisp Sweet Potato Chips with a lovely copper hue.

3. Keep a consistent medium heat. When you add the first batch of sweet potatoes, watch the thermometer— every time you add a batch of sweet potatoes, the oil temperature will drop. Adjust heat accordingly to maintain the temperature.

4. Once the chips finish frying for their allotted time, let the oil come back to 300° over medium heat. Proceed with the next batch. When each batch comes out of the oil, immediately sprinkle the chips with kosher salt. This helps the salt stick to the chips.

# Sweet Potato Chips

*The secret to crisp sweet potato chips is to fry them in small batches, in peanut oil, at a low temperature.*

**Makes:** 6 to 8 servings **Hands-on Time:** 40 min. **Total Time:** 40 min.

2 sweet potatoes, peeled (about 2 lb.)
  Peanut oil
  Kosher salt

Cut sweet potatoes into ⅟₁₆-inch-thick slices, using a mandoline. Pour peanut oil to depth of 3 inches into a Dutch oven; heat over medium-high heat to 300°. Fry potato slices, in small batches, stirring often, 4 to 4½ minutes or until crisp. Drain on a wire rack over paper towels. Immediately sprinkle with desired amount of kosher salt. Cool completely, and store in an airtight container at room temperature up to 2 days.

STEP 1

STEP 2

STEP 3

STEP 4

# Okra Rellenos

*(pictured on page 15)*

---

*Okra is a signature Southern ingredient whether fried, pickled, or grilled. Okra Rellenos are essentially fried okra filled with cheese. The recipe yields 2 dozen, but they'll go fast!*

**Makes:** 2 dozen    **Hands-on Time:** 40 min.    **Total Time:** 40 min.

- 4  oz. pepper Jack cheese
- 1  lb. fresh okra (4-inch-long pods)
- 1  cup self-rising flour
- ⅓  cup self-rising cornmeal
- 1  large egg
- ½  cup buttermilk
- ½  cup dark beer
-    Corn oil
- ½  tsp. salt
-    Salsa

**1.** Cut pepper Jack cheese into 3- x ¼-inch sticks.

**2.** Cut a lengthwise slit in each okra pod, cutting to but not through ends; push seeds aside. Stuff pods with cheese sticks, and set aside.

**3.** Combine flour and cornmeal in a large bowl; make a well in center of mixture.

**4.** Stir together egg, buttermilk, and beer; add to dry ingredients, stirring until smooth.

**5.** Pour oil to depth of 3 inches into a Dutch oven; heat to 375°. Dip stuffed okra in batter, coating well; fry, a few at a time, in hot oil until golden. Drain on paper towels. Sprinkle with salt; serve immediately with salsa.

## NORM'S NOTE
### Add Some Heat

Serve this Southern take on traditional chiles rellenos at your next party with salsa ranchera, a hybrid of hot sauce and salsa. Find it in the ethnic foods aisle of your grocery store; it's commonly sold in 7-oz. containers.

## NORM'S NOTE
### What's a Grit?

Grits are treasured like gold down here. They are steeped in tradition and are so versatile they can make an appearance in any meal from breakfast to supper, prepared in many ways from savory to sweet, simmered to fried, and almost anything in between. And, it's true, some self-respecting Southerners actually use quick-cooking grits. When frying grits, the quick-cooking grits are my preference. The finer texture has a more appealing mouth-feel when deep-fried in comparison to regular grits. And, of course, as they fry in hot oil, creamy grits actually do turn to gold.

# Bacon-Grits Fritters

**Makes:** about 32    **Hands-on Time:** 35 min.    **Total Time:** 4 hr., 40 min.

1   cup uncooked quick-cooking grits
4   cups milk
1   tsp. salt
1½  cups (6 oz.) shredded extra-sharp white Cheddar cheese
½   cup cooked and finely crumbled bacon (about 8 slices)
2   green onions, minced
½   tsp. freshly ground pepper
2   large eggs
3   cups panko (Japanese breadcrumbs)
    Vegetable oil

**1.** Prepare grits according to package directions, using 4 cups milk and 1 tsp. salt. Remove from heat, and let stand 5 minutes. Stir in cheese and next 3 ingredients, stirring until cheese is melted. Spoon mixture into a lightly greased 8-inch square baking dish or pan, and chill 4 to 24 hours.

**2.** Roll grits into 1½-inch balls. Whisk together eggs and ¼ cup water. Dip balls in egg wash, and roll in breadcrumbs.

**3.** Pour oil to depth of 3 inches into a large heavy skillet; heat over medium-high heat to 350°. Fry fritters, in batches, 3 to 4 minutes or until golden brown. Drain on paper towels. Keep fritters warm on a wire rack in a pan in a 225° oven up to 30 minutes. Serve warm.

> **Make ahead:** Prepare recipe as directed through Step 2. Cover and chill in a single layer up to 4 hours. Fry as directed. You may also prepare through Step 2 and freeze on a baking sheet for 30 minutes or until firm. Transfer to a zip-top plastic freezer bag, and freeze. Cook frozen fritters as directed in Step 3, increasing cooking time to 5 to 6 minutes or until golden and centers are thoroughly heated.

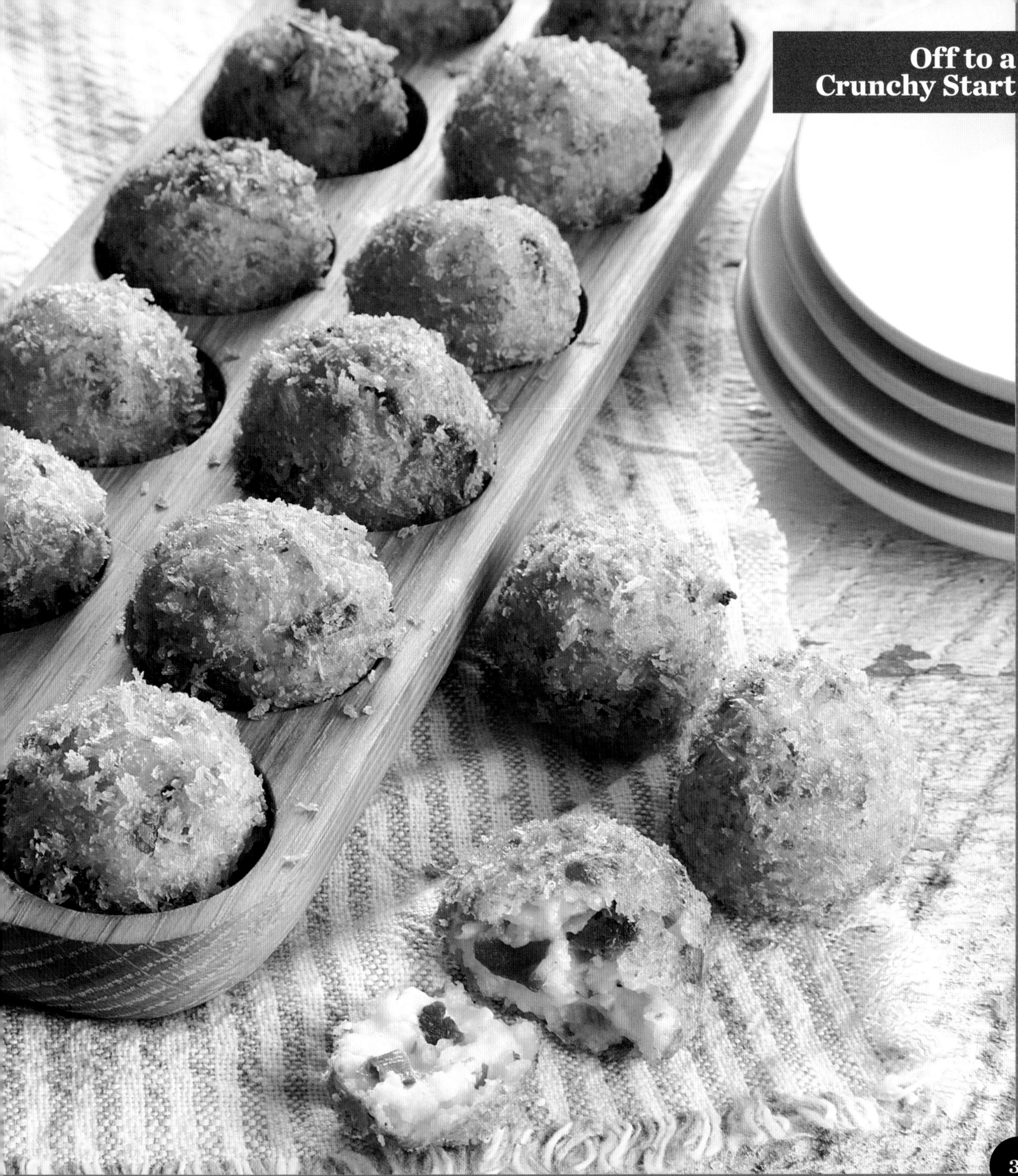

# Hoppin' John Hush Puppies

*A Lowcountry classic is transformed into a crispy, satisfying fritter.*

**Makes:** about 2 dozen    **Hands-on Time:** 40 min.    **Total Time:** 50 min., including relish

Peanut oil
1  (15-oz.) can seasoned field peas and snaps, drained and rinsed (about 1 cup)*
1  cup yellow self-rising cornmeal mix
¾  cup buttermilk
½  cup all-purpose flour
½  cup chopped country ham
½  cup cooked long-grain rice
½  cup sliced green onions, light green parts only
1  jalapeño pepper, seeded and diced
2  garlic cloves, pressed
1  tsp. baking powder
1  tsp. freshly ground pepper
2  large eggs, lightly beaten
Tomato-Corn Relish

**1.** Pour oil to depth of 3 inches into a large heavy skillet or Dutch oven; heat over medium-high heat to 350°.

**2.** Meanwhile, stir together field peas and next 11 ingredients in a large bowl.

**3.** Drop pea mixture by rounded tablespoonfuls into hot oil, and fry, in batches, 3 to 4 minutes or until hush puppies are golden brown. Drain on paper towels; keep warm. Serve with relish.

*1 (15.5-oz.) can seasoned black-eyed peas may be substituted.

## Tomato-Corn Relish

**Makes:** 1 cup
**Hands-on Time:** 10 min.
**Total Time:** 10 min.

1  thick bacon slice
1  cup fresh corn kernels (about 1 ear)
1  garlic clove, pressed
1  (8-oz.) jar green tomato relish
2  tsp. hot sauce
¼  tsp. salt

**1.** Cook bacon in a medium skillet over medium-high heat 3 minutes or until crisp; remove bacon, and drain on paper towels, reserving 1 Tbsp. drippings in skillet. Crumble bacon.

**2.** Sauté corn and garlic in hot drippings 3 minutes or until tender. Stir in tomato relish, next 2 ingredients, and bacon. Serve immediately.

# Andouille Corn Poppers

*These spicy, bite-sized versions of corn dogs are irresistible. You'll need about 30 minutes and 1 qt. of oil for frying them.*

**Makes:** 6 to 8 servings    **Hands-on Time:** 30 min.    **Total Time:** 30 min.

- 1 (8½-oz.) package corn muffin mix
- 1 large egg
- ½ cup buttermilk
- 1 tsp. Creole seasoning
- 1 lb. andouille sausage, cut into 1-inch slices*
  Peanut oil
  Creole mustard
  Cocktail sauce

**1.** Whisk together corn muffin mix and next 3 ingredients. Dip sausages slices in batter, coating well.

**2.** Pour oil to depth of 1 inch into a Dutch oven; heat over medium-high heat to 375°. Fry sausages, in batches, 1½ minutes on each side or until golden brown. Drain on paper towels. Keep warm on a wire rack in an aluminum foil-lined jelly-roll pan in a 200° oven. Serve with mustard and cocktail sauce.

*1 (16-oz.) package cocktail-size smoked sausages, drained, may be substituted. We tested with Bryan Cocktail Smokies.

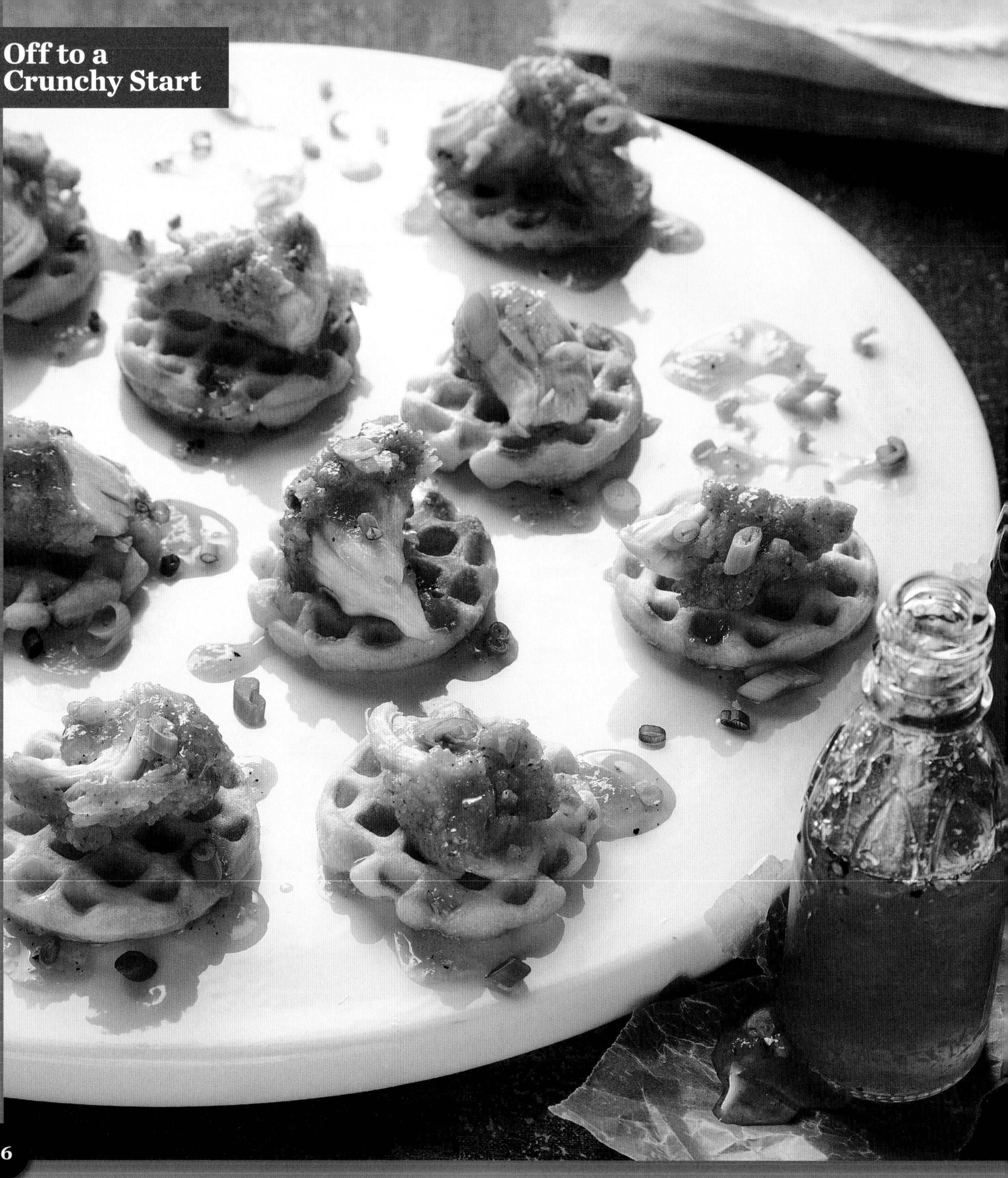

# Buttermilk Chicken and Waffles

*Keep waffles warm in a 200° oven up to 30 minutes before assembling.*

**Makes:** 14 to 16 appetizer servings    **Hands-on Time:** 50 min.    **Total Time:** 1 hr., 5 min., including syrup

1½  **cups all-purpose flour**
1  **Tbsp. sugar**
1½  **tsp. baking powder**
¾  **tsp. baking soda**
¾  **tsp. salt**
1¾  **cups buttermilk**
⅓  **cup butter, melted**
2  **large eggs**
12  **to 16 fried chicken breast tenders, cut into bite-size pieces**
   **Peach-Horseradish Maple Syrup**
   **Garnish: thinly sliced green onions**

**1.** Stir together first 5 ingredients in a large bowl. Whisk together buttermilk and next 2 ingredients in a small bowl; stir buttermilk mixture into flour mixture just until combined.

**2.** Cook batter in a preheated, oiled mini-style waffle iron 3½ to 4 minutes or until golden (about ½ Tbsp. batter per waffle). Top waffles with chicken, and drizzle with Peach-Horseradish Maple Syrup. Garnish, if desired.

**Note:** We tested with a Sunbeam Mini Waffle Maker. If you don't have a mini waffle iron, use ½ cup batter per waffle in a traditional (10- x 8½-inch) waffle iron, and cook 4 to 5 minutes or until golden; cut each waffle into fourths.

## Peach-Horseradish Maple Syrup

**Makes:** 1¼ cups
**Hands-on Time:** 5 min.
**Total Time:** 5 min.

1  **cup maple syrup**
¼  **cup peach preserves**
2  **tsp. prepared horseradish**
½  **tsp. coarsely ground pepper**
¼  **tsp. salt**

Stir together maple syrup, peach preserves, horseradish, pepper, and salt in a small microwave-safe bowl. Microwave at HIGH 30 seconds or until warm.

# Fried Chicken Bites

*Perfect for a picnic, these spicy fried chicken nuggets are great dipped in honey mustard or blue cheese dressing.*

**Makes:** 4 to 6 servings    **Hands-on Time:** 50 min.    **Total Time:** 50 min., plus 1 day for marinating

1½  tsp. to 1 Tbsp. ground red pepper
1½  tsp. ground chipotle chile pepper
1½  tsp. garlic powder
1½  tsp. dried crushed red pepper
1½  tsp. ground black pepper
¾   tsp. salt
½   tsp. paprika
2   lb. skinned and boned chicken breasts
2   cups buttermilk
3   bread slices, toasted
1   cup all-purpose flour
    Peanut oil
    Blue cheese dressing or honey mustard

**1.** Combine first 7 ingredients in a small bowl; reserve half of spice mixture. Cut chicken into 1-inch pieces. Place chicken in a medium bowl, and toss with remaining spice mixture until coated. Stir in buttermilk; cover and chill 24 hours.

**2.** Tear bread into pieces, and place in a food processor with reserved spice mixture. Process until mixture resembles cornmeal. Stir in flour. Remove chicken pieces from buttermilk, discarding buttermilk. Dredge chicken in breadcrumb mixture.

**3.** Pour oil to depth of 2 inches into a Dutch oven; heat to 350°. Fry chicken, in batches, 6 to 7 minutes on each side or until golden brown and done. Drain on a wire rack over paper towels. Sprinkle with salt to taste. Serve warm or cold with blue cheese dressing or honey mustard.

## Travel Ready

Chinese-style take-out boxes are an often overlooked but efficient way to take your food to go. The boxes are stackable, inexpensive, and disposable. They'll easily hold a few servings of Fried Chicken Bites and most of the traditional picnic sides. Pack up these bites with the Veggie Potato Salad on page 188, fresh diced watermelon with cherries and chopped fresh mint, and a bottle of sparkling lemonade for a simple summery picnic.

## Off to a Crunchy Start

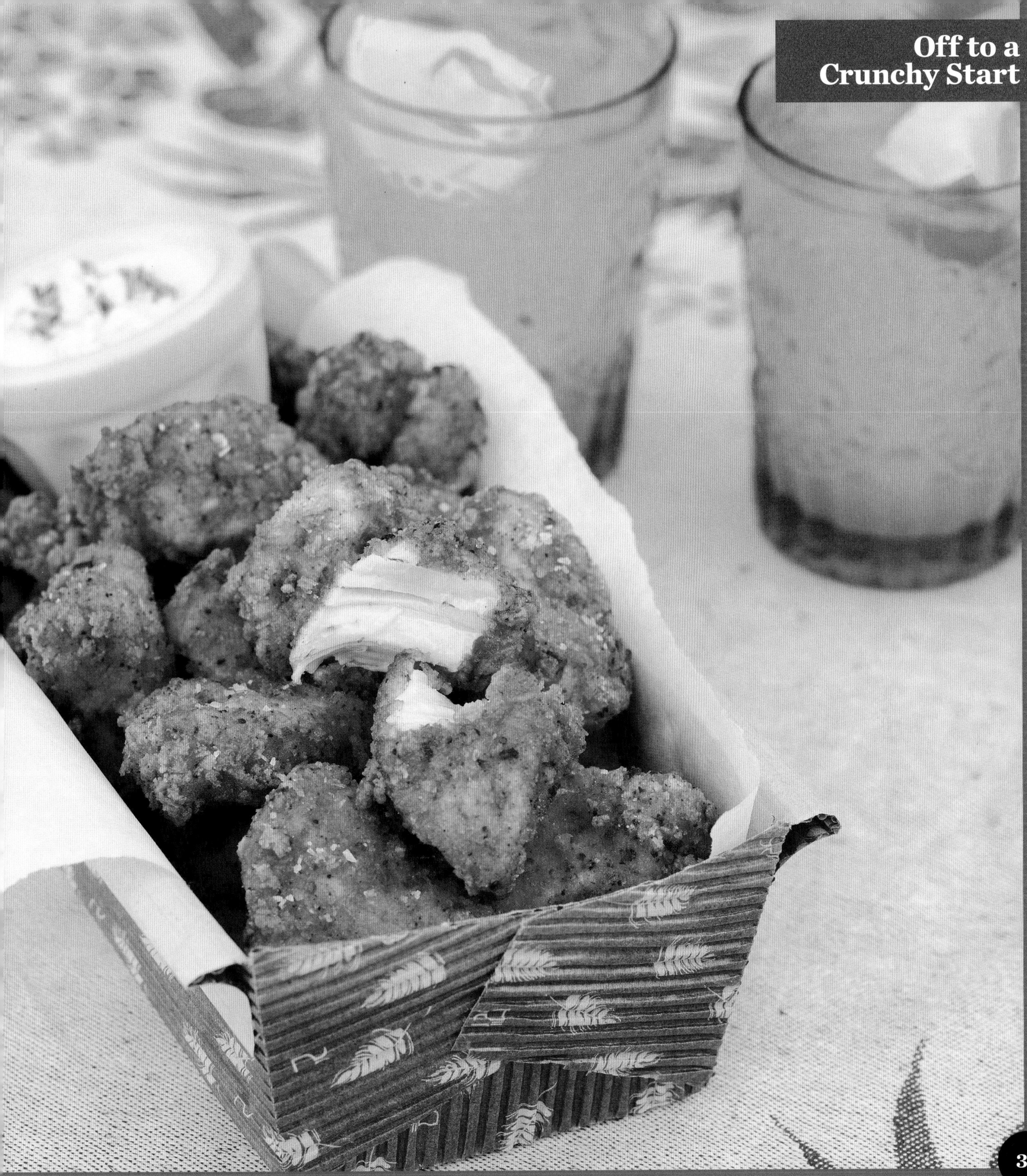

# Spicy Buffalo Wings

*Serve with plenty of cool beverages.*

**Makes:** 4 servings     **Hands-on Time:** 30 min.
**Total Time:** 55 min., including sauces

2½  lb. chicken wing pieces (wings already cut)
 2  tsp. salt
 ¾  tsp. ground black pepper
 ¼  tsp. ground red pepper
 ¼  tsp. onion powder
 1  cup all-purpose flour
     Vegetable oil
     Spicy Buffalo Sauce (page 246)
     Cool Ranch Sauce (page 245)
     Celery sticks

**1.** Sprinkle wings with salt and next 3 ingredients. Dredge in flour, shaking to remove excess.

**2.** Pour oil to depth of 2 inches into a large deep skillet; heat to 350°. Fry wings, in batches, 3 to 4 minutes on each side or until done. Drain on a wire rack over paper towels. Toss wings in Spicy Buffalo Sauce; serve immediately with Cool Ranch Sauce and celery sticks.

## HOW TO:
### Fry Wings

1. Sprinkle seasoning over chicken wings in a shallow dish; toss to coat. For extra flavor, cover and chill in refrigerator 2 to 3 hours.

2. Dredge seasoned wings in all-purpose flour, being sure to shake off excess flour to get a light coating.

3. Fry in batches of 5 to 6 wings per batch.

4. Remove wings from oil when their internal temperature reaches 165° with an instant-read thermometer. Drain on a wire rack over paper towels.

5. When all the wings are cooked, place in a large bowl and pour in Spicy Buffalo Sauce. Toss wings in sauce, thoroughly coating all sides.

**STEP 1**

**STEP 2**

**STEP 3**

**STEP 4**

**STEP 5**

# Mini Latkes with Salmon-Olive Relish

*The key to the best latkes is patting the potato-and-onion mixture very dry on paper towels before adding eggs and matzo meal.*

**Makes:** 8 servings    **Hands-on Time:** 44 min.    **Total Time:** 54 min., including relish

| | |
|---|---|
| 2 | **baking potatoes (about 1½ lb.), peeled** |
| 1 | **small sweet onion** |
| 2 | **large eggs, lightly beaten** |
| ⅓ | **cup unsalted matzo meal** |
| 1 | **tsp. kosher salt** |
| 1 | **tsp. coarsely ground pepper** |
| ¾ | **cup canola oil** |
| | **Kosher salt to taste (optional)** |
| | **Salmon-Olive Relish** |
| | **Garnish: chopped green onion** |

**1.** Grate potatoes and onion through large holes on a box grater. Pat grated potatoes and onion dry with paper towels.

**2.** Place potatoes and onion in a large bowl. Stir in lightly beaten eggs and next 3 ingredients.

**3.** Drop potato mixture by heaping tablespoonfuls into hot canola oil in a large deep skillet over medium-high heat; cook 2 to 4 minutes on each side or until golden brown. Drain latkes on paper towels, and sprinkle with kosher salt to taste, if desired. Top each latke with 1 tsp. Salmon-Olive Relish. Garnish, if desired. Serve immediately.

**Note:** To keep latkes warm before topping with relish, place on a wire rack on a baking sheet. Place in a 250° oven up to 30 minutes.

### Salmon-Olive Relish

*You can make this up to one day ahead; cover and refrigerate until ready to use.*

**Makes:** ¾ cup
**Hands-on Time:** 10 min.
**Total Time:** 10 min.

| | |
|---|---|
| 1 | **(4-oz.) package smoked salmon, diced** |
| 1 | **green onion, minced** |
| 3 | **oil-cured black olives, minced** |
| 1 | **tsp. extra virgin olive oil** |
| 1 | **tsp. fresh lemon juice** |

Stir together all ingredients.

## Off to a Crunchy Start

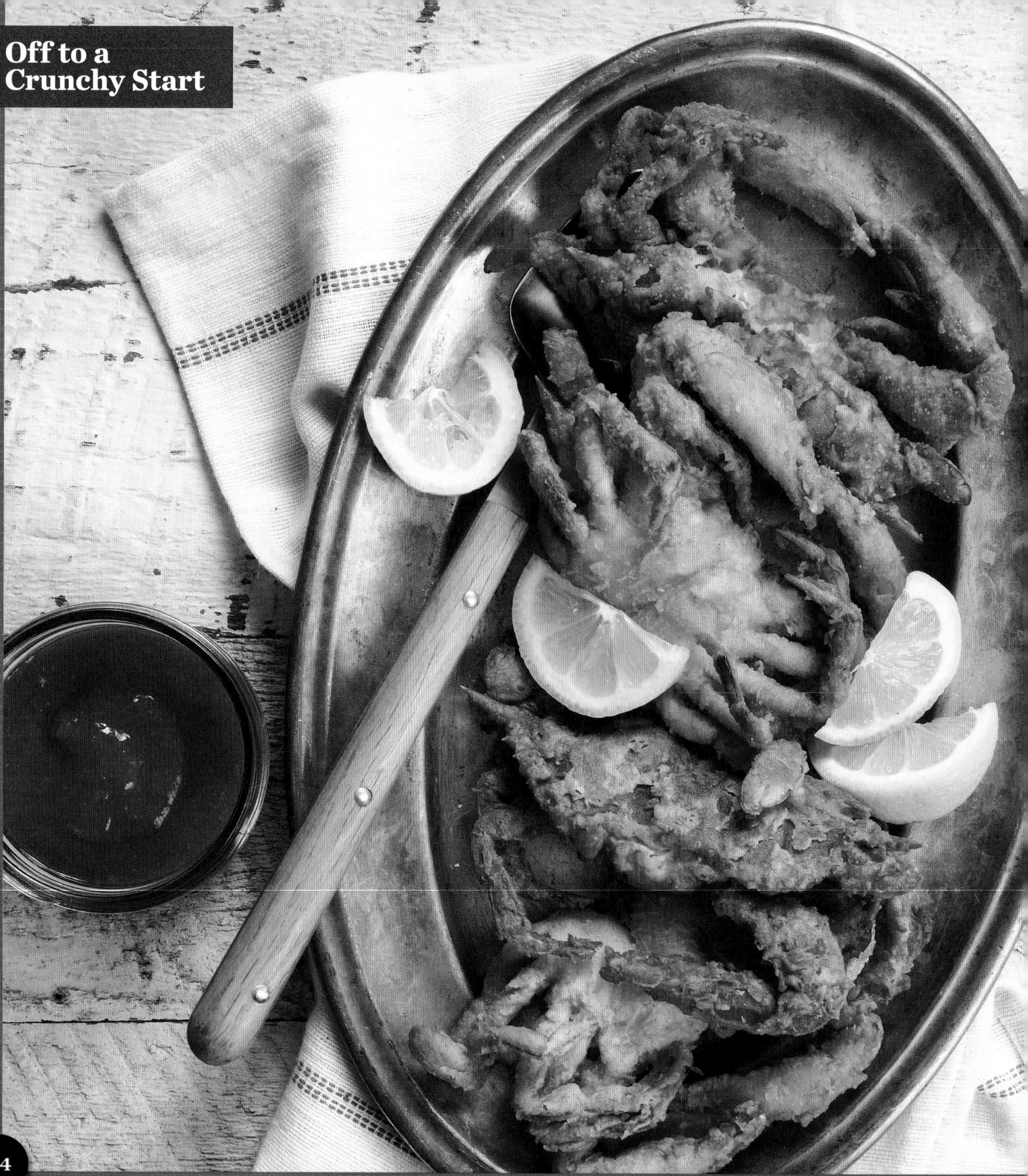

# Fried Soft-Shell Crab

**Makes:** 6 servings    **Hands-on Time:** 50 min.    **Total Time:** 50 min.

    Vegetable oil
1   (12-oz.) can evaporated milk
1   large egg
6   soft-shell crabs
1½  tsp. seasoned salt
1½  cups self-rising flour
    Garnish: lemon wedges
    Cocktail sauce

**1.** Pour oil to depth of 3 inches into a Dutch oven; heat to 360°. Whisk together milk, egg, and ¼ cup water in a large bowl.

**2.** Rinse crabs, and pat dry. Sprinkle crabs with seasoned salt. Dredge crabs in flour; dip in milk mixture, and dredge in flour again. Fry crabs, in batches, in hot oil 2 to 3 minutes on each side or until golden brown. Drain on a wire rack over paper towels. Garnish, if desired. Serve with cocktail sauce.

---

**Fried Shrimp:** Substitute 2 lb. peeled, large raw shrimp with tails for soft-shell crab. Prepare recipe as directed, heating oil to 325° and frying shrimp, in batches, 3 to 4 minutes or until golden brown.

**Fried Grouper:** Substitute 2 lb. grouper, cut into 2-inch fillets, for soft-shell crab. Prepare recipe as directed, heating oil to 350° and frying grouper, in batches, 3 minutes on each side or until golden brown.

**Fried Oysters:** Substitute 2 pt. fresh oysters, drained, for soft-shell crab. Prepare recipe as directed, frying oysters, in batches, 2 to 3 minutes or until golden brown. Serve immediately.

---

## NORM'S NOTE
### How to Buy Soft-Shell Crab

Blue crabs make their home in the waters of the Mid-Atlantic Chesapeake Bay, the Carolinas, and along the Gulf bordering Louisiana. Baited by fishermen or personally trapped off the pier, blue crabs are worth the time they take to catch. When buying soft-shell crabs, live ones are the best but they're not always easy to find. To select the tastiest, use your nose. When fresh, they smell clean and astrigent, like sea mist.

1. Shrimp sizes vary, but I like 26/30 count (per lb.) for a large shrimp. Start by peeling the shrimp and then devein them by making a ¼-inch slit down the back of the shrimp with a paring knife to pull out the vein.

2. Chill the egg mixture before pouring it over the shrimp to allow it to better coat the shrimp. Make sure that you mix the shrimp well so that it is coated with the mixture.

3. Coat the shrimp completely with the breading mixture. Gently shake off the excess breading.

4. A candy thermometer clips to the edge of the Dutch oven and allows you to see at eye level when the temperature reaches 325°.

5. The shrimp begin to float to the top when they are done. Make sure that they are brown on both sides before draining them.

# Bayou Fried Shrimp

*A squeeze of lemon and a dip in cocktail sauce are the only accessories these spicy shrimp really need.*

**Makes:** 6 to 8 servings    **Hands-on Time:** 30 min.    **Total Time:** 45 min.

- 3 lb. unpeeled, large raw shrimp
- 2 cups milk
- 1 large egg
- 1 Tbsp. yellow mustard
- 1 tsp. Cajun seasoning
- 1 (12-oz.) package fish fry mix
- 1 Tbsp. Cajun seasoning
- Vegetable oil
- Garnish: lemon wedges
- Cocktail sauce

**1.** Peel shrimp, leaving tails on. Butterfly shrimp by making a deep slit down back of each from large end to tail, cutting to but not through inside curve of shrimp. Devein shrimp, and place in a large bowl.

**2.** Whisk together milk and next 3 ingredients. Pour mixture over shrimp. Let stand at least 15 minutes or up to 1 hour.

**3.** Combine fish fry mix and 1 Tbsp. Cajun seasoning. Dredge shrimp in fish fry mixture, and shake off excess. Arrange on baking sheets.

**4.** Pour oil to depth of 3 inches into a Dutch oven; heat to 325°. Fry shrimp, in batches, 1½ minutes on each side or until golden brown; drain on wire racks over paper towels. Garnish, if desired. Serve with cocktail sauce.

**Note:** We tested with Zatarain's Wonderful Fish-Fri and Walker & Sons Cajun Seasoning.

STEP 1

STEP 2

STEP 3

STEP 4

STEP 5

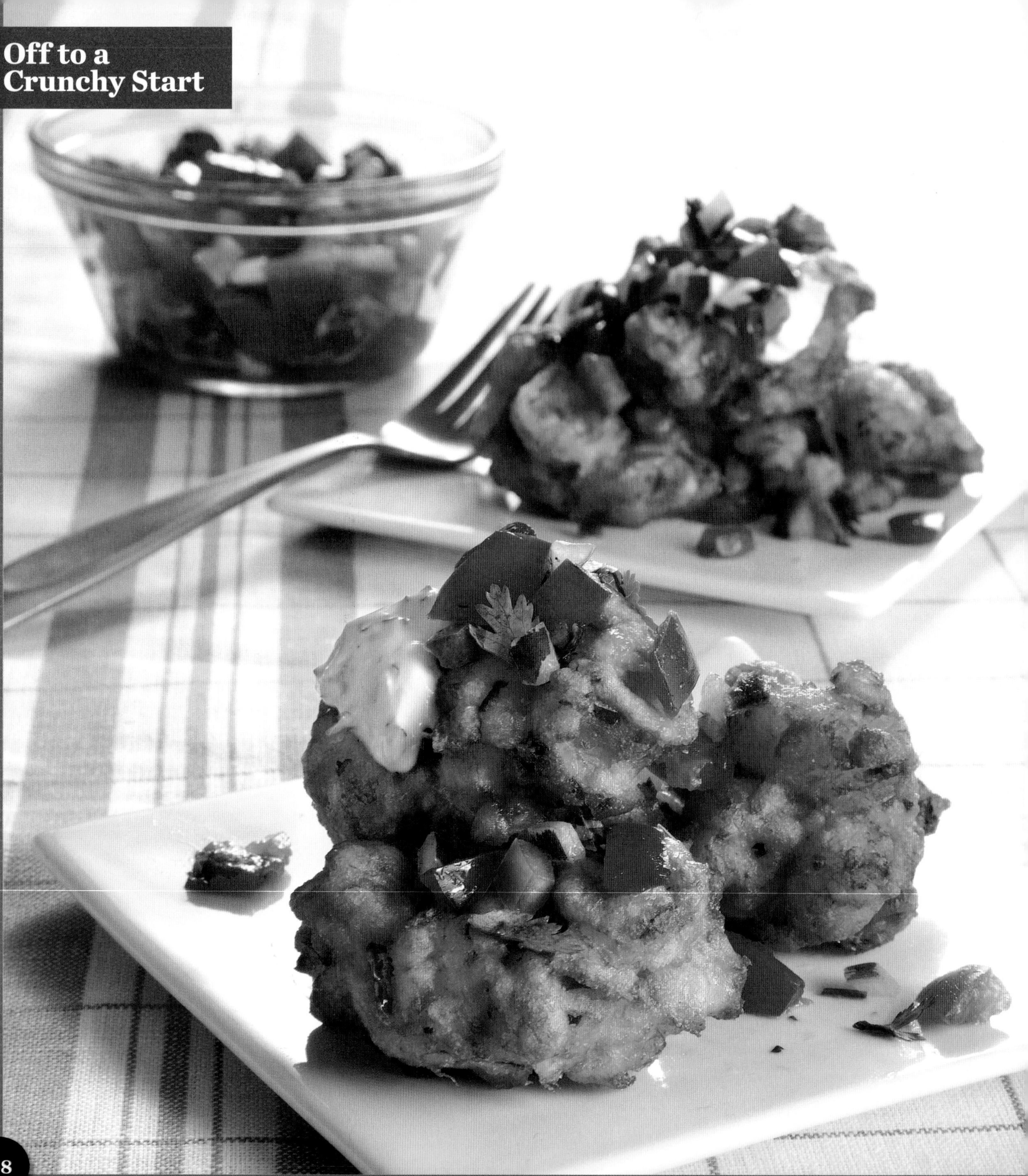

# Okra-Shrimp Beignets

**Makes:** about 30    **Hands-on Time:** 27 min.

**Total Time:** 47 min., including salsa and sour cream

     Vegetable oil
 2   cups sliced fresh okra
 ½   green bell pepper, diced
 ½   medium onion, diced
 1   large egg
 ½   cup all-purpose flour
 ¼   cup heavy cream
 1   jalapeño pepper, finely chopped
 ¾   tsp. salt
 ¾   tsp. freshly ground pepper
 ¼   lb. medium-size raw shrimp, peeled and coarsely chopped
     Fresh Tomato Salsa
     Cilantro Sour Cream

**1.** Pour oil to depth of 3 inches into a Dutch oven; heat to 350°.

**2.** Stir together okra and next 8 ingredients in a large bowl until well blended; stir in shrimp.

**3.** Drop batter by rounded tablespoonfuls into hot oil, and fry, in batches, 2 to 3 minutes on each side or until golden brown. Drain on a wire rack over paper towels. Serve with salsa and sour cream.

## Fresh Tomato Salsa

**Makes:** 4 servings

**Hands-on Time:** 15 min.

**Total Time:** 15 min.

 4   large plum tomatoes, seeded and chopped
 ¼   cup chopped fresh cilantro
 1   jalapeño pepper, seeded and finely diced
 3   Tbsp. finely diced red onion
 2½  Tbsp. fresh lime juice
 1   Tbsp. extra virgin olive oil
     Salt and pepper to taste

Stir together all ingredients.

## Cilantro Sour Cream

**Makes:** 1 cup

**Hands-on Time:** 5 min.

**Total Time:** 5 min.

 1   (8-oz.) container sour cream
 ¼   cup finely chopped fresh cilantro
 1   tsp. lime zest
 1   tsp. fresh lime juice
     Salt and pepper to taste

Stir together all ingredients.

## NORM'S NOTE
### A Savory Beignet?

Beignets are most commonly recognized as square pieces of fried dough, heavily coated with powdered sugar, and served alongside strong chicory coffee. This recipe is not that type of beignet. We took two Lowcountry favorites, okra and shrimp, and fried them into fritters that have the crispy and airy qualities of a good beignet, hence the name. Personally, I would swap the cup of coffee for a glass of fruity rosé wine.

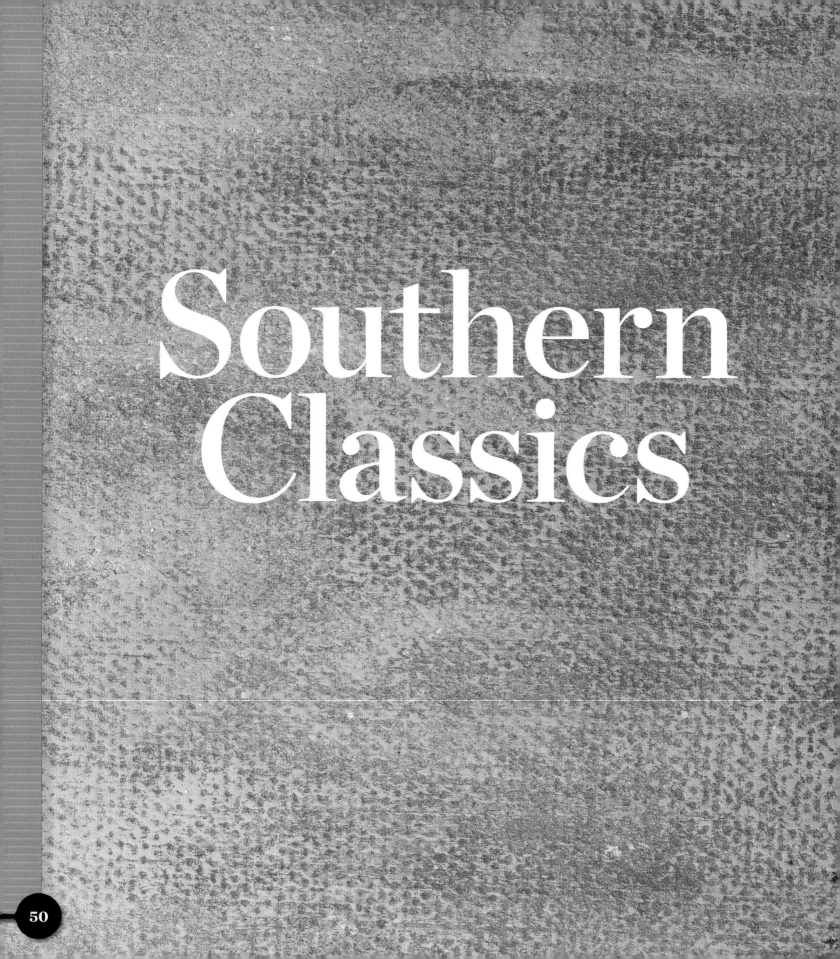

# Southern Classics

Fried Green
Tomatoes,
*page 54*

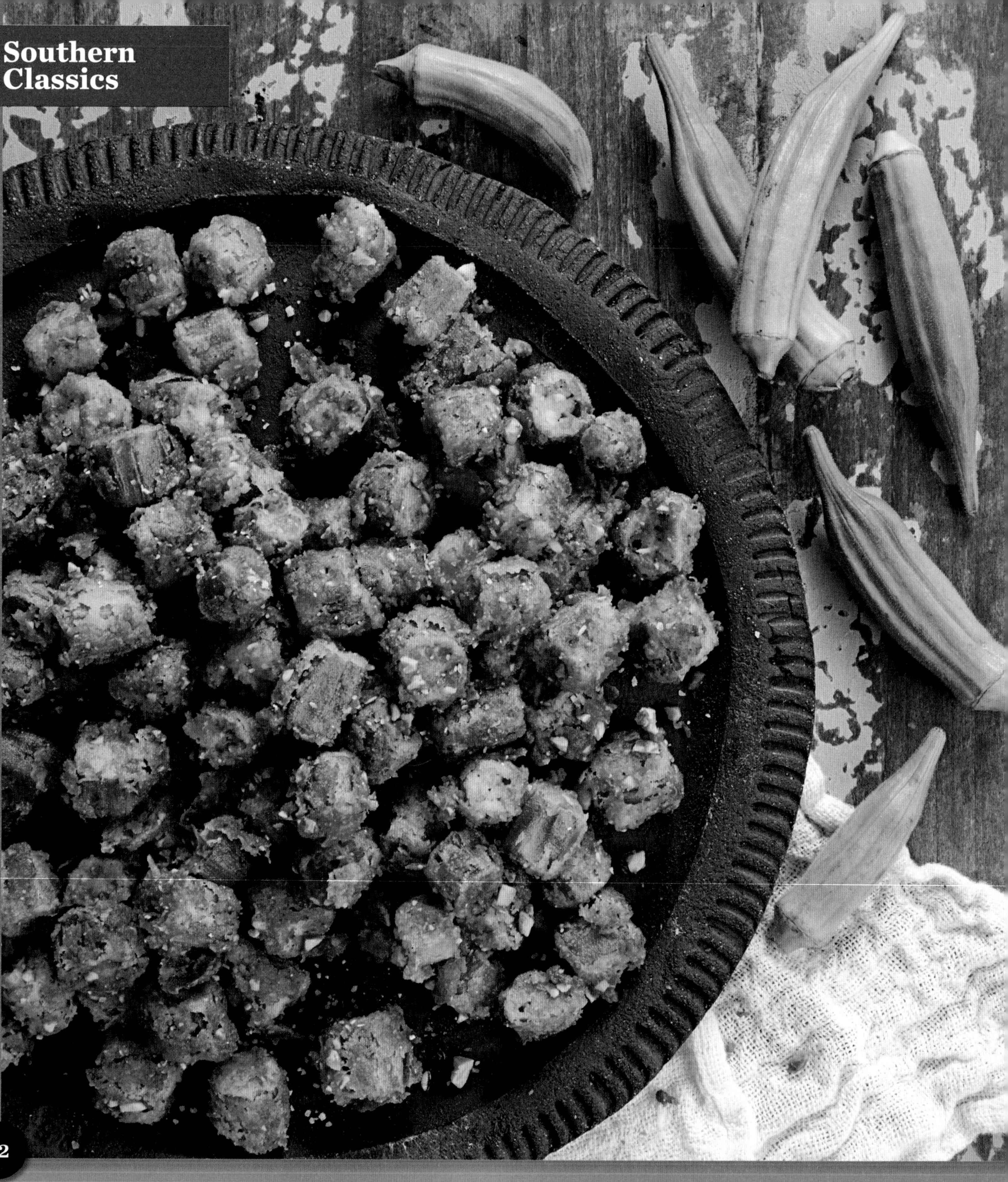

# Nutty Okra

*Pulse the peanuts in a food processor for easy chopping.*

**Makes:** 4 servings   **Hands-on Time:** 22 min.   **Total Time:** 42 min.

- 1 **lb. fresh okra, cut into ½-inch pieces***
- 1 **tsp. salt**
- 1 **egg white, lightly beaten**
- 1 **cup all-purpose baking mix**
- ½ **cup finely chopped salted dry-roasted peanuts**
- ½ **tsp. pepper**
- **Peanut oil**

**1.** Toss okra with salt, and let stand 20 minutes. Add egg white, stirring to coat. Stir together baking mix and next 2 ingredients in a large bowl. Add okra, tossing to coat; gently press peanut mixture onto okra, shaking off excess.

**2.** Pour oil to depth of 2 inches into a Dutch oven or cast-iron skillet; heat to 375°. Fry okra, in batches, 2 to 4 minutes or until golden; drain on paper towels.

*1 (16-oz.) package frozen cut okra, thawed, may be substituted.

## NORM'S NOTE
### Discover Purple Okra

My fellow Test Kitchen mate Pam Lolley introduced me to purple okra when she brought some down from her father's garden in Memphis.

As I received my plastic grocery bag filled with unusually beautiful varieties of familiar garden favorites, I was shocked to see the small, furry, purple pods lining the bottom. That evening I went home and cooked almost my entire bag. They were the most tender and tasty okra I ever had (sorry, Grandma Sue), and an even more amazing thing happened—they turned green when I cooked them.

Well, I have rarely seen them at farmers' markets, but the good news is the seeds aren't hard to get your hands on. So if you or someone you know has a green thumb, grab a seed packet next summer and wait for the precious pods to sprout.

### Fry Green Tomatoes

1. Remove tomato core using a paring or small utility knife.

2. Slice tomatoes ⅓ inch thick. For added flavor, sprinkle both sides of each slice with salt and pepper; let stand 30 minutes, then continue with breading process.

3. After dipping tomato slices in flour and egg mixture, gently press each side into cornmeal mixture to coat.

4. Shallow-fry 4 to 5 breaded tomato slices at a time in a large cast-iron skillet. When the slices begin to foam slightly and a golden-brown color peeks out from the edges, the tomatoes are ready to flip. Use tongs or a sturdy dinner fork to turn tomatoes over. You'll know they're ready to come out of the oil when you see the same foam and golden-brown color around the edges.

# Fried Green Tomatoes

*(pictured on page 51)*

**Makes:** 6 servings    **Hands-on Time:** 30 min.    **Total Time:** 30 min.

  1  large egg, lightly beaten
  ½  cup buttermilk
  ½  cup self-rising cornmeal mix
  ½  tsp. salt
  ½  tsp. pepper
  ½  cup all-purpose flour
  3  medium-size, firm green tomatoes, cut into ⅓-inch-thick slices (about 1¼ lb.)
     Vegetable oil

**1.** Whisk together egg and buttermilk. Combine cornmeal mix, salt, pepper, and ¼ cup flour in a shallow dish. Dredge tomato slices in remaining ¼ cup flour; dip in egg mixture, and dredge in cornmeal mixture.

**2.** Pour oil to depth of ½ inch into a large cast-iron skillet; heat to 375° over medium-high heat. Drop tomatoes, in batches, into hot oil, and cook 2 minutes on each side or until golden. Drain on paper towels. Sprinkle hot tomatoes with salt to taste.

**STEP 1**

**STEP 2**

**STEP 3**

**STEP 4**

**TRY THIS TWIST!**

**Fried Green Tomatoes with Shrimp Rémoulade:** Place 2 to 3 Fried Green Tomatoes on individual serving plates. Top each with 1½ Tbsp. Rémoulade Sauce (page 245) and 3 medium-size, peeled, cooked shrimp. Garnish with fresh pea shoots or arugula, if desired.

# Hot-Water Cornbread

*Prepare this cornbread at the last minute so you can serve it piping hot.*

**Makes:** 8 patties    **Hands-on Time:** 21 min.    **Total Time:** 21 min.

 2  cups white cornmeal
 ¼  tsp. baking powder
 1¼ tsp. salt
 1  tsp. sugar
 ¼  cup half-and-half
 1  Tbsp. vegetable oil
 ¾  to 1¼ cups boiling water
    Vegetable oil

**1.** Combine cornmeal and next 3 ingredients in a bowl; stir in half-and-half and 1 Tbsp. oil. Gradually add boiling water, stirring until batter is the consistency of grits.

**2.** Pour oil to depth of ½ inch into a large heavy skillet; place over medium-high heat. Scoop batter into a ¼-cup measure; drop into hot oil, and fry, in batches, 3 minutes on each side or until golden. Drain well on paper towels. Serve immediately.

**Note:** Stone-ground (coarsely ground) cornmeal requires more liquid.

---

**TRY THESE TWISTS!**

**Country Ham Hot-Water Cornbread:** Stir in 1 to 2 cups finely chopped country ham after adding boiling water.

**Bacon-Cheddar Hot-Water Cornbread:** Stir in 8 slices cooked and crumbled bacon, 1 cup shredded sharp Cheddar cheese, and 4 minced green onions after adding boiling water.

**Southwestern Hot-Water Cornbread:** Stir in 1 seeded and minced jalapeño pepper; 1 cup Mexican cheese blend; 1 cup frozen whole kernel corn, thawed; and ¼ cup minced fresh cilantro after adding boiling water.

**Baked Hot-Water Cornbread:** Preheat oven to 475°. Omit skillet procedure. Pour ⅓ cup vegetable oil into a 15- x 10-inch jelly-roll pan, spreading to edges. Drop batter as directed onto pan. Bake for 12 to 15 minutes. Turn cakes, and bake 5 more minutes or until golden brown.

---

## NORM'S NOTE
### How I Learned to Make Hot-Water Cornbread

I learned to make hot water cornbread with my aunts. First, Aunt Harriet took the helm, and out came the 12-inch cast-iron skillet and all the other necessities. Her instruction: Make sure the water is at a hard boil before pouring it into the "meal," add the right pinch of salt, and stir in a tablespoon or two of finely chopped sweet onion into the mix. After the "meal" was fried, Aunt Harriet smiled and said, "That's how it's done, baby."

After her sister had left, Aunt Icelia came over to the stove and asked, "Do you really want to know how to make cornbread?" She added a tablespoon of bacon grease into the "meal" for flavor. She gave me visual cues as to when the oil was ready: "Look for the ribbons," she said. She demonstrated how to form the corn patties so that you have a crisp exterior and moist and fluffy interior, and pointed out when the patties were just the right shade of radiant golden brown. Easing the last morsels out of the oil, she placed them on neatly arranged paper towels to drain.

# Grannie's Cracklin' Cornbread

*This traditional Southern cornbread calls for just five ingredients.*

**Makes:** 8 to 10 servings    **Hands-on Time:** 10 min.    **Total Time:** 39 min.

¼  cup butter
2½  cups self-rising cornmeal mix
2½  cups buttermilk
2  large eggs, lightly beaten
1  cup cracklings*
   Softened butter

**1.** Preheat oven to 425°. Place butter in a 9-inch cast-iron skillet, and heat in a 425° oven 4 minutes.

**2.** Place cornmeal mix in a large bowl; make a well in center of mixture.

**3.** Stir together buttermilk, eggs, and cracklings; add to dry ingredients, stirring just until moistened. Pour over melted butter in hot skillet.

**4.** Bake at 425° for 25 to 30 minutes or until golden brown. Serve with softened butter.

*1 cup cooked, crumbled bacon (12 to 15 slices) may be substituted for cracklings.

---

**TRY THIS TWIST!**
**Grannie's Cracklin' Cakes:**
Prepare batter as directed at left; stir in ¼ cup butter, melted. Heat a large skillet coated with cooking spray over medium-high heat. Spoon about ¼ cup batter for each cake into skillet; cook, in batches, 2 to 3 minutes on each side or until golden.

# Shrimp and Okra Hush Puppies

*Creole seasoning, okra, and shrimp add a delightful Southern taste and texture to these addictive cornbread bites.*

**Makes:** 8 servings (about 2½ dozen)     **Hands-on Time:** 25 min.
**Total Time:** 30 min.

- 1 **cup self-rising yellow cornmeal mix**
- ½ **cup self-rising flour**
- 1 **cup peeled, medium-size raw shrimp, chopped**
- 1 **tsp. Creole seasoning**
- ½ **cup frozen diced onion, red and green bell pepper, and celery, thawed***
- ½ **cup frozen cut okra, thawed and chopped**
- 1 **large egg, lightly beaten**
- ¾ **cup beer**
  - **Canola oil**
  - **Garnish: lemon wedges**

**1.** Stir together cornmeal mix and flour in a large bowl until combined.

**2.** Sprinkle shrimp with Creole seasoning. Add shrimp, onion mixture, and okra to cornmeal mixture. Stir in egg and beer just until moistened. Let stand 5 to 7 minutes.

**3.** Pour oil to depth of 4 inches into a Dutch oven; heat to 350°. Drop batter by level tablespoonfuls into hot oil, and fry, in batches, 2 to 2½ minutes on each side or until golden brown. Drain on a wire rack over paper towels; serve immediately. Garnish, if desired.

**Note:** Keep fried hush puppies warm in a 225° oven for up to 15 minutes. We tested with McKenzie's Seasoning Blend for diced onion, red and green bell pepper, and celery.

## NORM'S NOTE
### Size It Right

A rough chop of the shrimp and okra works best for this recipe. Cutting each shrimp and okra pod into four to five pieces gives these "puppies" a bit more substance. Use a small ice cream scoop or large soup spoon to best portion out this thick batter, helping you to get a fair portion of okra and shrimp in each hush puppy.

# Crab Cake Hush Puppies

*This "hush puppy" is probably not a "hush puppy" in the traditional sense. Think of these fried critters as handheld crab cakes.*

**Makes:** about 32    **Hands-on Time:** 25 min.    **Total Time:** 35 min.

1   cup self-rising white cornmeal mix
½   cup self-rising flour
3   green onions, thinly sliced
½   cup finely chopped red bell pepper
1   Tbsp. sugar
¼   tsp. salt
8   oz. fresh lump crabmeat, drained and picked
1   large egg
¾   cup beer
    Vegetable oil
    Rémoulade Sauce (page 245)
    Mike's Cocktail Sauce (page 250)

Stir together cornmeal mix, flour, green onions, bell pepper, sugar, and salt in a large bowl. Stir in crabmeat, egg, and beer just until moistened. Let stand 10 minutes. Pour oil to depth of 2 inches into a Dutch oven; heat to 360°. Drop batter by tablespoonfuls into hot oil, and fry, in batches, 2 to 3 minutes or until golden brown, turning once. Serve with Rémoulade Sauce or Mike's Cocktail Sauce.

# Chicken-Fried Steak with Redeye Gravy

*Ground red pepper, hot sauce, and buttermilk punch up the flavor in this recipe. Serve alongside mashed potatoes.*

**Makes:** 4 servings    **Hands-on Time:** 45 min.    **Total Time:** 2 hr., 30 min., including gravy

- 4 (4-oz.) rib-eye steaks
- 3 cups all-purpose flour
- 1 tsp. baking powder
- ½ tsp. baking soda
- ¼ tsp. ground red pepper
- 2 large eggs
- 2 cups buttermilk
- ½ tsp. hot sauce
- 1 tsp. salt
- ¼ tsp. freshly ground black pepper
- 3 cups vegetable oil
- Redeye Gravy (page 250)

**1.** Place steaks between 2 sheets of heavy-duty plastic wrap, and flatten to ¼-inch thickness, using flat side of a meat mallet. Lightly pound steak, using textured side of meat mallet. Wrap tightly with plastic wrap, and chill 1 hour.

**2.** Combine flour and next 3 ingredients in a bowl. Whisk together eggs and next 2 ingredients in a separate bowl. Sprinkle both sides of steaks with salt and black pepper.

**3.** Dip steaks in egg mixture, and dredge in flour mixture, shaking off excess. Repeat procedure 2 more times.

**4.** Fry steaks, 1 at a time, in hot oil in a nonstick skillet over medium-high heat 4 to 6 minutes on each side or until golden. Drain on a wire rack in a jelly-roll pan. Serve with gravy.

# Easy Pork Grillades over Gouda Grits

*Any time is a perfect time for Grillades and Grits. They make a delicious and filling breakfast, lunch, or dinner.*

**Makes:** 6 servings    **Hands-on Time:** 55 min.    **Total Time:** 1 hr., 25 min., including grits

**Gouda Grits**

1¼ lb. boneless pork loin chops
¼ cup all-purpose flour
2 tsp. Old Bay seasoning
4 Tbsp. olive oil, divided
1 cup chopped celery
½ cup chopped green bell pepper
½ cup chopped red bell pepper
2 cups sliced baby portobello mushrooms
1 (14.5-oz.) can diced tomatoes with garlic and onion
½ cup low-sodium chicken broth
1½ tsp. chopped fresh or ½ tsp. dried thyme
¾ tsp. chopped fresh or ¼ tsp. dried oregano
¼ to ½ tsp. dried crushed red pepper
¼ tsp. salt

**1.** Prepare Gouda Grits; keep warm.

**2.** Trim fat from pork chops, and cut pork crosswise into thin strips. Combine flour and Old Bay seasoning; dredge pork in flour mixture.

**3.** Cook half of pork in 2 Tbsp. hot oil in a large skillet over medium-high heat 3 minutes on each side or until browned.

**4.** Repeat procedure with 1 Tbsp. oil and remaining pork. Remove pork from skillet.

**5.** Sauté celery and bell peppers in remaining 1 Tbsp. oil in skillet 30 seconds. Add mushrooms, and sauté 2 minutes. Add tomatoes and next 5 ingredients; cook over medium heat 5 minutes. Add pork; cover, reduce heat, and simmer 5 minutes. Serve over Gouda Grits.

*Gouda Grits*

**Makes:** 8 servings
**Hands-on Time:** 10 min.
**Total Time:** 30 min.

4 cups chicken broth
1 cup whipping cream
1 tsp. salt
¼ tsp. freshly ground pepper
2 cups uncooked quick-cooking grits
2 cups (8 oz.) shredded Gouda cheese
½ cup buttermilk
¼ cup butter
2 tsp. hot sauce

Bring first 4 ingredients and 4 cups water to a boil in a Dutch oven over high heat; whisk in grits, reduce heat to medium-low, and simmer, stirring occasionally, 15 minutes or until thickened. Remove from heat, and stir in Gouda and remaining ingredients.

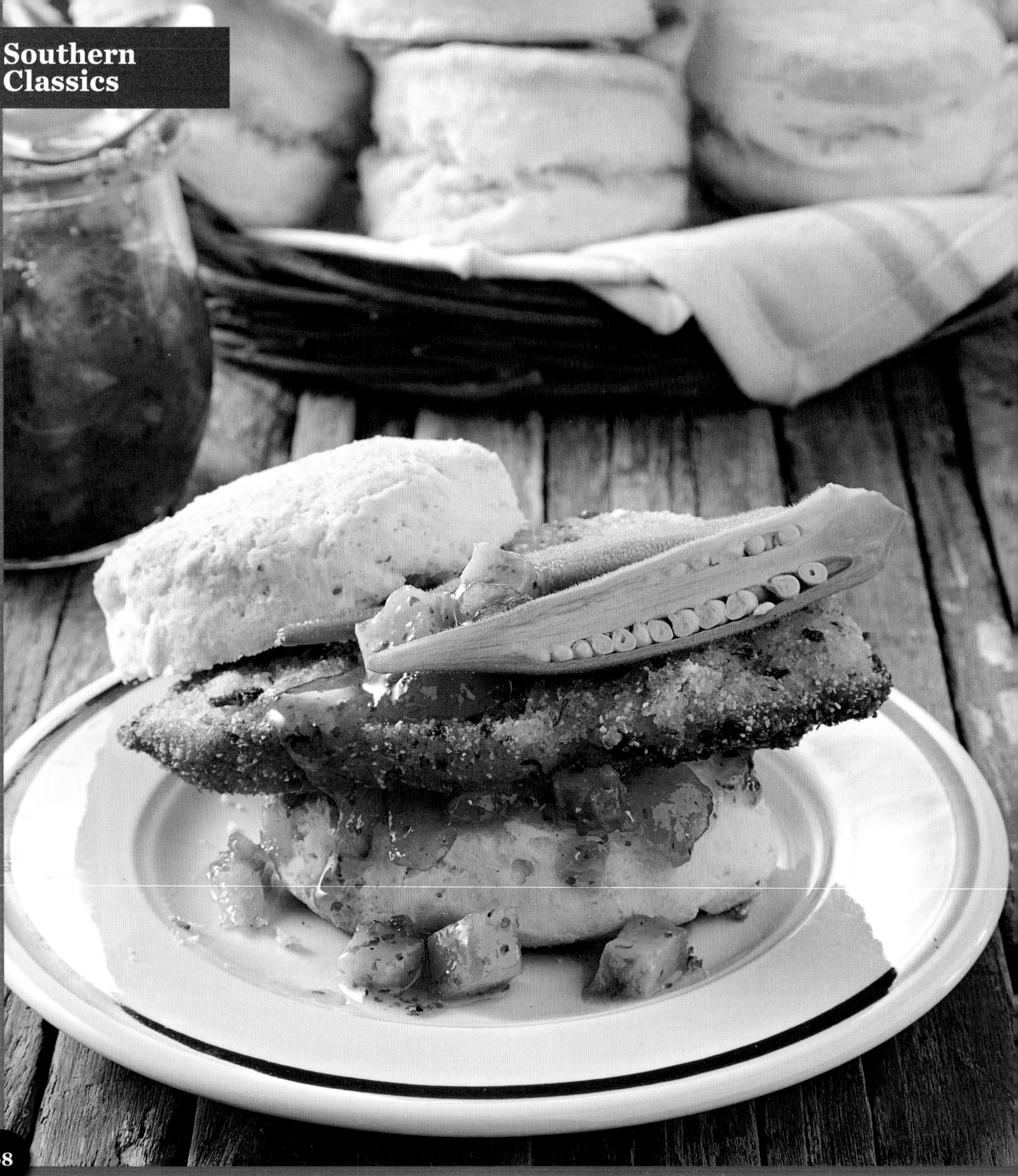

# Chicken Biscuit

**Makes:** 1 serving

- 1 **Crispy Chicken Cutlet**
  **Mustard-Peach Preserves**
  **(page 246)**
  **Pickled okra**
- 1 **Cornbread Biscuit**

Place Crispy Chicken Cutlet, Mustard-Peach Preserves, and pickled okra on a Cornbread Biscuit.

## Crispy Chicken Cutlets

*If your cutlets are thick, put them between sheets of plastic wrap, and flatten to ½ inch thick using a rolling pin.*

**Makes:** about 16 servings
**Hands-on Time:** 30 min.
**Total Time:** 8 hr., 30 min.

- 8 **(4-oz.) chicken breast cutlets, cut in half crosswise**
- 2 **cups dill pickle juice from jar**
- 2 **large eggs**
- ¾ **cup self-rising cornmeal mix**
- ¾ **cup fine, dry breadcrumbs**
- ¼ **cup finely chopped fresh parsley**
- 1 **tsp. pepper**
- ½ **tsp. salt**
- 1 **cup peanut oil**

**1.** Combine first 2 ingredients in a 1-gal. zip-top plastic freezer bag. Seal bag, pressing out most of air, and chill 8 hours.

**2.** Whisk together eggs and 3 Tbsp. water in a shallow bowl. Combine cornmeal mix and next 3 ingredients in a second shallow bowl. Remove chicken from marinade, discarding marinade; sprinkle chicken with salt. Dip chicken in egg mixture, and dredge in cornmeal mixture, pressing firmly to adhere.

**3.** Heat oil in a large nonstick skillet over medium-high heat. Add chicken, and cook, in batches, 2 to 3 minutes on each side or until done.

## Cornbread Biscuits

*Add your own signature spin with a few teaspoons of your favorite herb, such as thyme or rosemary.*

**Makes:** about 15 biscuits
**Hands-on Time:** 35 min.
**Total Time:** 58 min.

- 3 **cups self-rising soft-wheat flour**
- ½ **cup yellow self-rising cornmeal mix**
- ¼ **cup cold butter, cut into pieces**
- ¼ **cup shortening, cut into pieces**
- 1½ **cups buttermilk**
- 1 **tsp. yellow cornmeal**
- 2 **Tbsp. butter, melted**

**1.** Preheat oven to 500°. Whisk together first 2 ingredients in a large bowl. Cut in cold butter and shortening with a pastry blender or fork until mixture resembles small peas and dough is crumbly. Cover and chill 10 minutes. Add buttermilk, stirring just until dry ingredients are moistened.

**2.** Turn dough out onto a heavily floured surface; knead 3 or 4 times. Pat dough into a ¾-inch-thick circle.

**3.** Cut dough with a well-floured 2½-inch round cutter, rerolling scraps as needed. Sprinkle cornmeal on ungreased baking sheets; place biscuits on baking sheets. Lightly brush tops with 2 Tbsp. melted butter.

**4.** Bake at 500° for 13 to 15 minutes or until golden brown.

**Note:** We tested with White Lily Bleached Self-Rising Flour.

## Select the Best Fried Chicken

This recipe really is the best fried chicken recipe *Southern Living* has published—well, for now, anyway. We kept the ingredients simple but improved our technique. Brining the chicken overnight allows the salt to penetrate the meat, a quick tumble in plain flour keeps the crust light, and a shallow fry in a cast-iron skillet provides the ideal texture.

## MAKE IT A MEAL

Since we kept our fried chicken simple, make the meal complete with Browned-Butter Mashed Potatoes (page 156) and Green Beans with Caramelized Shallots (page 151). For a lighter option, serve alongside Lucky Black-eyed Pea Salad (page 152).

# Our Best Southern Fried Chicken

**Makes:** 4 servings  **Hands-on Time:** 55 min.  **Total Time:** 8 hr., 55 min.

- 1 **Tbsp. salt**
- 1 **(2- to 2½-lb.) cut-up whole chicken**
- 1 **tsp. salt**
- 1 **tsp. pepper**
- 1 **cup all-purpose flour**
- 2 **cups vegetable oil**
- ¼ **cup bacon drippings**
  **Garnish: oregano**

**1.** Combine 3 qt. water and 1 Tbsp. salt in a large bowl; add chicken. Cover and chill 8 hours. Drain chicken; rinse with cold water, and pat dry.

**2.** Combine 1 tsp. salt and pepper; sprinkle half of pepper mixture evenly over chicken. Combine remaining pepper mixture and flour in a large zip-top plastic freezer bag. Place 2 pieces of chicken in bag; seal. Shake to evenly coat. Remove chicken, and repeat procedure with remaining chicken, 2 pieces at a time.

**3.** Combine vegetable oil and bacon drippings in a 12-inch cast-iron skillet or chicken fryer; heat to 360°. Add chicken, a few pieces at a time, skin sides down. Cover and cook 6 minutes; uncover and cook 9 minutes.

**4.** Turn chicken pieces; cover and cook 6 minutes. Uncover and cook 5 to 9 minutes, turning pieces during last 3 minutes for even browning, if necessary. Drain on paper towels. Garnish, if desired

**Note:** For best results, keep the oil temperature between 300° to 325° as you fry the chicken. Also, you may substitute 2 cups buttermilk for the saltwater solution used to soak the chicken pieces. Proceed as directed.

## HOW TO:
### Fry Catfish

1. Thoroughly coat all fillets with a mixture of buttermilk and hot sauce. It adds a depth of flavor that the catfish soaks up.

2. Carefully remove each fillet from the buttermilk mixture using a long, wide spatula, allowing the excess mixture to drip off. This will prevent breading from becoming gummy.

3. Lay each fillet in prepared cornmeal mixture, gently pressing on each side. A light coating is all you need.

4. Fry no more than 3 fillets per batch. Remove fillets from oil using tongs, grasping in the center to prevent breaking.

# Classic Fried Catfish

*For an extra-crispy crust, use stone-ground yellow cornmeal. The secret to this recipe is maintaining an oil temperature of 360° for a crispy, golden crust.*

**Makes:** 6 to 8 servings   **Hands-on Time:** 20 min.   **Total Time:** 8 hr., 30 min.

1½  cups buttermilk
¼   tsp. hot sauce
6   (4- to 6-oz.) catfish fillets
⅓   cup plain yellow cornmeal
⅓   cup masa harina (corn flour)*
⅓   cup all-purpose flour
2   tsp. salt
1   tsp. ground black pepper
1   tsp. ground red pepper
¼   tsp. garlic powder
    Peanut oil
    Garnish: lemon slices

**1.** Whisk together buttermilk and hot sauce. Place catfish in a single layer in a 13- x 9-inch baking dish; pour buttermilk mixture over fish. Cover and chill 8 hours, turning once.

**2.** Combine cornmeal and next 6 ingredients in a shallow dish.

**3.** Let fish stand at room temperature 10 minutes. Remove from buttermilk mixture, allowing excess to drip off. Dredge fish in cornmeal mixture, shaking off excess.

**4.** Pour oil to depth of 2 inches into a large, deep cast-iron or heavy-duty skillet; heat to 360°.

**5.** Fry fish, in batches, 2 minutes on each side or until golden brown. Transfer to a wire rack on a paper towel-lined jelly-roll pan. Keep warm in a 225° oven until ready to serve. Garnish, if desired. Serve with your favorite tartar sauce.

*All-purpose flour or plain yellow cornmeal may be substituted.

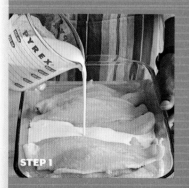

**STEP 1**

**STEP 2**

**STEP 3**

**STEP 4**

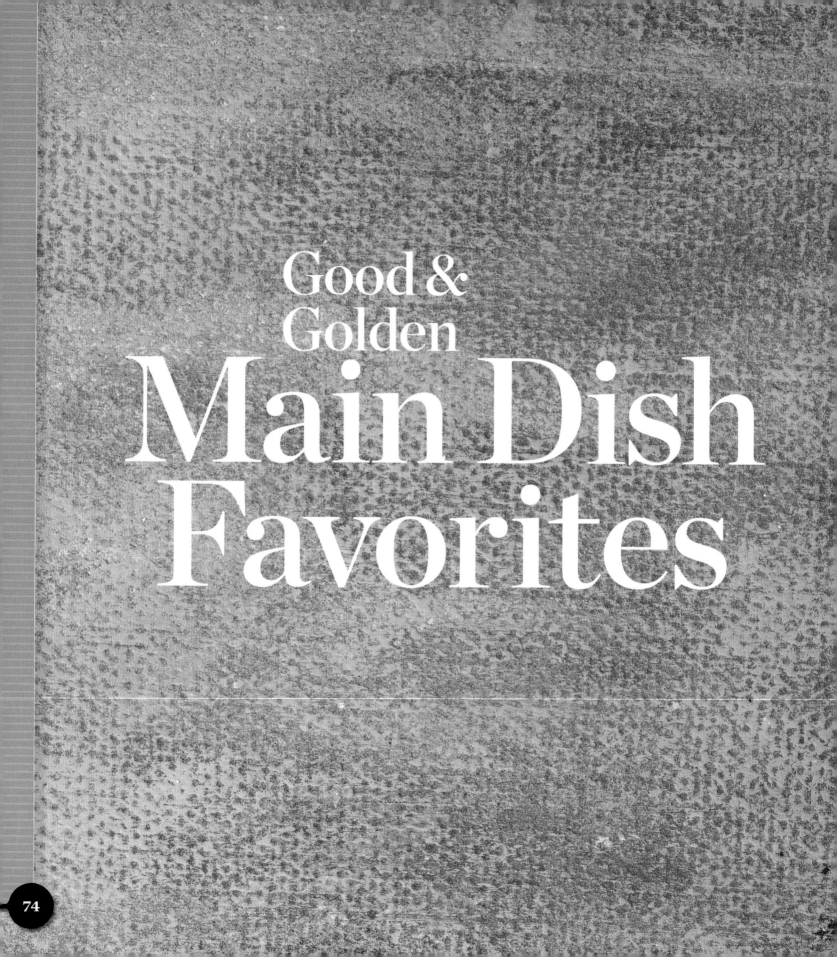

# Good & Golden
# Main Dish Favorites

Cajun-Seasoned
Pan-Fried
Pork Chops,
*page 86*

# Fried Okra Tacos

Tortillas
Shredded lettuce
Buttermilk Fried Okra
Fresh Tomato Salsa
Hot sauce

Fill warm tortillas with shredded lettuce, hot Buttermilk Fried Okra, and Fresh Tomato Salsa. Serve with hot sauce.

## Buttermilk Fried Okra

*A sprinkling of sugar in the cornmeal coating caramelizes as the okra cooks, creating a crisp, golden crust.*

**Makes:** 8 cups
**Hands-on Time:** 30 min.
**Total Time:** 30 min.

- 1  lb. fresh okra, cut into ½-inch-thick slices
- ¾  cup buttermilk
- 1½ cups self-rising white cornmeal mix
- 1  tsp. salt
- 1  tsp. sugar
- ¼  tsp. ground red pepper
     Vegetable oil

**1.** Stir together okra and buttermilk in a large bowl. Stir together cornmeal mix and next 3 ingredients in a separate large bowl. Remove okra from buttermilk, in batches, using a slotted spoon, discarding buttermilk. Dredge in cornmeal mixture, and place in a wire-mesh strainer. Shake off excess.

**2.** Pour oil to depth of 1 inch into a large, deep cast-iron skillet or Dutch oven; heat to 375°. Fry okra, in batches, 4 minutes or until golden, turning once. Drain on paper towels.

## Fresh Tomato Salsa

**Makes:** about 5 cups
**Hands-on Time:** 15 min.
**Total Time:** 15 min.

- 3  cups seeded and diced tomatoes (about 1½ lb.)
- 1  large avocado, diced
- 1  small green bell pepper, diced
- ½  cup chopped green onions
- ⅓  cup chopped fresh cilantro
- 1½ tsp. balsamic vinegar
- ½  tsp. seasoned salt
     Table salt to taste

Stir together diced tomatoes and next 6 ingredients. Season with table salt to taste.

# Fried Green Tomato Po'boys

*After splitting each baguette, try spreading a layer of mayonnaise or softened butter on the cut sides, then slide underneath the broiler for a moment.*

French bread baguettes
Rémoulade Sauce (page 245)
Shredded lettuce
Fried Green Tomatoes (page 54)
Cooked bacon
Avocado slices

Cut baguettes into 6-inch lengths. Split each lengthwise, cutting to but not through the other side; spread with Rémoulade Sauce. Layer with lettuce, Fried Green Tomatoes, bacon, and avocado.

## NORM'S NOTE
### Try My Salty Secret

Lightly salt both sides of the eggplant with a teaspoon or so of kosher salt, and let it stand 15 minutes to help draw out moisture from the eggplant slices. Less moisture before frying means a reduced chance of getting soggy, spongy, or oily fried eggplant slices and increases the chance of getting crisp, meaty ones. Be sure to pat both sides with paper towels after the stand time to soak up excess moisture, and then proceed with the recipe as directed.

# Crispy Eggplant with Tomatoes and Mozzarella

*Use smaller eggplants, which are less bitter. Look for eggplants with a small, round dimple versus the deep, long groove in the bottom.*

**Makes:** 8 servings    **Hands-on Time:** 36 min.    **Total Time:** 36 min.

- 3  large eggs
- 3  medium tomatoes
- 1  small eggplant, cut into ¼-inch-thick rounds (about 1 lb.)
- 2  cups crushed tortilla chips
- 1  cup vegetable oil
    Salt and pepper to taste
- 1  (8-oz.) package fresh mozzarella cheese, cut into 8 (¼-inch-thick) rounds
- ¼  cup firmly packed fresh basil leaves, torn
    Balsamic vinegar

**1.** Whisk together eggs and 1 Tbsp. water until blended.

**2.** Cut tomatoes into 16 (⅛-inch-thick) slices. Place tomatoes in a single layer on paper towels.

**3.** Dredge eggplant in ½ cup crushed tortilla chips; dip in egg mixture, and dredge in remaining 1½ cups crushed tortilla chips.

**4.** Cook eggplant, in batches, in hot oil in a 10-inch (3-inch-deep) skillet over medium heat 3 to 4 minutes on each side or until golden brown. Place on a wire rack, and sprinkle with salt and pepper to taste.

**5.** Cut cheese rounds in half. Arrange eggplant, cheese, and tomatoes on a serving platter; sprinkle with basil, and drizzle with balsamic vinegar. Sprinkle with salt and pepper to taste.

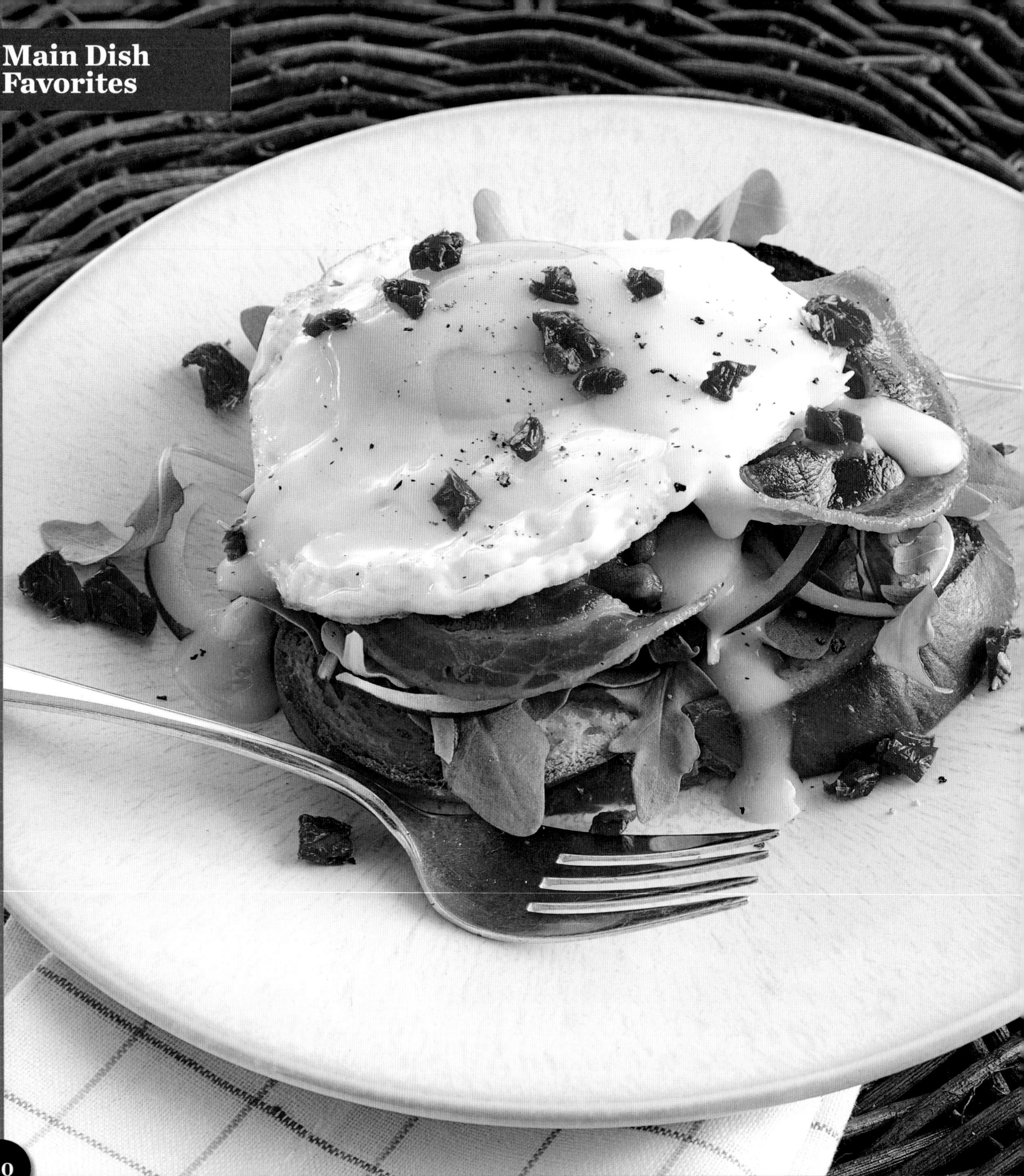

# Fried Egg Sandwiches

*A nonstick skillet or well-seasoned cast-iron skillet is vital to making flawless fried eggs. Keep the heat an even medium, and give the skillet a little shake here and there to make sure the eggs are not sticking. Gently turn eggs over with a spatula and continue cooking, shaking the pan every so often.*

**Makes:** 4 servings  **Hands-on Time:** 25 min.  **Total Time:** 27 min.

- 4  (½-inch-thick) challah bread slices
- 2  Tbsp. butter, melted
- 1  (0.9-oz.) envelope hollandaise sauce mix
- ¼  tsp. lemon zest
- 1½  tsp. fresh lemon juice, divided
- 2  cups loosely packed arugula
- ½  cup loosely packed fresh flat-leaf parsley leaves
- ¼  cup thinly sliced red onion
- 3  tsp. extra virgin olive oil, divided
- 4  large eggs
- ¼  tsp. kosher salt
- ¼  tsp. freshly ground pepper
- 12  thin pancetta slices, cooked
- 2  Tbsp. chopped sun-dried tomatoes

**1.** Preheat broiler with oven rack 5 to 6 inches from heat. Brush both sides of bread with butter; place on an aluminum foil-lined broiler pan. Broil 1 to 2 minutes on each side or until lightly toasted.

**2.** Prepare hollandaise sauce according to package directions; stir in zest and ½ tsp. lemon juice. Keep warm.

**3.** Toss together arugula, next 2 ingredients, 2 tsp. olive oil, and remaining 1 tsp. lemon juice.

**4.** Heat remaining 1 tsp. olive oil in a large nonstick skillet over medium heat. Gently break eggs into hot skillet; sprinkle with salt and pepper. Cook 2 to 3 minutes on each side or to desired degree of doneness.

**5.** Top bread slices with arugula mixture, pancetta slices, and fried eggs. Spoon hollandaise sauce over each egg, and sprinkle with tomatoes. Serve immediately.

## NORM'S NOTE
### Serve This Sandwich Any Time

Fried Egg Sandwiches are my go-to recipe for a quick and easy meal. I've made them for breakfast, brunch, lunch, dinner, and even for very late-night nibbles with friends. They contain all the elements of a great meal in a manageable portion size. I love the fact that these sandwiches are open-faced and require a knife and fork; that way I feel a bit more civilized when eating them at 2 o'clock in the morning with a glass of Champagne. Hey, fried eggs and Champagne know no seasons at my house.

## MAKE IT A MEAL

Serve this true Southern icon with roasted and seasoned butternut squash and mixed salad greens. If you need a sweet ending for your meal, serve the Peanut Butter-Banana Icebox Pie (page 211).

# Tyler's Country-Fried Steak with Uncle Ellis' Cornmeal Gravy

*This down-home classic came to us from Tyler Brown of the Capitol Grille in Nashville, Tennessee. The restaurant's chef de cuisine grew up in Cleveland, Mississippi, and the cornmeal gravy is inspired by something he enjoyed as a child.*

**Makes:** 6 servings   **Hands-on Time:** 15 min.   **Total Time:** 1 hr., 5 min.

- 6 (6-oz.) top sirloin steaks, cubed
- 1 tsp. kosher salt
- ¼ tsp. freshly ground pepper
- 3 cups all-purpose flour
- 1½ cups finely crushed round buttery crackers
- 6 Tbsp. chopped fresh marjoram
- 3 large eggs
- 2 cups buttermilk
  Vegetable oil
  Uncle Ellis' Cornmeal Gravy (page 250)
  Garnishes: fresh thyme leaves, freshly ground pepper

**1.** Sprinkle cubed steaks with salt and pepper. Combine flour, crackers, and marjoram in a shallow dish. Whisk eggs and buttermilk in a bowl.

**2.** Dip steaks in egg mixture; dredge in cracker mixture. Repeat procedure.

**3.** Pour oil to depth of 1½ inches into a large heavy skillet. Heat to 325°. Fry steaks, in batches, 5 to 7 minutes on each side or until golden. Drain on a wire rack in a jelly-roll pan. Serve with gravy. Garnish, if desired.

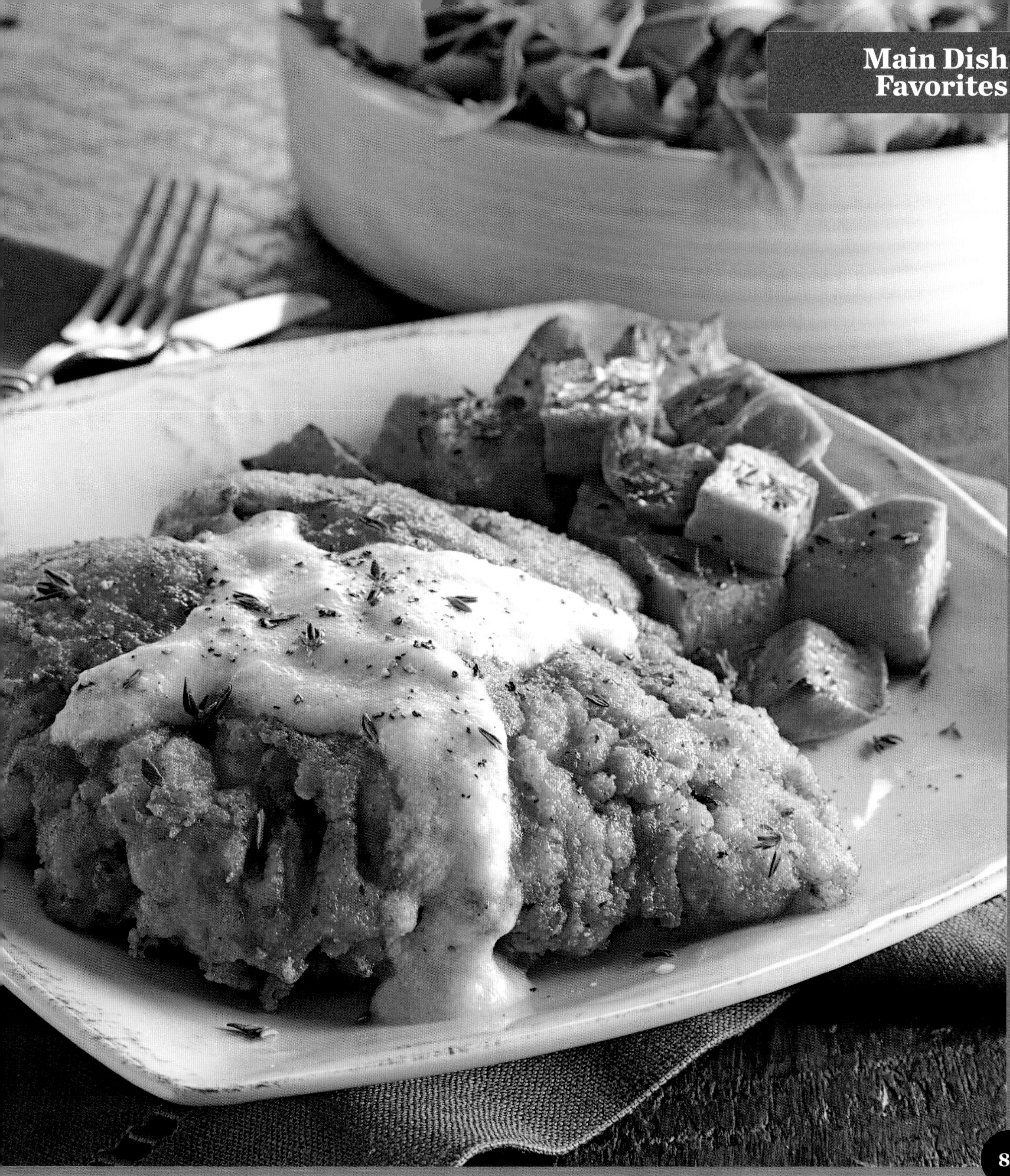

# Taquitos with Pork Picadillo

*I like to fry with flour tortillas rather than corn. I find them easier to fill, roll, and secure; plus they tend to fry up a bit more airy and crisp than their corn cousins.*

**Makes:** 6 to 8 servings   **Hands-on Time:** 15 min.   **Total Time:** 33 min.

12 **(6-inch) flour tortillas**
1 **lb. chopped cooked pork***
2 **Tbsp. vegetable oil, divided**
1 **medium onion, chopped**
4 **garlic cloves, minced**
3 **jalapeño peppers, seeded and chopped**
¼ **cup tomato paste**
¼ **cup red wine vinegar**
1 **tsp. pepper**
½ **tsp. salt**
¼ **cup chopped fresh cilantro**
1 **cup (4 oz.) shredded Monterey Jack cheese**
**Vegetable oil**
**Toppings: shredded lettuce, salsa, cilantro, finely chopped red onion**

**1.** Heat tortillas according to package directions. Cut tortillas into circles with a 3-inch cutter. Put tortilla circles on a plate, and cover with a towel; set aside.

**2.** Cook pork in a large nonstick skillet in 1 Tbsp. hot vegetable oil over medium heat 5 minutes or until lightly browned, stirring constantly. Remove pork from pan, and drain on paper towels. Wipe skillet clean.

**3.** Sauté onion, garlic, and peppers in remaining 1 Tbsp. hot oil over medium-high heat 3 to 4 minutes or until onion is tender. Stir in pork, tomato paste, vinegar, pepper, and salt; cook, stirring occasionally, 2 to 3 minutes. Remove from heat, and stir in cilantro.

**4.** Spoon 2 Tbsp. pork mixture down center of each tortilla circle; top evenly with cheese. Roll up, and secure with a wooden pick.

**5.** Pour vegetable oil to depth of 1½ inches into a large heavy skillet. Fry taquitos, in batches, in hot oil (350°) over medium-high heat 1 to 2 minutes or until golden brown. Remove wooden picks, and serve immediately. Serve with desired toppings.

*1 lb. chopped or shredded pork (without sauce) from your favorite barbecue restaurant can be used.

# Cajun-Seasoned Pan-Fried Pork Chops

*(pictured on page 75)*

___

*Cajun seasoning adds a bit of zip to the breading of this Southern specialty.*

**Makes:** 4 servings   **Hands-on Time:** 26 min.   **Total Time:** 26 min.

- 4  (8-oz.) bone-in center-cut pork chops
- 1½  tsp. Cajun seasoning*
- 3  Tbsp. self-rising flour
- ½  cup plain yellow cornmeal
- 1  Tbsp. butter
- 2  Tbsp. olive oil
-   Lemon (optional)
-   Garnishes: fresh parsley leaves, lemon wedges

**1.** Sprinkle pork chops with 1 tsp. seasoning. Combine flour, cornmeal, and remaining ½ tsp. seasoning. Dredge pork chops in cornmeal mixture, shaking off excess.

**2.** Melt butter with oil in a large skillet over medium-high heat; add pork chops, and cook 8 to 10 minutes on each side or until done. Squeeze juice from lemon over pork chops, and garnish, if desired. Serve immediately.

*Creole seasoning may be substituted.

# Sage-and-Pecan Pork Tenderloin Cutlets

**Makes:** 4 servings  **Hands-on Time:** 35 min.  **Total Time:** 51 min.

- 1 cup red wine vinegar
- 5 Tbsp. seedless blackberry preserves
- ½ tsp. salt
- 1 lb. pork tenderloin
- ¾ cup fine, dry breadcrumbs
- ½ cup finely chopped pecans
- 2 tsp. rubbed sage
- 2 large eggs, beaten
- 4 tsp. olive oil
  **Garnish: fresh blackberries**

**1.** Bring vinegar to a boil in a small saucepan over medium-high heat. Reduce heat to medium, and cook 6 minutes or until reduced by half. Stir in preserves, and cook 5 minutes. Stir in salt.

**2.** Remove silver skin from tenderloin, leaving a thin layer of fat. Cut pork into 8 slices. Place pork between 2 sheets of plastic wrap, and flatten to ¼-inch thickness, using a rolling pin or flat side of a meat mallet.

**3.** Stir together breadcrumbs, pecans, and sage in a shallow bowl.

**4.** Dredge pork in breadcrumb mixture, dip in beaten eggs, and dredge again in breadcrumb mixture.

**5.** Cook 4 pork slices in 2 tsp. hot oil in a large nonstick skillet over medium heat 8 minutes or until done, turning every 2 minutes. Repeat procedure with remaining pork and oil. Serve with vinegar mixture, and garnish, if desired.

## HOW TO:
### Pan-Fry Pork Cutlets

**1.** Remove silver skin by gently piercing just underneath the silver skin with a paring knife and carefully dragging the knife under the surface of the silver skin, making sure not to remove much of the meat.

**2.** Cut tenderloin into 8 slices, about 1 inch thick. Gently flatten each slice between 2 sheets of plastic wrap using a rolling pin, the flat side of a meat mallet, or a heavy-bottom skillet.

**3.** "Double dredge" the flattened pork slices by coating in breadcrumb mixture, dipping in beaten eggs, and finally coating once more in breadcrumb mixture. The "double dredge" ensures the slices have a thick crust.

**4.** When pan-frying the pork slices, turn them often (about every 2 minutes) to prevent pecans from becoming overly toasted and bitter.

STEP 1

STEP 2

STEP 3

STEP 4

# Buttermilk Fried Chicken

*Soaking the chicken overnight in buttermilk keeps it extra tender and juicy. The pieces quickly brown in a skillet and then get a fuss-free finish in the oven. Hot baked biscuits are the ideal partner for Buttermilk Fried Chicken. Make sure those fluffy gems get a coat of melted butter on the tops right out of the oven.*

**Makes:** 4 servings  **Hands-on Time:** 40 min.  **Total Time:** 9 hr., 10 min.

1 **(3¾-lb.) cut-up whole chicken**
3 **cups buttermilk**
2 **tsp. salt**
2 **tsp. pepper**
2 **cups all-purpose flour**
  **Vegetable oil**
  **Peanut oil**

**1.** Combine chicken and buttermilk in a large nonmetal bowl; cover and chill 8 to 12 hours. Drain chicken, discarding buttermilk.

**2.** Preheat oven to 350°. Combine salt and pepper; sprinkle half of salt mixture over chicken. Combine remaining salt mixture and flour in a large zip-top plastic freezer bag.

**3.** Place 2 pieces of chicken in bag; seal bag, and shake to coat. Remove chicken. Repeat procedure with remaining chicken.

**4.** Pour oil to depth of ¼ inch into a large skillet. Fry chicken pieces, in 2 batches, in hot oil over medium-high heat 5 to 6 minutes on each side or until browned. Place chicken on a wire rack in a jelly-roll pan. Bake at 350° for 30 minutes or until done.

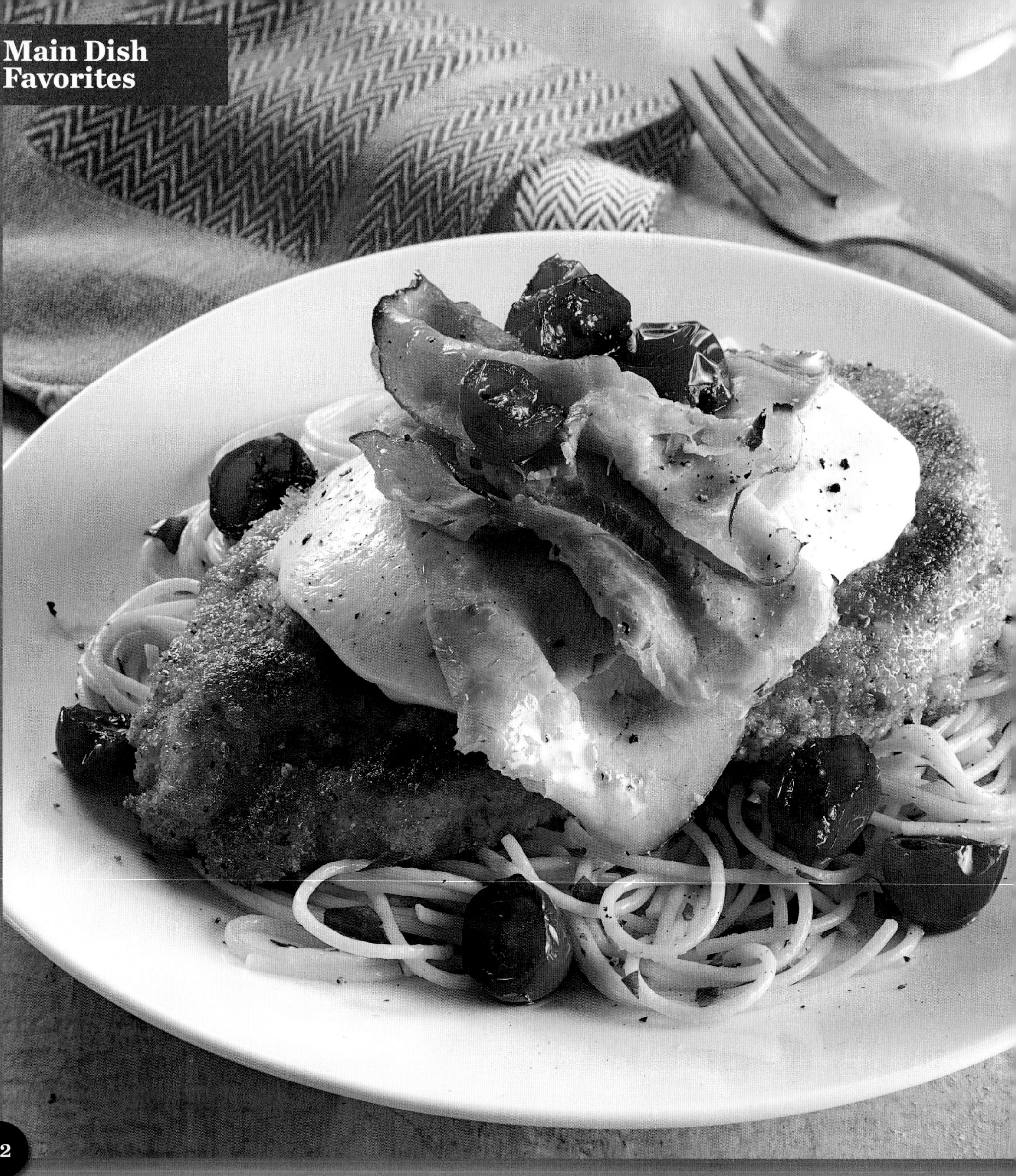

# Pan-Fried Chicken-and-Ham Parmesan

**Makes:** 4 servings    **Hands-on Time:** 18 min.

**Total Time:** 1 hr., 9 min., including pasta and tomatoes

- 4  **(6-oz.) skinned and boned chicken breasts**
- 1  **tsp. salt**
- ½  **tsp. pepper**
- 1  **large egg**
- ¼  **cup all-purpose flour**
- ⅔  **cup Italian-seasoned breadcrumbs**
- 2  **Tbsp. olive oil**
- 4  **(1-oz.) fresh mozzarella cheese slices**
- 8  **thinly sliced smoked deli ham slices (about ¼ lb.)**
  **Garlic-Herb Pasta**
  **Sautéed Grape Tomatoes**
  **Garnish: freshly ground pepper**

**1.** Preheat oven to 350°. Sprinkle chicken with salt and pepper. Whisk together egg and 2 Tbsp. water. Dredge chicken in flour; dip in egg mixture, and dredge in breadcrumbs, shaking off excess.

**2.** Cook chicken in hot oil in a large oven-proof skillet over medium-high heat 3 to 4 minutes on each side or until golden. Top chicken with cheese and ham.

**3.** Bake chicken in skillet at 350° for 8 minutes or until cheese is melted. Serve over Garlic-Herb Pasta; top with Sautéed Grape Tomatoes. Sprinkle with freshly ground pepper.

### Garlic-Herb Pasta:

Cook 8 oz. vermicelli according to package directions; drain. Toss with ¼ cup Garlic-Herb Butter. Season with salt to taste. Makes: 4 servings. Hands-on Time: 5 min.; Total Time: 15 min.

### Garlic-Herb Butter:

Stir together ½ cup softened butter; 1 large garlic clove, pressed; ⅔ cup chopped fresh basil; ¼ cup chopped fresh parsley; and ¼ tsp. salt until well blended. Use immediately, or cover and chill up to 3 days. For longer storage, form into a log or press into ice cube trays, and wrap tightly with plastic wrap; freeze up to 1 month. Makes: ½ cup. Hands-on Time: 15 min.; Total Time: 15 min.

### Sautéed Grape Tomatoes:

Sauté 1 pt. grape tomatoes, halved; 1 Tbsp. light brown sugar; 3 Tbsp. balsamic vinegar; and ¼ tsp. salt in 1 tsp. olive oil in a small skillet over medium-high heat 2 to 3 minutes or until thoroughly heated. Remove from heat, and stir in 2 Tbsp. thinly sliced fresh basil. Makes: 4 servings. Hands-on Time: 13 min.; Total Time: 13 min.

## MAKE IT A MEAL

When serving a rich recipe that includes a hearty starch like Pan-Fried Chicken-and-Ham Parmesan, I organize my meal so that I can have something light and refreshing at the beginning and end to get the full flavor of the main dish. Start the meal with sliced English cucumber, thinly sliced red onion and celery, parsley leaves, and shaved Parmesan, tossed with a splash of Champagne vinegar and a wisp of extra virgin olive oil. Then have your fill of the main dish, and finish with Citrus-Walnut Salad on page 176 to cleanse your palate before dessert and coffee.

# Fried Chicken Thighs and Biscuits

*Drizzling chicken thighs with honey while warm and topping with chopped pickled green tomatoes enhances the flavor of the tender biscuit and crunchy chicken, adding a touch of sweetness and zesty tang.*

**Makes:** 8 servings    **Hands-on Time:** 40 min.    **Total Time:** 1 hr., 5 min.

**Fried Chicken Thighs**

- 8 skinned and boned chicken thighs (about 2¼ lb.)
- 1 tsp. salt
- ½ tsp. pepper
- ⅛ tsp. onion powder
- 1 cup buttermilk
- 1 large egg
  Vegetable oil
- 2 cups all-purpose flour

**Biscuits**

- 2 cups bread flour
- 2 cups all-purpose flour
- 2 Tbsp. baking powder
- 2 Tbsp. sugar
- 1 tsp. salt
- 1 cup butter, cut into small cubes
- 1½ cups buttermilk
- 1 large egg
  Parchment paper

**Toppings**

  Chopped pickled green tomatoes, honey

**1.** Prepare Chicken: Sprinkle chicken thighs with salt and next 2 ingredients. Whisk together 1 cup buttermilk and 1 egg in a large bowl; add chicken, tossing to coat.

**2.** Pour oil to depth of 1 inch into a large cast-iron skillet; heat to 325°. Place flour in a shallow dish; dredge chicken in flour, shaking off excess. Fry chicken, in 2 batches, 5 to 6 minutes on each side or until golden brown and done. Drain on a wire rack over paper towels, and keep warm.

**3.** Prepare Biscuits: Combine bread flour and next 4 ingredients in a large bowl. Place cubed butter in a zip-top plastic freezer bag. Freeze flour mixture and butter separately 10 minutes or until well chilled. Whisk together 1½ cups buttermilk and 1 egg in a small bowl.

**4.** Cut chilled butter into flour mixture with a pastry blender or fork until crumbly. Add buttermilk mixture, stirring just until dry ingredients are moistened.

**5.** Preheat oven to 450°. Turn dough out onto a lightly floured surface, and knead lightly 3 to 4 times. Pat or roll dough to 1-inch thickness; cut into 8 squares, and place on a parchment paper-lined baking sheet.

**6.** Bake at 450° for 15 to 16 minutes or until golden brown. Split biscuits; fill each with 1 cooked chicken thigh and desired toppings.

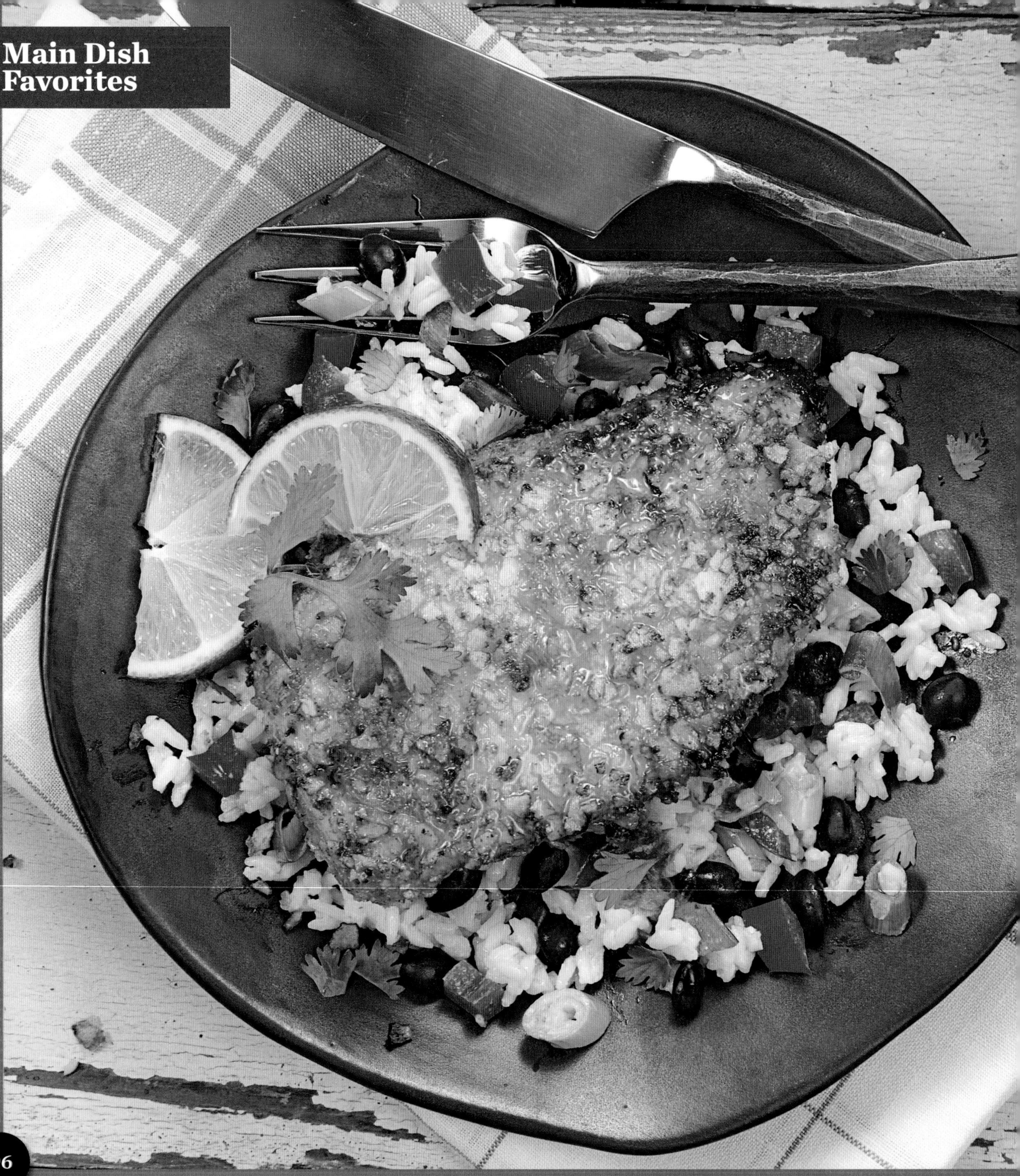

# Honey-Lime Chicken with Coconut-Black Bean Rice

*For a quick Caribbean-style dessert to go with your meal, pick up a package of frozen sweet plantains and ice cream. Quickly heat the plantains in the microwave, and top with a couple of scoops of ice cream.*

**Makes:** 6 servings
**Hands-on Time:** 35 min.
**Total Time:** 35 min.

  1  **(13.5-oz.) can coconut milk**
1½  **tsp. salt, divided**
  1  **cup uncooked long-grain rice**
  6  **(4-oz.) chicken breast cutlets**
¼  **tsp. freshly ground pepper**
¾  **cup finely crushed tortilla chips**
¼  **cup honey**
  1  **tsp. lime zest**
⅓  **cup fresh lime juice**
¼  **cup extra virgin olive oil**
  1  **(15.5-oz.) can seasoned black beans, drained and rinsed**

½  **cup chopped red bell pepper**
⅓  **cup sliced green onions**
¼  **cup chopped fresh cilantro**
    **Garnishes: lime slices, fresh cilantro sprigs**

**1.** Bring coconut milk and 1 tsp. salt to a boil over medium-high heat; stir in rice. Cover, reduce heat to low, and simmer 20 minutes or until rice is tender.

**2.** Meanwhile, sprinkle chicken with pepper and remaining ½ tsp. salt. Place crushed tortilla chips in a shallow bowl. Whisk together honey and next 2 ingredients in a second shallow bowl. Reserve 2 Tbsp. honey mixture. Dip chicken in remaining honey mixture, allowing excess to drip off. Dredge in crushed chips.

**3.** Cook half of chicken in 2 Tbsp. hot oil in a large nonstick skillet over medium-high heat 2 minutes on each side or until done. Repeat procedure with remaining chicken and oil. Spoon reserved honey mixture over chicken.

**4.** Stir black beans and next 2 ingredients into rice; spoon onto serving plates. Top with chicken and cilantro. Garnish, if desired.

# Chicken Parmesan Pizza

**Makes:** 4 servings
**Hands-on Time:** 4 min.
**Total Time:** 20 min.

  1  **(10-oz.) package frozen garlic bread loaf**
½  **cup canned pizza sauce**
  6  **deli fried chicken strips**
  1  **cup (4 oz.) shredded Italian three-cheese blend**
  2  **Tbsp. chopped fresh parsley**

**1.** Preheat oven to 400°. Arrange garlic bread, buttered sides up, on a baking sheet. Bake at 400° for 8 to 9 minutes or until bread is lightly browned. Spread pizza sauce over garlic bread.

**2.** Cut chicken strips into ½-inch pieces, and arrange over pizza sauce. Sprinkle with cheese and parsley.

**3.** Bake at 400° for 8 to 10 minutes or until cheese melts. Serve immediately.

# Pecan-Crusted Chicken and Tortellini with Herbed Butter Sauce

*As this recipe already comes with a starchy side, cook up a skillet of Pan-Fried Okra, Onion, and Tomatoes (page 115) to complete the meal.*

**Makes:** 4 servings    **Hands-on Time:** 30 min.    **Total Time:** 30 min.

- 2 (9-oz.) packages refrigerated cheese-filled tortellini
- 4 (4-oz.) chicken breast cutlets
- ½ tsp. salt
- ¼ tsp. freshly ground pepper
- ¾ cup finely chopped pecans
- 1 large egg, lightly beaten
- 3 Tbsp. olive oil
- ½ cup butter
- 3 garlic cloves, thinly sliced
- 3 Tbsp. chopped fresh basil
- 3 Tbsp. chopped fresh parsley
- ¼ cup (1 oz.) shredded Parmesan cheese

**1.** Prepare tortellini according to package directions.

**2.** Meanwhile, sprinkle chicken with salt and pepper. Place pecans in a shallow bowl. Place egg in a second bowl. Dip chicken in egg, allowing excess to drip off. Dredge chicken in pecans, pressing firmly to adhere.

**3.** Cook chicken in hot oil in a large nonstick skillet over medium-high heat 2 minutes on each side or until done. Remove from skillet; wipe skillet clean.

**4.** Melt butter in skillet over medium heat. Add garlic, and sauté 5 to 7 minutes or until garlic is caramel colored and butter begins to turn golden brown. Immediately remove from heat, and stir in basil, parsley, and hot cooked tortellini. Sprinkle with cheese. Serve immediately with chicken.

# Turkey Piccata

*Pull out your largest nonstick skillet for this recipe. (An electric one would be great.) Don't crowd the pan, and add each turkey cutlet slowly so temperature will stay hot.*

**Makes:** 4 to 6 servings    **Hands-on Time:** 30 min.    **Total Time:** 30 min.

- 1  lb. boneless turkey breast cutlets*
- ½  cup all-purpose flour
- 1  tsp. salt
- 1  tsp. white pepper
- 3  Tbsp. butter, divided
- 2  Tbsp. olive oil
- ½  cup dry white wine
- ⅓  cup fresh lemon juice
- 1  Tbsp. drained capers
- 6  lemon slices
- 1  Tbsp. chopped fresh flat-leaf parsley

**1.** Place turkey between 2 sheets of heavy-duty plastic wrap, and flatten to ¼-inch thickness, using a rolling pin or the flat side of a meat mallet.

**2.** Combine flour, salt, and pepper in a shallow dish. Dredge turkey cutlets in flour mixture.

**3.** Melt 1 Tbsp. butter in 1 Tbsp. olive oil in a large nonstick skillet over medium-high heat. Add half of turkey, and cook 2 to 3 minutes on each side or until golden brown. Remove turkey from skillet, and place on a wire rack in a jelly-roll pan in a 200° oven to keep warm. Repeat with remaining turkey, 1 Tbsp. butter, and 1 Tbsp. oil as needed.

**4.** Stir wine and next 3 ingredients into skillet, and cook over medium-high heat 2 minutes or until sauce is slightly thickened. Remove from heat; stir in remaining 1 Tbsp. butter. Place turkey on a serving platter; pour sauce over turkey, and sprinkle evenly with parsley.

*1 lb. boneless, skinless chicken thighs or thin-cut boneless pork chops may be substituted.

## MAKE IT A MEAL

I love serving Turkey Piccata over roasted fingerling potato halves. To make them, toss together 1 (24-oz.) bag fingerling potatoes, halved; 1 garlic clove, pressed; a couple of table-spoons of extra virgin olive oil; and a heavy pinch of kosher salt and freshly ground pepper on a 15- x 10-inch jelly-roll pan. Bake potatoes at 400°, stirring occasionally, 45 minutes or until tender and golden brown. I generally skip greens or a salad because I want to savor the flavor of the sauce and the heavenly texture of the pan-seared meat. However, if I want something green to go with the piccata, I'll toss in an 8-oz. package of trimmed fresh French green beans (haricots verts) with the potatoes during the final 15 minutes of bake time.

# Two-Alarm Deep-Fried Turkey

*You'll need about 3 to 4 gallons of oil to completely submerge your turkey. Make sure you don't overfill your turkey fryer.*

**Makes:** 10 to 12 servings    **Hands-on Time:** 15 min.    **Total Time:** 1 hr., 15 min.

- 2  **Tbsp. kosher salt**
- 1  **Tbsp. salt-free spicy seasoning blend**
- 1  **tsp. garlic powder**
- 1  **tsp. onion powder**
- 1  **tsp. dried crushed red pepper**
- 1  **(12- to 14-lb.) frozen whole turkey, thawed**
- 2  **Tbsp. vegetable oil**
   **Peanut oil**
   **Garnish: fresh herbs**

**1.** Stir together first 5 ingredients.

**2.** Remove giblets and neck from turkey, and, if desired, reserve for another use. Rinse turkey with cold water. Drain cavity well; pat dry. Rub turkey evenly with 2 Tbsp. vegetable oil. Loosen and lift skin from turkey breasts with fingers without totally detaching skin; spread one-fourth of salt mixture evenly underneath. Carefully replace skin. Sprinkle additional one-fourth of salt mixture inside cavity; rub into cavity. Sprinkle remaining salt mixture evenly on skin; rub into skin. Place turkey on fryer rod.

**3.** Pour peanut oil into a deep propane turkey fryer, pouring 10 to 12 inches below top of fryer. Heat to 300° over a medium-low flame according to manufacturer's instructions. Carefully lower turkey into hot oil with rod attachment.

**4.** Fry 45 minutes or until a meat thermometer inserted in thickest portion of thigh registers 165°. (Keep oil temperature between 300° to 325°.) Remove turkey from oil; drain and let stand 15 minutes before slicing. Garnish, if desired.

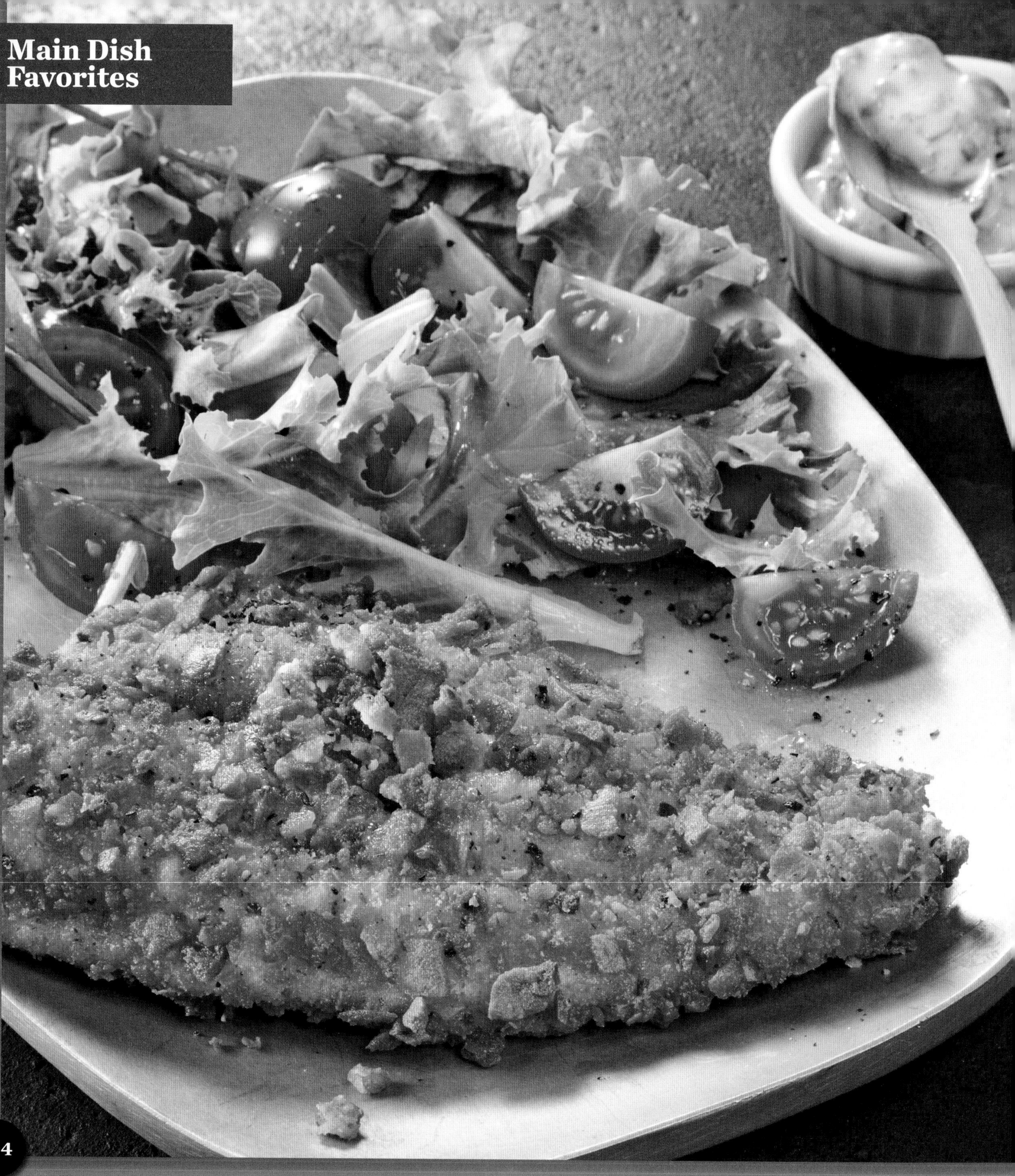

# Tuscan Catfish with Sun-Dried Tomato Aïoli

*Getting a tablespoon of Italian herb blend ground by hand can take some wrist work and a little time, but the flavor payoff is well worth the effort. Grind the seasoning over a small sheet of parchment paper so it's easier to see how much you have and how much more you need to grind. When you have enough, gently crease the paper and pour seasoning into flour.*

**Makes:** 6 servings    **Hands-on Time:** 25 min.    **Total Time:** 35 min., including aïoli

- 6 (6-oz.) catfish fillets
- ½ tsp. salt
- ½ tsp. freshly ground pepper
- 2 cups firmly packed pesto and sun-dried pita chips
- 2 cups all-purpose flour
- 1 Tbsp. freshly ground Italian herb blend grinder
- 2 large eggs, lightly beaten
  Vegetable oil
  Sun-Dried Tomato Aïoli

**1.** Sprinkle catfish with salt and pepper.

**2.** Pulse pita chips in a food processor 6 to 8 times or until coarsely chopped. Place in a shallow dish or pie plate.

**3.** Stir together flour and Italian herb blend in another shallow dish or pie plate. Stir together eggs and ⅓ cup water in a third shallow dish or pie plate.

**4.** Dredge catfish in flour mixture, shaking off excess. Dip in egg mixture, shaking off excess. Dredge in pita chips, pressing mixture into catfish to coat thoroughly.

**5.** Pour oil to depth of 1 inch into a large deep skillet; heat to 350°. Fry catfish, in batches, 4 to 5 minutes on each side or until golden brown. Drain on paper towels. Serve with Sun-Dried Tomato Aïoli.

### Sun-Dried Tomato Aïoli

**Makes:** 1½ cups
**Hands-on Time:** 10 min.
**Total Time:** 10 min.

- ¼ cup sun-dried tomatoes in oil
- 2 garlic cloves, finely minced
- 1 Tbsp. minced fresh basil leaves
- 1 Tbsp. lemon juice
- 1 Tbsp. Dijon mustard
- 1 cup mayonnaise

Process first 5 ingredients in a food processor 30 seconds or until combined. Add mayonnaise, and process 15 seconds or until smooth. Cover and chill until ready to serve.

# Fritto Misto Po'boys

*Pepperoncini and sliced green tomatoes brighten our take on the Italian "mixed fry" seafood combo. If you have any leftover batter, simply discard it.*

**Makes:** 8 servings    **Hands-on Time:** 35 min.    **Total Time:** 45 min., including coleslaw

- 1½ lb. unpeeled, large raw Gulf shrimp
- 3 tsp. Creole seasoning, divided
- 1 cup jarred pepperoncini salad peppers
- 1 (8-oz.) package tempura batter mix
- 1 cup cold light beer
- 1 Tbsp. lemon zest
- 1 Tbsp. hot sauce
- Vegetable oil
- Cajun Coleslaw
- 8 hoagie rolls, split and toasted
- 1 green tomato, sliced

**1.** Peel shrimp; devein, if desired. Sprinkle with 1 tsp. Creole seasoning.

**2.** Pat peppers dry with paper towels.

**3.** Whisk together tempura batter mix, next 3 ingredients, and remaining 2 tsp. Creole seasoning in a large bowl; let stand 5 minutes.

**4.** Meanwhile, pour oil to depth of 3 inches into a Dutch oven; heat over medium-high heat to 350°.

**5.** Dip shrimp and peppers into batter. Shake off excess. Fry, in batches, 2 to 3 minutes or until golden. Drain on a wire rack over paper towels.

**6.** Spoon Cajun Coleslaw onto rolls. Layer with tomato slices, shrimp, and peppers.

### Cajun Coleslaw

**Makes:** 8 servings    **Hands-on Time:** 5 min.    **Total Time:** 5 min.

Stir together 1 cup mayonnaise, ½ cup red pepper jelly, 6 Tbsp. Creole mustard, and ½ tsp. salt in a large bowl. Reserve half of mixture. Add 1 (16-oz.) package coleslaw mix to remaining mayonnaise mixture, stirring until well coated. Serve reserved mayo mixture with po'boys.

# Tempura Shrimp Tacos

*Make the coleslaw up to 24 hours in advance to jump-start this recipe.*

**Makes:** 6 servings    **Hands-on Time:** 35 min.
**Total Time:** 1 hr., 15 min., including coleslaw

- 1  **lb. unpeeled, large raw shrimp**
- 1  **cup tempura batter mix**
- ¾  **cup cold light beer**
- 2  **tsp. fajita seasoning mix**
- **Vegetable oil**
- 12  **(6-inch) fajita-size flour tortillas, warmed**
- **Mexi-Coleslaw Mix**
- **Toppings: chopped tomatoes, sliced avocados, chopped fresh cilantro**

**1.** Peel shrimp; devein, if desired.

**2.** Whisk together tempura batter mix, beer, and fajita seasoning in a large bowl; let stand 5 minutes.

**3.** Pour oil to depth of 2 inches into a Dutch oven; heat to 325°. Dip shrimp in tempura batter, shaking off excess. Fry shrimp, in batches, 1 to 2 minutes on each side or until golden; drain on a wire rack over paper towels.

**4.** Serve in warm tortillas with Mexi-Coleslaw Mix and desired toppings.

**Note:** We tested with McCormick Golden Dipt Tempura Seafood Batter Mix.

### Mexi-Coleslaw Mix

**Makes:** 6 servings    **Hands-on Time:** 10 min.    **Total Time:** 40 min.

- 2  **Tbsp. chopped fresh cilantro**
- 3  **Tbsp. mayonnaise**
- 1  **Tbsp. fresh lime juice**
- ½  **tsp. fajita seasoning**
- ½  **(16-oz.) package shredded coleslaw mix**
- **Salt to taste**

Stir together cilantro, mayonnaise, lime juice, and fajita seasoning in a large bowl; add coleslaw mix, stirring to coat. Season with salt to taste. Cover and chill 30 minutes to 24 hours.

## MAKE IT A MEAL

Complete the Latin American theme of Tempura Shrimp Tacos and serve with Avocado Fruit Salad (page 172). Finish your meal with a dessert of Oven-Baked Churros (page 199) and a cup of rich hot chocolate spiced with a touch of cinnamon.

# Fried Soft-Shell Crabs Benedict

*Pass the Bloody Marys: This Chesapeake staple now stars for brunch.*

**Makes:** 6 servings  **Hands-on Time:** 30 min.  **Total Time:** 40 min.

Vegetable oil
1 (12-oz.) can evaporated milk
7 large eggs, divided
6 soft-shell crabs
1½ tsp. seasoned salt
1½ cups self-rising flour
6 (¾-inch-thick) French bread loaf slices
2 Tbsp. butter, melted
1 (0.9-oz.) envelope hollandaise sauce mix
1 cup milk
1 Tbsp. lemon juice
½ tsp. white vinegar
2 cups loosely packed baby arugula
2 Tbsp. chopped fresh chives

**1.** Pour oil to depth of 3 inches into a Dutch oven; heat to 360°. Whisk together evaporated milk, 1 egg, and ¼ cup water in a large bowl.

**2.** Rinse crabs, pat dry, and sprinkle with seasoned salt. Dredge crabs in flour; dip in evaporated milk mixture, and dredge in flour again. Fry crabs, in 2 batches, in hot oil 2 minutes on each side or until golden brown. Drain on a wire rack over paper towels. Keep warm.

**3.** Preheat oven to 375°. Brush 1 side of each bread slice with butter. Bake bread slices, buttered sides up, 5 minutes or until toasted.

**4.** Prepare hollandaise sauce mix according to package directions, omitting butter and using 1 cup milk and 1 Tbsp. lemon juice.

**5.** Pour water to depth of 2 inches into a large saucepan. Bring to a boil; reduce heat, and maintain at a light simmer. Add vinegar. Break remaining 6 eggs, and slip into water, 1 at a time, as close as possible to surface. Simmer 3 to 5 minutes or to desired degree of doneness. Remove with a slotted spoon. Trim edges, if desired.

**6.** Top bread slices with arugula, fried crabs, poached eggs, and hollandaise sauce. Sprinkle with chives and salt and pepper to taste.

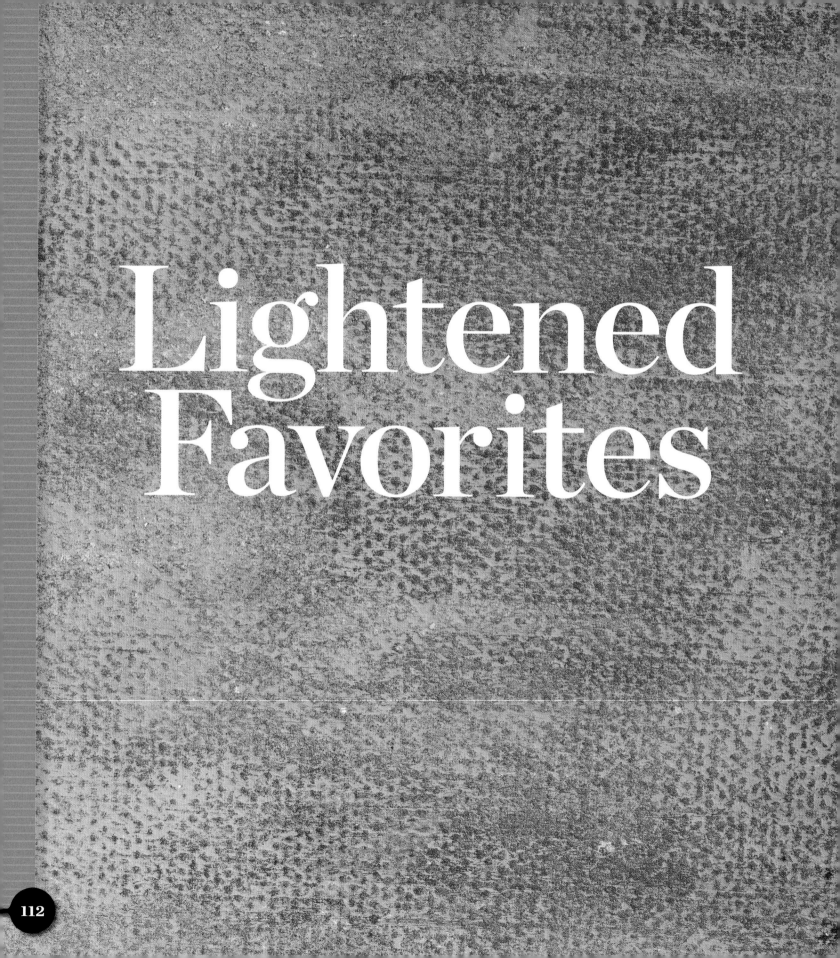

# Lightened Favorites

Lightened-Up
Fried Green
Tomatoes,
*page 116*

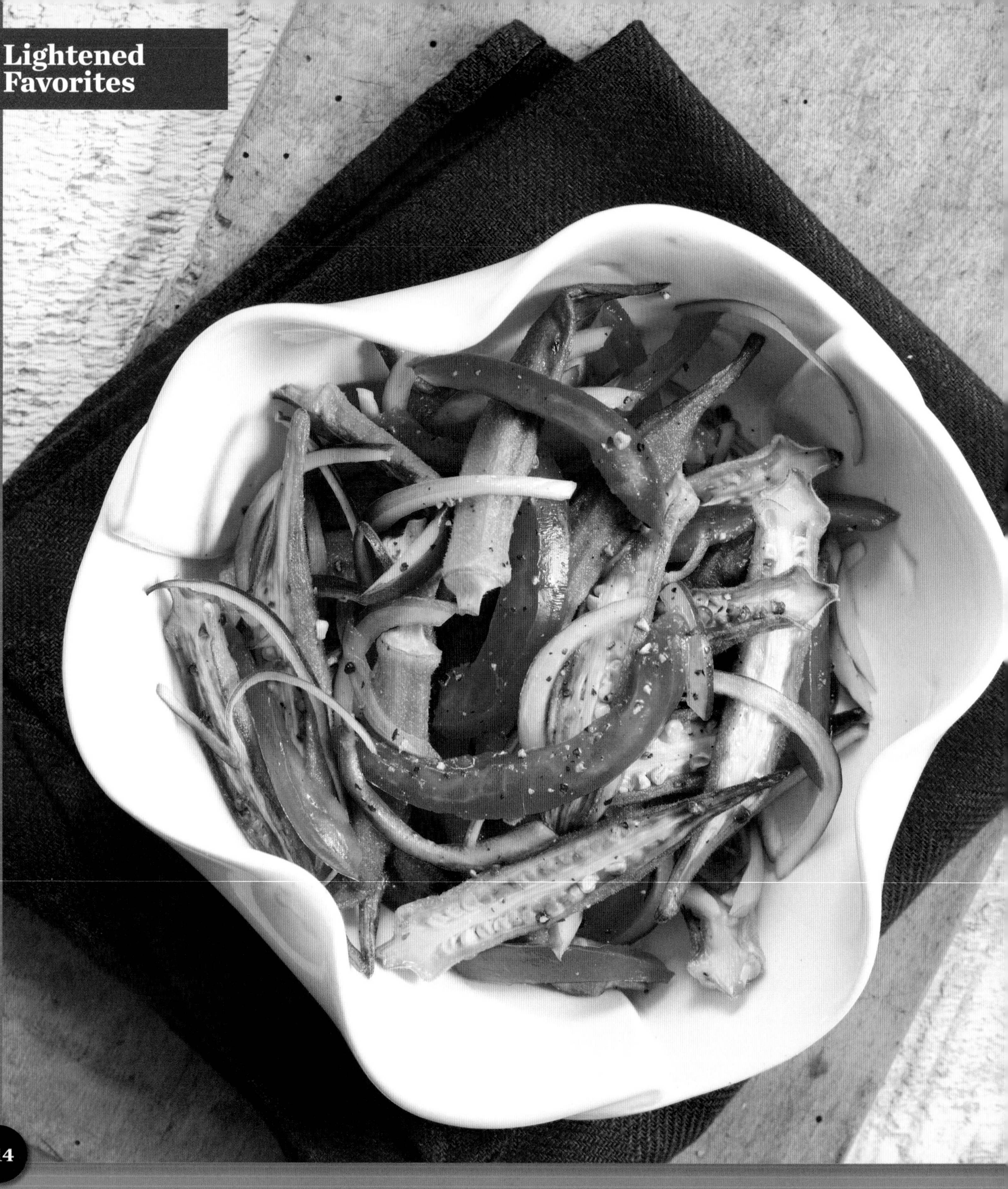

# Pan-Fried Okra, Onion, and Tomatoes

*Tender okra pods, zesty red onion, and juicy tomatoes come together in this light and healthy Southern stir-fry.*

**Makes:** 8 servings  **Hands-on Time:** 10 min.  **Total Time:** 28 min.

- 2 lb. fresh okra
- ½ cup vegetable oil
- 1 medium-size red onion, thinly sliced
- 2 large tomatoes, seeded and thinly sliced
- 2 Tbsp. lime juice
- 1½ tsp. salt
- 1½ tsp. pepper
- 1 tsp. chicken bouillon granules

**1.** Cut okra in half lengthwise.

**2.** Pour ¼ cup oil into a large skillet over medium-high heat. Cook okra in hot oil, in batches, 6 minutes or until browned, turning occasionally. Remove from skillet, and drain well on paper towels. Repeat with remaining okra, adding remaining ¼ cup oil as needed. Cool.

**3.** Stir together onion and next 5 ingredients in a large bowl. Add okra, tossing to coat. Serve at room temperature.

**Per serving:** Calories 172; Fat 14.3g (sat 1.5g, mono 6g, poly 6g); Protein 2.9g; Carb 11.6g; Fiber 4.5g; Chol 0mg; Iron 1mg; Sodium 500mg; Calc 102mg

## NORM'S NOTE
### Cast-Iron Can-Do

A cast-iron skillet is probably the most valuable piece of cookware you can own. It can do a multitude of jobs, and with minor upkeep it will last a lifetime. For example, stir-frying requires high heat to get the vegetables to cook and brown quickly while preserving their texture and fresh taste. In place of a wok, I often use a cast-iron skillet for stir-frying because it can handle the high heat needed and sits flat on the stove without wobbling to and fro.

A large (10- to 12-inch) well-seasoned cast-iron skillet easily meets the cooking demands of most jobs on the stove or in the oven. I prefer using a 12-inch skillet because it provides enough room to cook food for a crowd; plus, it's possible to whip up a stack of pan-cakes in a single pan. I end up using mine just about every time I set foot in the kitchen; to me it's the perfect tool, and it just gets better with age.

# Lightened-Up Fried Green Tomatoes

*(pictured on page 113)*

*Finally, a crispy and crunchy Southern delight without deep-frying. You're welcome.*

**Makes:** about 20 slices
**Hands-on Time:** 30 min.
**Total Time:** 40 min.

- 4   medium-size green tomatoes (about 1⅓ lb.)
- ½   tsp. salt
- ½   tsp. pepper
- 1   cup self-rising white cornmeal mix
- ½   cup panko (Japanese breadcrumbs)
- ½   cup all-purpose flour
- 4   egg whites
- 3   Tbsp. olive oil

**1.** Cut tomatoes into ½-inch-thick slices; sprinkle with salt and pepper. Let stand 10 minutes.

**2.** Combine cornmeal mix and panko in a shallow dish or pie plate. Place flour in a second shallow dish or pie plate. Whisk egg whites in a medium bowl until foamy. Dredge tomato slices in flour, shaking off excess. Dip in egg whites, and dredge in cornmeal mixture.

**3.** Cook half of tomato slices in 1½ Tbsp. hot oil in a nonstick skillet over medium heat 4 to 5 minutes on each side or until golden brown. Season with salt to taste. Place on a wire rack in a jelly-roll pan, and keep warm in a 225° oven. Repeat procedure with remaining tomato slices and oil.

**Per serving:** Calories 65; Fat 2.2g (sat 0.3g, mono 1.6g, poly 0.2g); Protein 2.1g; Carb 9.3g; Fiber 0.6g; Chol 0mg; Iron 0.5mg; Sodium 157mg; Calc 16mg

# Sesame Won Ton Crisps

*Although we liked the color contrast of the white and black sesame seeds, feel free to omit one and double the other. Sesame seeds are best stored in the refrigerator for up to three months.*

**Makes:** 12 pieces
**Hands-on Time:** 5 min.
**Total Time:** 10 min.

- 12   won ton wrappers
- 1   Tbsp. melted butter
- ½   tsp. white sesame seeds
- ½   tsp. black sesame seeds
- ¼   tsp. kosher salt

**1.** Preheat oven to 425°. Place won ton wrappers on an ungreased baking sheet. Brush 1 side of each wrapper with melted butter; sprinkle with sesame seeds and salt.

**2.** Bake at 425° for 5 to 6 minutes or until golden brown.

**Note:** Won ton wrappers can be found in the refrigerated section of most supermarkets.

**Per serving:** Calories 33; Fat 1.2g (sat 0.7g, mono 0.3g, poly 0.2g); Protein 0.9g; Carb 4.7g; Fiber 0.2g; Chol 3mg; Iron 0.3mg; Sodium 93mg; Calc 4mg

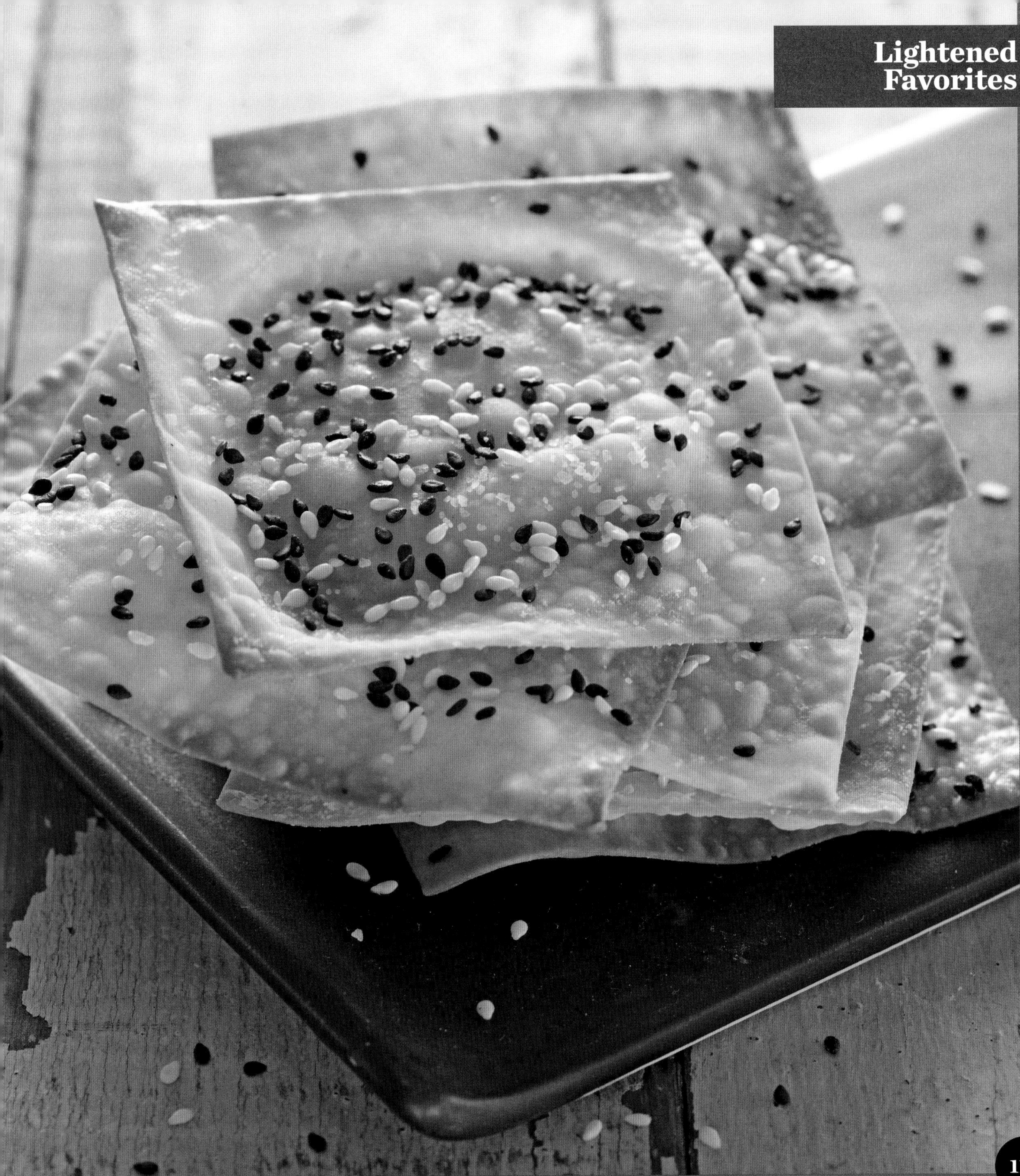

Italian-Parmesan Oven Fries

# From-Scratch Oven Fries

*Whether you leave the potato skin on or remove it, cut into strips or wedges, these are some of the tastiest potatoes you'll ever eat.*

**Makes:** 4 servings    **Hands-on Time:** 9 min.    **Total Time:** 44 min.

1½  lb. medium-size baking potatoes, peeled and cut into ½-inch-thick strips
1  Tbsp. vegetable oil
½  tsp. kosher or table salt
   Ketchup (optional)

**1.** Preheat oven to 450°. Rinse potatoes in cold water. Drain and pat dry. Toss together potatoes, oil, and salt in a large bowl.

**2.** Place a lightly greased wire rack in a jelly-roll pan. Arrange potatoes in a single layer on wire rack.

**3.** Bake at 450° for 35 to 40 minutes or until browned, turning once with tongs. Serve immediately with ketchup, if desired.

**Note:** Nutritional analysis does not include ketchup.

**Per serving:** Calories 152; Fat 3.6g (sat 0.5g, mono 0.8g, poly 2.3g); Protein 2.6g; Carb 28.2g; Fiber 2g; Chol 0mg; Iron 0.5mg; Sodium 247mg; Calc 7mg

---

**TRY THESE TWISTS!** Three more ways to enjoy our From-Scratch Oven Fries.

**Buffalo Oven Fries:** Omit salt. Toss 2 tsp. mesquite seasoning, 1 tsp. hot sauce, ½ tsp. celery salt, and ½ tsp. garlic powder with potatoes and vegetable oil; bake as directed. Serve with blue cheese dressing and bottled hot wing sauce, if desired.

**Per serving (including 2 Tbsp. blue cheese dressing; not including wing sauce):** Calories 211; Fat 8.8g (sat 1.8g, mono 1.3g, poly 4g); Protein 4.2g; Carb 32.4g; Fiber 2.1g; Chol 5mg; Iron 0.5mg; Sodium 537mg; Calc 44mg

**Italian-Parmesan Oven Fries:** Toss 2 tsp. freshly ground Italian seasoning with potato mixture, and bake as directed. Sprinkle warm fries with 2 Tbsp. grated Parmesan cheese. Serve with marinara sauce, if desired.

**Per serving (including ¼ cup marinara sauce):** Calories 258; Fat 11.7g (sat 2g, mono 5.8g, poly 3.3g); Protein 5.4g; Carb 35.6g; Fiber 4.3g; Chol 3mg; Iron 1.3mg; Sodium 489mg; Calc 95mg

**Spicy Cheese Oven Fries:** Toss a pinch of ground red pepper with potato mixture, and bake as directed. Sprinkle with ⅓ cup (1½ oz.) shredded reduced-fat pepper Jack cheese. Bake 1 more minute or until cheese is melted. Serve with ketchup, if desired.

**Per serving (not including ketchup):** Calories 184; Fat 5.9g (sat 1.9g, mono 0.8g, poly 2.3g); Protein 5.3g; Carb 28.9g; Fiber 2g; Chol 8mg; Iron 0.5mg; Sodium 230mg; Calc 83mg

## HOW TO:
### *Make Sweet Potato Fries*

**1. Brush foil-lined pan with olive oil, and heat in oven at 425° for 5 minutes. This gives the outside of the potatoes a quick sear when added to the hot pan, helping develop the rich color and texture of deep-fried sweet potatoes.**

**2. Peel potatoes, and cut into uniform strips. Sweet potatoes can be quite firm and require a bit of pressure to cut. Cut a thin slice off one long side to provide a flat base to prevent the potato from rolling while cutting.**

**3. Once potatoes are cut, add them to a large zip-top plastic freezer bag with seasonings and remaining oil. Seal bag, and shake back and forth to coat all potato strips evenly.**

**4. Using an oven mitt or a thick towel, remove hot pan from oven, and place on a wire rack or heat-resistant surface. Arrange potato strips in a single layer, giving fries ample separation to encourage proper browning.**

## Spicy Sweet Potato Fries

**Makes:** 4 servings
**Hands-on Time:** 15 min.
**Total Time:** 35 min.

- 1 Tbsp. olive oil, divided
- 2 large sweet potatoes (about 1¼ lb.)
- 1 tsp. brown sugar
- ¼ tsp. salt
- ¼ tsp. chili powder

**1.** Preheat oven to 425°. Brush an aluminum foil-lined jelly-roll pan with 2 tsp. olive oil. Heat pan in a 425° oven 5 minutes.

**2.** Peel sweet potatoes, and cut into 3- x ½-inch strips. Combine strips, brown sugar, salt, chili powder, and remaining 1 tsp. oil in a large zip-top plastic freezer bag, tossing to coat.

**3.** Place strips in a single layer in prepared pan. Bake at 425° for 20 minutes or until crisp, turning after 10 minutes.

**Per serving:** Calories 117; Fat 3.5g (sat 0.5g, mono 2.5g, poly 0.4g); Protein 1.5g; Carb 20.3g; Fiber 2.8g; Chol 0mg; Iron 0.8mg; Sodium 183mg; Calc 31mg

## "Fried" Rings

**Makes:** 3 servings
**Hands-on Time:** 20 min.
**Total Time:** 32 min.

- ½ cup low-fat buttermilk
- 1 egg white
- 1 large sweet onion
- ½ cup all-purpose flour
- 2 Tbsp. olive oil
  Vegetable cooking spray
- ½ tsp. coarse kosher salt

**1.** Preheat oven to 400°. Whisk together buttermilk and egg white until blended. Cut onion into ¼-inch-thick slices, and separate into rings. Select largest 12, and dredge in flour; dip into buttermilk mixture, coating well. Dredge again in flour.

**2.** Heat 2 tsp. oil at a time in a 10-inch skillet over medium-high heat. Fry onion rings in batches in hot oil 1 minute on each side or until golden. Place fried onion rings on an aluminum foil-lined baking sheet coated with cooking spray. Bake at 400° for 3 minutes. Turn onion rings, and bake 3 more minutes. Remove from oven; sprinkle with salt.

**Per serving:** Calories 119; Fat 5.9g (sat 0.9g, mono 4.1g, poly 0.7g); Protein 3.1g; Carb 13.6g; Fiber 1g; Chol 1mg; Iron 0.6mg; Sodium 345mg; Calc 24mg

STEP 1

STEP 2

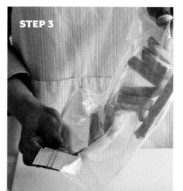

STEP 3

STEP 4

# Chicken-Fried Steak

*The crispy coating on this Chicken-Fried Steak is achieved from crushed saltine crackers, and 45 is the perfect number to get it just right.*

**Makes:** 6 servings    **Hands-on Time:** 15 min.    **Total Time:** 23 min., including gravy

6   (4-oz.) cubed steaks (1½ lb.)
½   tsp. salt
½   tsp. pepper
¼   cup all-purpose flour
½   cup egg substitute
45  saltine crackers, crushed
    (1 sleeve plus 7 crackers)
    Vegetable cooking spray
    Cream Gravy

**1.** Sprinkle steaks with salt and pepper. Dredge steaks in flour; dip in egg substitute, and dredge in crushed crackers. Lightly coat steaks on each side with cooking spray.

**2.** Cook steaks, in batches, in a hot nonstick skillet over medium heat 3 to 4 minutes on each side or until golden, turning twice. Transfer steaks to a wire rack in a jelly-roll pan. Keep warm in a 225° oven. Serve with Cream Gravy.

**Per serving (not including gravy):**
Calories 315; Fat 11.9g (sat 3.9g, mono 5g, poly 1.1g) Protein 29.3g; Carb 20.3g; Fiber 0.9g; Chol 65mg; Iron 4.1mg; Sodium 369mg; Calc 43mg

## Cream Gravy

**Makes:** 6 servings
**Hands-on Time:** 10 min.
**Total Time:** 10 min.

1½  cups 1% low-fat milk
¼   cup all-purpose flour
1   Tbsp. low-sodium jarred
    chicken soup base
½   tsp. pepper

Gradually whisk milk into flour until smooth; cook over medium heat, whisking constantly, 3 to 5 minutes or until mixture is thickened and bubbly. Whisk in soup base and pepper.

**Per serving:** Calories 55; Fat 0.9g (sat 0.5g, mono 0.2g, poly 0.1g); Protein 3.2g; Carb 8.3g; Fiber 0.2g; Chol 4mg; Iron 0.3mg; Sodium 126mg; Calc 77mg

## MAKE IT A MEAL

Green Beans with Goat Cheese, Tomatoes, and Almonds (page 184) and simple mashed potatoes are all this lightened classic needs to be complete. Well, the cream gravy doesn't hurt, either.

## MAKE IT A MEAL

Serve Tortilla-Crusted Pork with Mango Salad (page 176) or Hearts of Palm and Jicama Salad (page 179). Sometimes, I'll quickly char corn tortillas in a cast-iron skillet and use them to make tacos. Use the pork as the base, and top with your choice of salsa and a few heavy dashes of Mexican-style hot sauce.

## FRY IT SAFELY

### Make the Right Oil Choice

In addition to being a healthy choice for frying foods, canola oil is also a safe choice because it has a high smoke point. An oil will begin smoking at its smoke point, giving foods an unpleasant flavor and potentially setting off the kitchen smoke alarm.

# Tortilla-Crusted Pork

*Let the pork sear evenly on each side to allow the coating to reach maximum crispness.*

**Makes:** 6 servings  **Hands-on Time:** 32 min.
**Total Time:** 1 hr., 47 min., including Pico de Gallo

- 2 lb. pork tenderloin
- ½ cup finely crushed blue-corn tortilla chips
- ½ cup finely crushed tortilla chips
- 1 Tbsp. coarsely ground pepper
- ½ tsp. chili powder
- ½ tsp. salt
- ¼ tsp. ground cumin
- 3 Tbsp. extra virgin olive oil, divided
  Pico de Gallo
  Garnishes: fresh cilantro sprigs, sliced jalapeños

**1.** Remove silver skin from tenderloin, leaving a thin layer of fat. Cut tenderloin into 1-inch-thick medallions.

**2.** Combine blue-corn tortilla chips and next 5 ingredients in a bowl. Brush pork medallions with 1½ Tbsp. olive oil, and dredge in tortilla chip mixture, pressing mixture into medallions on all sides to thoroughly coat.

**3.** Cook pork medallions in remaining 1½ Tbsp. hot oil in a large skillet over medium heat 6 minutes on each side or until done. Serve with Pico de Gallo. Garnish, if desired.

**Per serving (not including Pico de Gallo):** Calories 262; Fat 12.5g (sat 2.8g, mono 7.3g, poly 1.6g); Protein 32.4g; Carb 4.1g; Fiber 0.6g; Chol 98mg; Iron 2mg; Sodium 262mg; Calc 21mg

### Pico de Gallo

*Pico de Gallo is best when made the day you plan to serve it. Use extra to serve atop a fried egg or in an omelet.*

**Makes:** 3 cups
**Hands-on Time:** 15 min.
**Total Time:** 1 hr., 15 min.

- 2 medium tomatoes, seeded and diced
- 1 medium-size ripe avocado, diced
- ¼ cup diced white onion
- 1 serrano or jalapeño pepper, seeded and finely chopped
- 2 Tbsp. lime juice
- 1 Tbsp. extra virgin olive oil
  Salt to taste

Toss together first 6 ingredients in a medium bowl. Cover and chill 1 hour. Season with salt to taste.

**Per serving:** Calories 83; Fat 6.9g (sat 0.9g, mono 4.5g, poly 0.9g); Protein 1.2g; Carb 6g; Fiber 2.8g; Chol 0mg; Iron 0.4mg; Sodium 6mg; Calc 12mg

# Crispy Oven-Fried Drumsticks

*These oven-fried drumsticks have a satisfyingly crunchy texture. We loved the flavor results when we used ½ tsp. red pepper. Use ¼ tsp. for kids.*

**Makes:** 4 servings    **Hands-on Time:** 15 min.
**Total Time:** 40 min., including preserves

- 3    cups cornflakes cereal, crushed
- ⅓    cup grated Parmesan cheese
- ½    tsp. salt
- ¼    to ½ tsp. ground red pepper
- ¼    tsp. freshly ground black pepper
- ¾    cup fat-free buttermilk
- 8    chicken drumsticks (about 2 lb.), skinned
       Vegetable cooking spray
       Peach-Pepper Preserves (page 246; optional)

**1.** Preheat oven to 425°. Combine first 5 ingredients in a large zip-top plastic freezer bag; seal and shake well to combine.

**2.** Pour buttermilk into a shallow bowl. Dip 2 drumsticks in buttermilk, and place in bag. Seal and shake well, coating drumsticks completely. Place drumsticks on an aluminum foil-lined baking sheet coated with cooking spray. Repeat procedure with remaining drumsticks. Sprinkle remaining cornflakes mixture evenly over drumsticks on baking sheet. Lightly coat with cooking spray.

**3.** Bake at 425° for 25 to 30 minutes or until drumsticks are well browned and done. Serve immediately with Peach-Pepper Preserves, if desired.

**Per serving:** Calories 324; Fat 7.8g (sat 2.6g, mono 2.4g, poly 1.5g); Protein 40.7g; Carb 21.3g; Fiber 1g; Chol 137mg; Iron 5.9mg; Sodium 790mg; Calc 150mg

## NORM'S NOTE
### How to Get Crunchy, Crispy, Oven-Fried Food

Use "oven-frying" to achieve the textural qualities of fried foods while using less fat. Getting the crispy, crunchy coatings and moist interiors of fried foods we love takes a bit of finesse and some help from items that are already crunchy, such as crackers, chips, even breakfast cereals. Giving "oven-fried" foods a tumble in these items and coating with cooking spray allows the exterior to brown evenly while baking, keeping the fat to a minimum and the crunch to a maximum.

# Pecan-Crusted Chicken Tenders

*Crunchy chicken fingers get faux-fry flavor after a quick bake in the oven. The saltines add crunch and the pecans add nutty flavor. Pair with a side and your choice of sauce for dipping.*

**Makes:** 8 servings   **Hands-on Time:** 15 min.   **Total Time:** 33 min.

- 16  **saltine crackers, finely crushed**
- ¼  **cup pecans, ground**
- 2  **tsp. paprika**
- ½  **tsp. salt**
- ½  **tsp. pepper**
- 2  **egg whites**
  **Vegetable cooking spray**
- 1½  **lb. chicken tenders**
- ¼  **cup all-purpose flour**

**1.** Preheat oven to 425°. Stir together crushed crackers and next 4 ingredients.

**2.** Whisk egg whites just until foamy.

**3.** Place a wire rack coated with cooking spray in a parchment paper-lined 15- x 10-inch jelly-roll pan.

**4.** Dredge chicken tenders in flour; dip in egg white, and dredge in saltine mixture. Lightly coat chicken on each side with cooking spray; arrange chicken on wire rack.

**5.** Bake at 425° for 18 to 20 minutes or until golden brown, turning once after 12 minutes.

**Per serving:** Calories 152; Fat 4.3g (sat 0.3g, mono 1.6g, poly 0.7g); Protein 19.5g; Carb 8g; Fiber 0.8g; Chol 46mg; Iron 1.2mg; Sodium 494mg; Calc 9mg

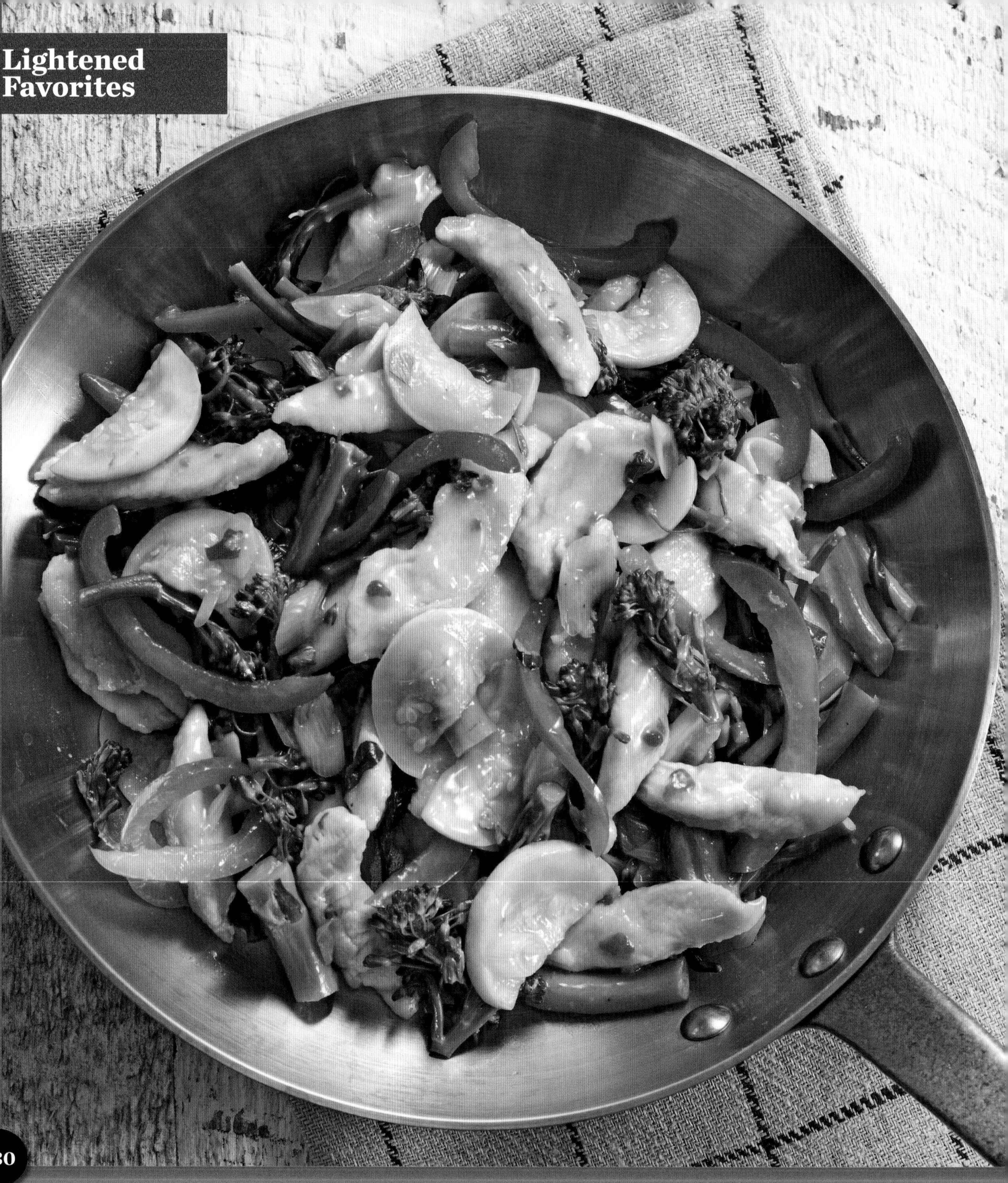

# Chicken-and-Veggie Stir-Fry

*Tossing the chicken strips in cornstarch does two things: It helps the chicken become a rich golden brown, and it provides a foundation for a velvety sauce when liquid is added. You can substitute medium-sized shrimp or thinly sliced beef for chicken.*

**Makes:** 4 servings    **Hands-on Time:** 30 min.    **Total Time:** 30 min.

- 1  **lb. skinned and boned chicken breasts, cut into thin strips**
- ½  **tsp. salt**
- ¼  **cup cornstarch**
- 4  **Tbsp. vegetable oil, divided**
- ½  **lb. Broccolini, cut into 1-inch pieces**
- 1  **cup chicken broth, divided**
- 1  **red bell pepper, cut into thin strips**
- 1  **small yellow squash, thinly sliced into half moons**
- ¼  **cup sliced green onions**
- 2  **tsp. cornstarch**
- 1  **Tbsp. fresh lime juice**
- 1½  **tsp. soy sauce**
- 1  **tsp. Asian chili-garlic sauce**
  **Hot cooked rice**

**1.** Sprinkle chicken with salt; toss with ¼ cup cornstarch.

**2.** Stir-fry chicken in 3 Tbsp. hot oil in a large skillet or wok over medium-high heat 5 to 6 minutes or until golden brown and done. Transfer to a plate, using a slotted spoon; keep warm. Add Broccolini and ¼ cup broth; cover and cook 1 to 2 minutes or until crisp-tender. Transfer to plate with chicken, using slotted spoon.

**3.** Add remaining 1 Tbsp. oil to skillet. Sauté bell pepper and next 2 ingredients in hot oil 2 minutes or until crisp-tender.

**4.** Whisk together 2 tsp. cornstarch and remaining ¾ cup broth until cornstarch dissolves. Add broth mixture, chicken, and Broccolini (with any accumulated juices) to bell pepper mixture in skillet. Cook, stirring often, 1 minute or until liquid thickens. Stir in lime juice and next 2 ingredients. Serve over hot cooked rice.

**Per serving:** Calories 330; Fat 15.2g (sat 1.9g, mono 6.4g, poly 6.4g); Protein 29.7g; Carb 17.4g; Fiber 2.4g; Chol 66mg; Iron 1.9mg; Sodium 627mg; Calc 70mg

## HOW TO:

### Prepare Coconut Shrimp

1. Peel and devein shrimp in a medium-size bowl, leaving the tails on the shrimp.

2. Whisk egg whites in a separate bowl just until foamy. The egg whites need to be thick enough to stick to the shrimp.

3. After seasoning shrimp, dip into egg whites, and dredge shrimp in coconut mixture, gently pressing mixture onto both sides.

4. Arrange shrimp on a wire rack in a 15- x 10-inch jelly-roll pan, and coat both sides with cooking spray to make the shrimp crispy without added calories.

5. Bake shrimp 10 to 12 minutes or until pink, turning once after 8 minutes so that they brown evenly on both sides.

# Coconut Shrimp

**Makes:** 4 servings    **Hands-on Time:** 20 min.    **Total Time:** 30 min.

- 1½ **lb. unpeeled, large raw shrimp**
  **Vegetable cooking spray**
- 2 **egg whites**
- ¼ **cup cornstarch**
- 1 **Tbsp. Caribbean jerk seasoning**
- 1 **cup sweetened flaked coconut**
- 1 **cup panko (Japanese breadcrumbs)**
- 1 **tsp. paprika**
  **Pineapple Salsa (optional)**

**1.** Preheat oven to 425°. Peel shrimp, leaving tails on; devein, if desired.

**2.** Place a wire rack coated with cooking spray in a 15- x 10-inch jelly-roll pan.

**3.** Whisk egg whites just until foamy.

**4.** Stir together cornstarch and jerk seasoning in a shallow dish. Stir together coconut, Japanese breadcrumbs, and paprika in another shallow dish.

**5.** Dredge shrimp, 1 at a time, in cornstarch mixture; dip in egg whites, and dredge in coconut mixture, pressing gently with fingers. Lightly coat shrimp on each side with cooking spray; arrange shrimp on wire rack.

**6.** Bake at 425° for 10 to 12 minutes or just until shrimp turn pink, turning once after 8 minutes. Serve with Pineapple Salsa, if desired.

**Per serving (not including salsa):**
Calories 363; Fat: 8.9g (sat 5.4g, mono 0.7g, poly 1.2g); Protein 39g; Carb 28.8g; Fiber 2.6g; Chol 259mg; Iron 4.5mg; Sodium 601mg; Calc 93mg

### Pineapple Salsa

**Makes:** 1 cup
**Hands-on Time:** 6 min.
**Total Time:** 6 min.

- ¾ **cup chopped fresh pineapple**
- 2 **Tbsp. diced green bell pepper**
- 2 **Tbsp. diced red onion**
- 1 **Tbsp. fresh lime juice**

Stir together all ingredients in a small bowl.

**Per serving:** Calories 19; Fat 0.1g (sat 0g, mono 0g, poly 0g); Protein 0.3g; Carb 5.1g; Fiber 0.6g; Chol 0mg; Iron 0.1mg; Sodium 1mg; Calc 6mg

STEP 1    STEP 2

STEP 3

STEP 4

STEP 5

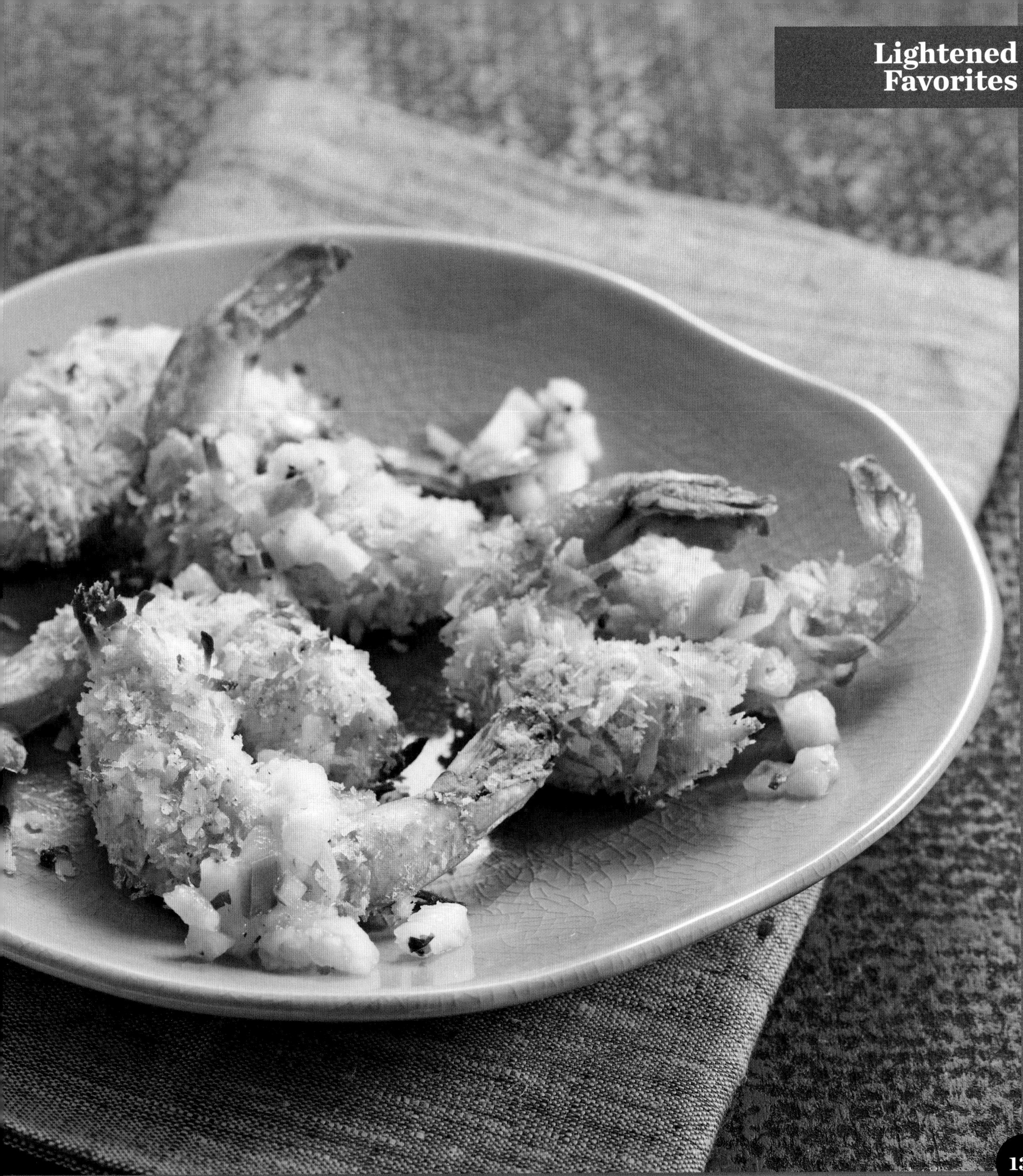

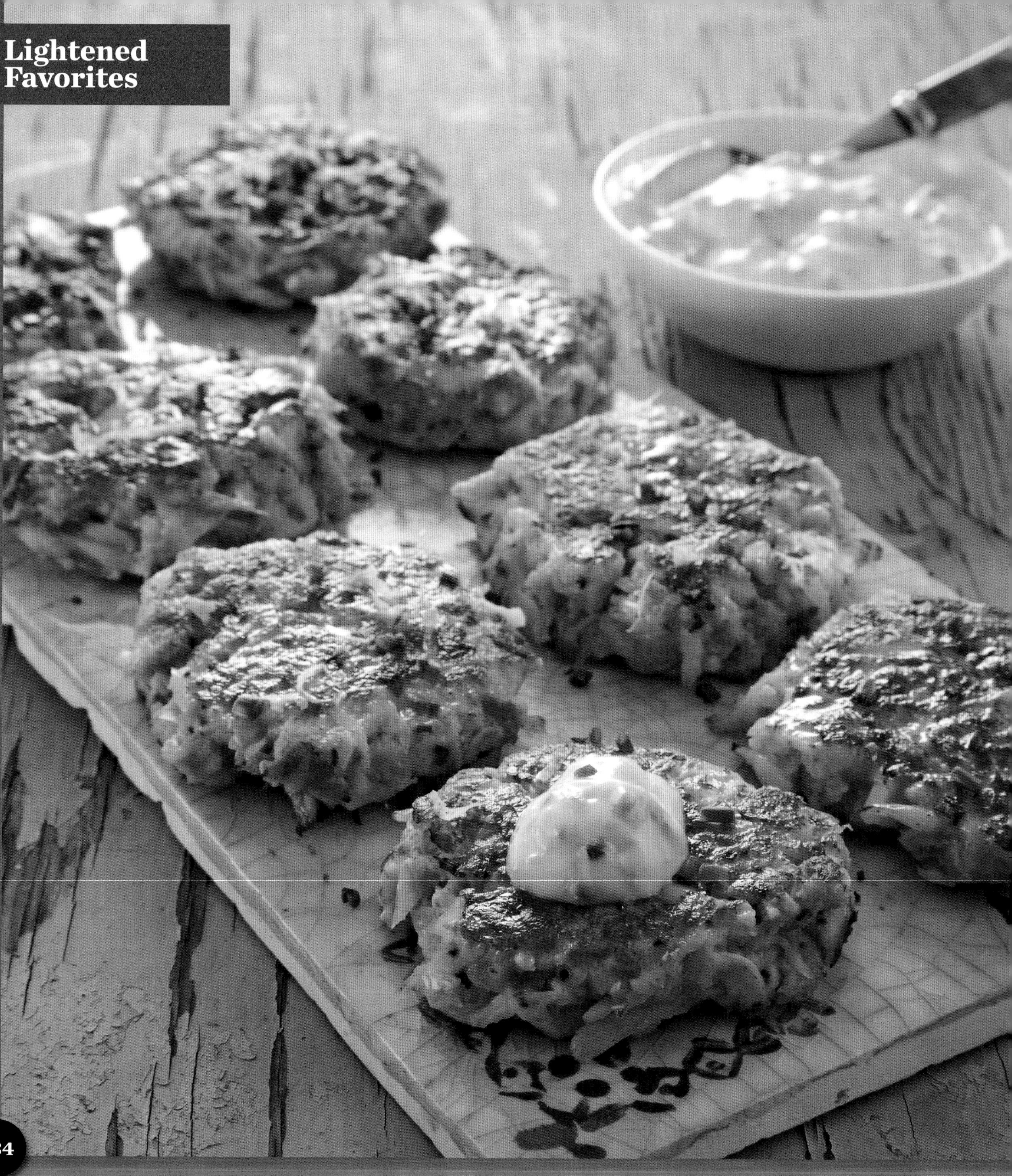

# Mini Crab Cakes with Garlic-Chive Sauce

*Cook these Mid-Atlantic beauties over medium-low heat to ensure a deep golden crust without overcooking the delicate crab.*

**Makes:** 16 cakes     **Hands-on Time:** 28 min.     **Total Time:** 28 min.

- 1 (8-oz.) package fresh lump crabmeat, drained
- 3 whole grain white bread slices
- ⅓ cup light mayonnaise
- 2 Tbsp. fresh chives, chopped
- 1 tsp. Old Bay seasoning
- 1 tsp. Worcestershire sauce
- 2 large eggs, lightly beaten
  Vegetable cooking spray
  Salt to taste
  Garlic-Chive Sauce
  Garnishes: chopped chives, lemon zest

**1.** Pick crabmeat, removing any bits of shell. Pulse bread slices in a blender or food processor 5 times or until finely crumbled. (Yield should be about 1½ cups.)

**2.** Stir together mayonnaise and next 4 ingredients in a large bowl. Gently stir in breadcrumbs and crabmeat. Shape mixture into 16 (2-inch) cakes (about 2 Tbsp. each).

**3.** Cook cakes, in batches, on a hot, large griddle or nonstick skillet coated with cooking spray over medium-low heat 4 minutes on each side or until golden brown. Season with salt to taste. (Keep cakes warm in a 200° oven for up to 30 minutes.) Serve with Garlic-Chive Sauce. Garnish, if desired.

**Note:** We tested with Sara Lee Soft & Smooth Whole Grain White Bread.

**Note:** Nutritional analysis does not include salt to taste.

**Per serving:** Calories 67; Fat 3.7g (sat 1.3g, mono 0.2g, poly 0.1g); Protein 4.2g; Carb 4.3g; Fiber 0.4g; Chol 41mg; Iron 0.3mg; Sodium 238mg; Calc 12mg

### Garlic-Chive Sauce

**Makes:** 1 cup
**Hands-on Time:** 10 min.
**Total Time:** 40 min.

- ¾ cup light sour cream*
- 1 garlic clove, minced
- 1 Tbsp. chopped fresh chives
- ¾ tsp. lemon zest
- 1½ Tbsp. fresh lemon juice
- ¼ tsp. salt
- ⅛ tsp. pepper

Stir together all ingredients in a small bowl. Cover and chill 30 minutes before serving.

*Light mayonnaise may be substituted.

**Per serving:** Calories 16; Fat 0.9g (sat 0.7g, mono 0g, poly 0g); Protein 0.8g; Carb 1g; Fiber 0g; Chol 0mg; Iron 0mg; Sodium 46mg; Calc 1mg

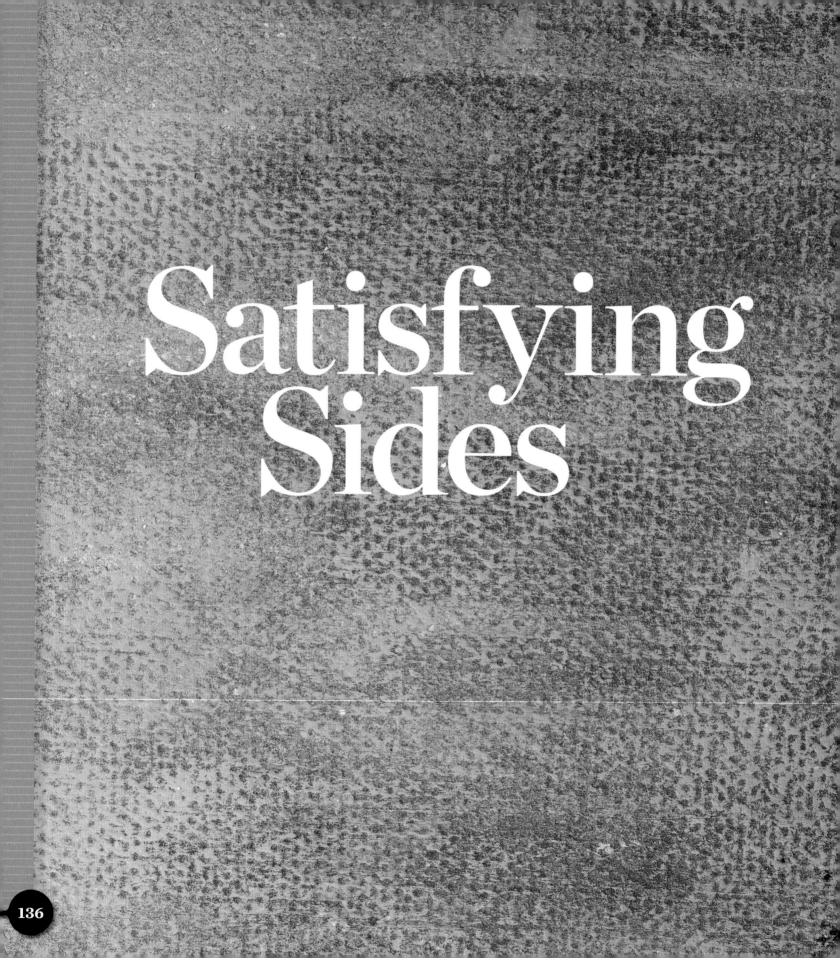

# Satisfying Sides

Grilled Jalapeño-Lime Corn on the Cob, *page 139*

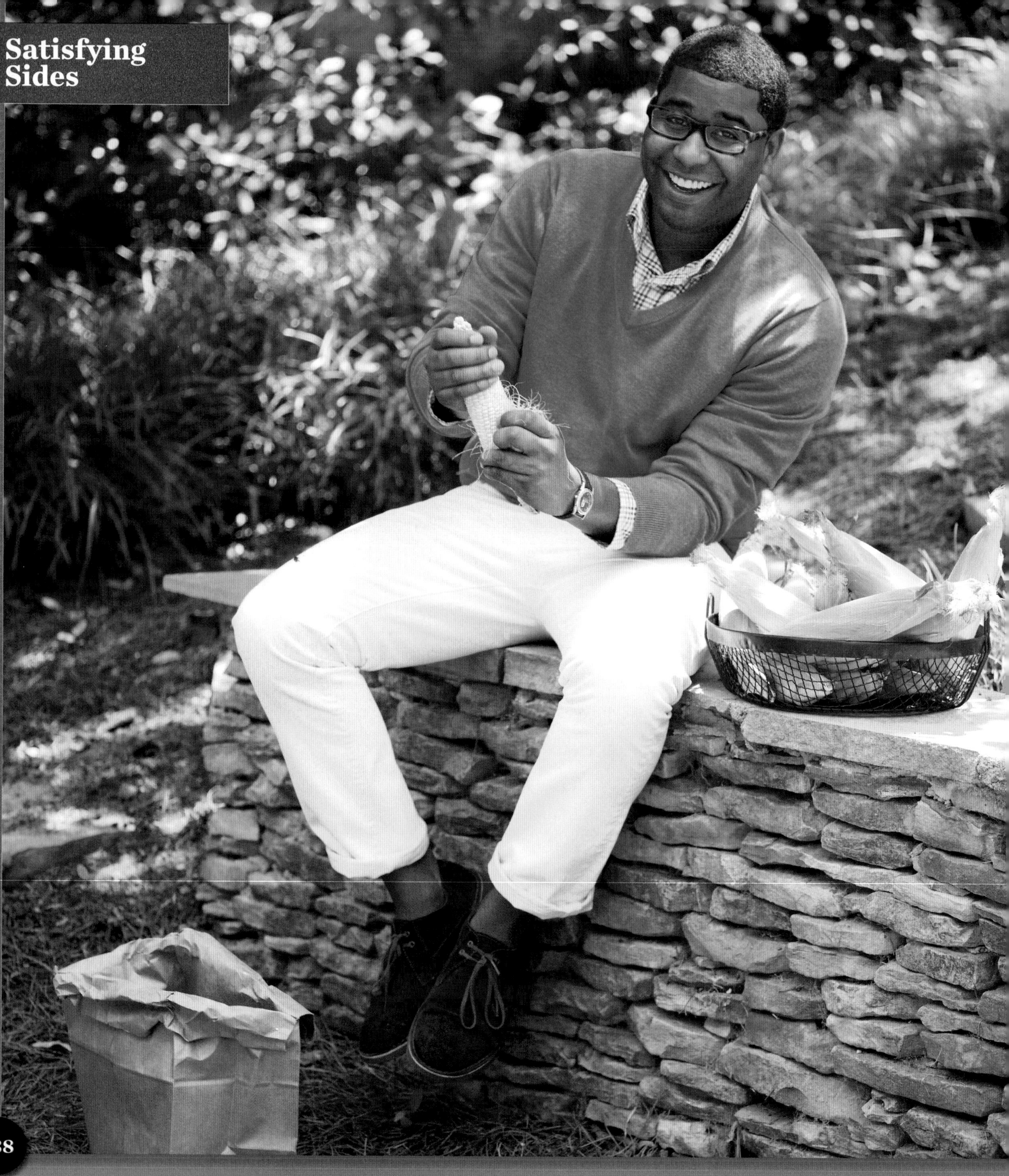

# Grilled Jalapeño-Lime Corn on the Cob

*(pictured on page 137)*

**Makes:** 8 servings
**Hands-on Time:** 30 min.
**Total Time:** 30 min.

- 8 ears fresh corn, husks removed
  Vegetable cooking spray
  Salt and freshly ground pepper
- ½ cup butter, softened
- 1 jalapeño pepper, seeded and minced
- 1 small garlic clove, pressed
- 1 Tbsp. lime zest
- 1 Tbsp. fresh lime juice
- 2 tsp. chopped fresh cilantro
  Garnish: lime zest

**1.** Preheat grill to 350° to 400° (medium-high) heat. Coat corn lightly with cooking spray. Sprinkle with desired amount of salt and pepper. Grill corn, covered with grill lid, 15 minutes or until golden brown, turning occasionally.

**2.** Meanwhile, stir together butter and next 5 ingredients. Remove corn from grill, and serve with butter mixture. Garnish, if desired.

# Fried Confetti Corn

*Sweet, creamy, and decadently rich, this fried corn would be great nestled next to a piece of fried chicken and a side of greens.*

**Makes:** 8 servings
**Hands-on Time:** 30 min.
**Total Time:** 30 min.

- 8 bacon slices
- 6 cups fresh sweet corn kernels (about 8 ears)
- 1 cup diced sweet onion
- ½ cup chopped red bell pepper
- ½ cup chopped green bell pepper
- 1 (8-oz.) package cream cheese, cubed
- ½ cup half-and-half
- 1 tsp. sugar
- 1 tsp. salt
- 1 tsp. pepper

**1.** Cook bacon in a large skillet over medium-high heat 6 to 8 minutes or until crisp. Remove bacon, and drain on paper towels, reserving 2 Tbsp. drippings in skillet. Coarsely crumble bacon.

**2.** Sauté corn and next 3 ingredients in hot drippings in skillet over medium-high heat 6 minutes or until tender. Add cream cheese and half-and-half, stirring until cream cheese melts. Stir in sugar and next 2 ingredients. Transfer to a serving dish, and top with bacon.

## NORM'S NOTE
### Add a Cajun Twist

Use spicy, smoky Alabama-produced Conecuh sausage to add depth and character to this traditional Louisiana side dish, maque choux. It's a take on the area's beloved jambalaya. Andouille sausage or tasso would make an acceptable substitute if Conecuh sausage is not available in your area.

# Okra and Corn Maque Choux

*Add velvety richness to this recipe by stirring in a tablespoon of butter and ¼ cup chicken broth during the last few minutes of cooking.*

**Makes:** 8 servings    **Hands-on Time:** 18 min.    **Total Time:** 18 min.

¼  lb. spicy smoked sausage, diced
½  cup chopped sweet onion
½  cup chopped green bell pepper
2  garlic cloves, minced
3  cups fresh corn kernels
1  cup sliced fresh okra
1  cup peeled, seeded, and diced tomato (½ lb.)
    Salt and freshly ground pepper to taste

Sauté sausage in a large skillet over medium-high heat 3 minutes or until browned. Add onion, bell pepper, and garlic, and sauté 5 minutes or until tender. Add corn, okra, and tomato; cook, stirring often, 10 minutes. Season with salt and pepper to taste.

**Note:** We tested with Conecuh Original Spicy and Hot Smoked Sausage.

# Lela's Hush Puppies

*If you were raised on fried hush puppies made with a mix of all-purpose flour and cornmeal, you'll be pleasantly surprised by the airy texture and bold flavors of this all-cornmeal version.*

**Makes:** 6 to 8 servings    **Hands-on Time:** 34 min.    **Total Time:** 1 hr., 4 min.

2¼  cups self-rising white cornmeal mix
½  cup chopped green bell pepper
½  medium onion, chopped
1  tsp. salt
¼  tsp. ground red pepper
½  tsp. ground black pepper
1  cup buttermilk
2  large eggs
    Vegetable oil

**1.** Combine first 6 ingredients in a bowl; make a well in center of mixture.

**2.** Whisk together buttermilk and eggs; add to dry ingredients, stirring just until moistened. Let mixture stand 30 minutes.

**3.** Pour oil to depth of 2 inches into a Dutch oven; heat to 375°.

**4.** Drop batter by heaping teaspoonfuls into hot oil. Fry, in batches, 2 minutes on each side or until golden. Drain on wire racks over paper towels; serve hot.

## NORM'S NOTE
### Make Light Hush Puppies

Be sure to let the cornmeal mixture stand after adding the buttermilk and eggs. This stand time allows the baking powder in the flour and the acid in the buttermilk to combine and release gases that make the hush puppies light and airy.

Take note that the cast-iron skillet size of this recipe is 8 inches. This smaller size yields a thick inch-and-a-half wedge when baked and cut. If you happen to have the more common 10-inch cast-iron skillet, you'll need to decrease the bake time by 3 to 5 minutes. Expect a thinner sub-one-inch wedge when cut, but trust that the taste will be just as delicious.

# Buttermilk Cornbread

*Bake your cornbread in a well-seasoned cast-iron skillet to ensure that it has a crispy crust. You can also add a little zip to this recipe by tossing in chopped jalapeño.*

**Makes:** 8 servings    **Hands-on Time:** 5 min.    **Total Time:** 35 min.

1¼  cups all-purpose flour
 1  cup plus 3 Tbsp. plain white cornmeal
 ¼  cup sugar
 1  Tbsp. baking powder
 1  tsp. salt
 ¼  cup butter, melted
 2  large eggs
 1  cup buttermilk

**1.** Preheat oven to 400°. Lightly grease an 8-inch cast-iron skillet, and heat in oven 5 minutes.

**2.** Meanwhile, whisk together first 5 ingredients in a bowl; whisk in melted butter. Add eggs and buttermilk, whisking just until smooth.

**3.** Pour batter into hot skillet. Bake at 400° for 30 to 33 minutes or until golden brown.

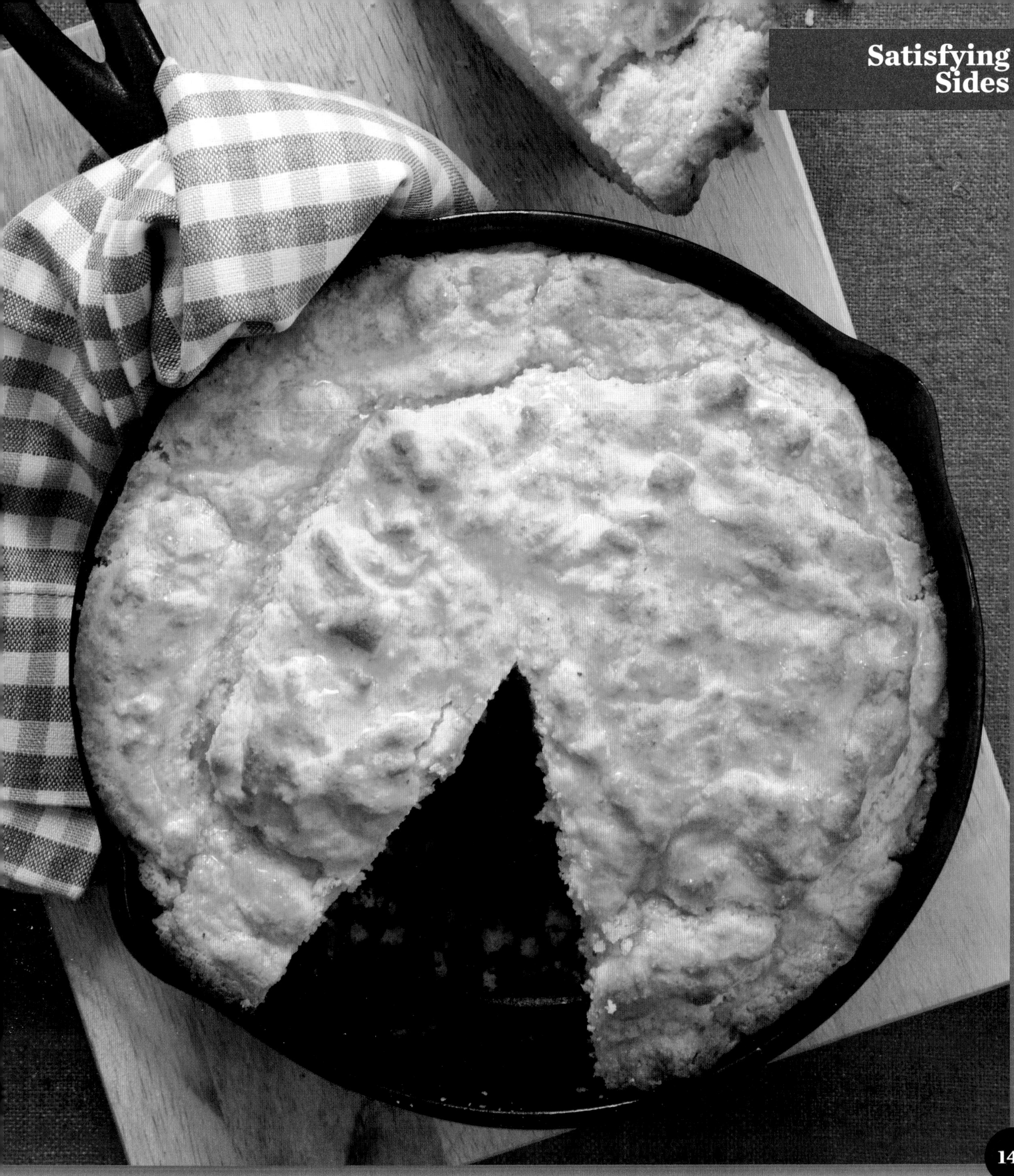

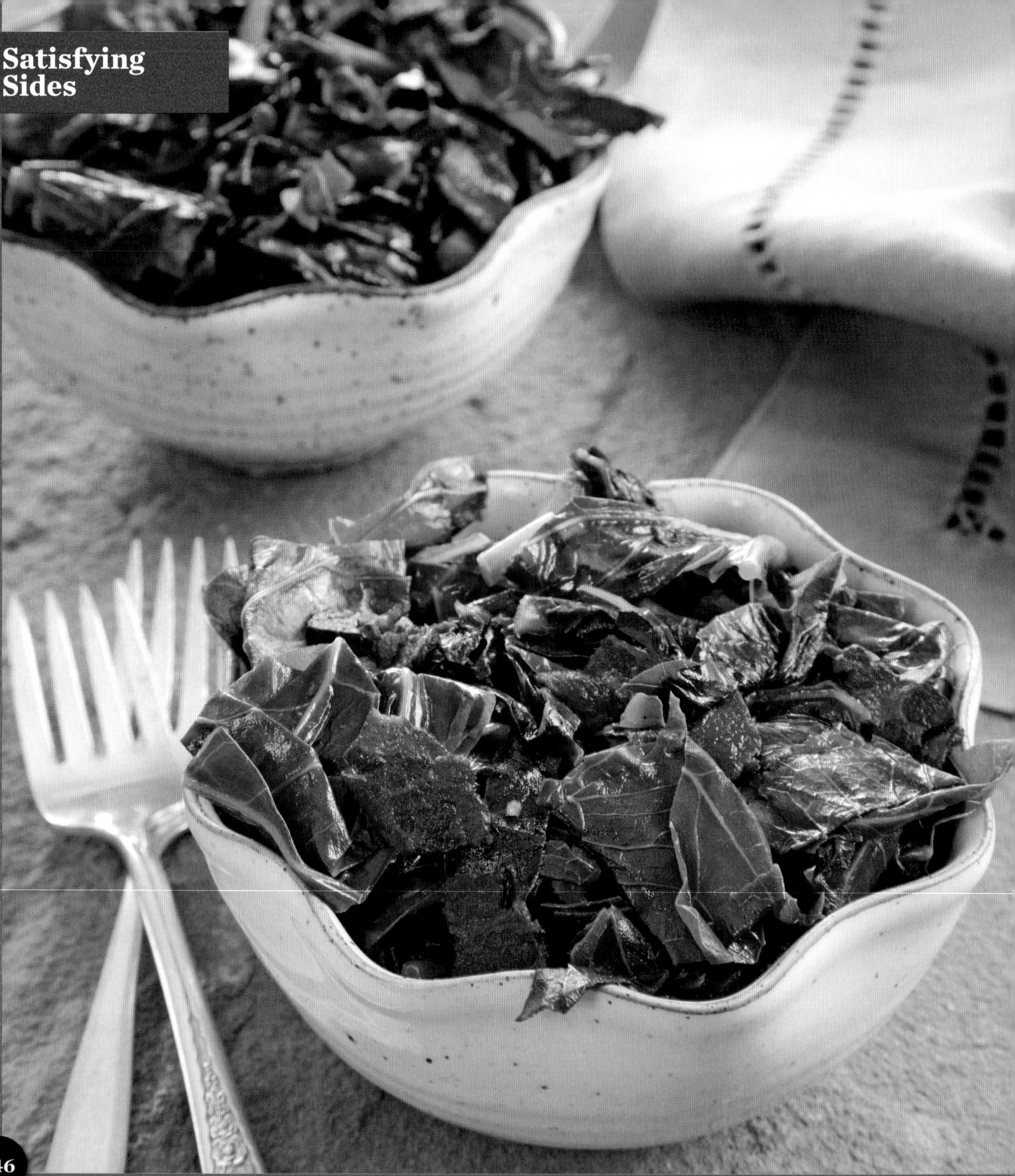

# Bacon and Bourbon Collards

*You'll need the largest Dutch oven you have to hold this "mess o' greens." A 7.5-qt. size provides ample space.*

**Makes:** 10 servings   **Hands-on Time:** 40 min.   **Total Time:** 1 hr., 40 min.

- 4   thick bacon slices
- 3   Tbsp. butter
- 1   large sweet onion, diced
- 1   (12-oz.) bottle ale beer
- ½   cup firmly packed brown sugar
- ½   cup bourbon
- 1   tsp. dried crushed red pepper
- 6   lb. fresh collard greens, trimmed and chopped
- ½   cup cider vinegar
- 1   tsp. salt
- ½   tsp. pepper

**1.** Cut bacon crosswise into ¼-inch strips. Melt butter in a large Dutch oven over medium heat; add bacon, and cook, stirring often, 8 minutes or until crisp. Drain bacon on paper towels, reserving drippings in skillet. Sauté onion in hot drippings 3 minutes or until onion is tender. Stir in bacon, ale, and next 3 ingredients; cook 3 minutes or until mixture is reduced by one-fourth.

**2.** Add collards, in batches, and cook, stirring occasionally, 5 minutes or until wilted. Reduce heat to medium-low; cover and cook 1 hour or to desired degree of doneness. Stir in vinegar, salt, and pepper.

## NORM'S NOTE
### Discover a Shortcut for Collards

Washing, trimming, and chopping 6 pounds of collards takes a bit of patience to get the job done. If short on time or the energy needed to tackle the task, there is another option. Fresh collards are now sold washed, chopped, and bagged for your convenience in many grocery stores. They are usually found neighboring prepackaged lettuces and bagged salad mixes.

# Fried Cucumbers

*Crispy fried Kirbys are an ideal mate to your next hamburger.*

**Makes:** about 5½ to 6 dozen   **Hands-on Time:** 37 min.   **Total Time:** 57 min.

4  small Kirby cucumbers (about 1 lb.), cut into ⅛- to ¼-inch-thick slices
1  tsp. kosher salt, divided
¾  cup cornstarch
½  cup self-rising white cornmeal mix
¼  tsp. ground black pepper
¼  tsp. ground red pepper
¾  cup lemon-lime soft drink
1  large egg, lightly beaten
   Vegetable oil
   Ranch dressing or desired sauce

**1.** Arrange cucumber slices between layers of paper towels. Sprinkle with ½ tsp. kosher salt, and let stand 20 minutes.

**2.** Combine cornstarch and next 3 ingredients. Stir in soft drink and egg. Dip cucumber slices into batter.

**3.** Pour oil to depth of ½ inch into a large cast-iron or heavy skillet; heat to 375°. Fry cucumbers, 6 to 8 at a time, about 1½ minutes on each side or until golden. Drain on paper towels. Sprinkle with remaining ½ tsp. kosher salt, and serve immediately with dressing or sauce.

**Note:** We tested with White Lily Self-Rising White Cornmeal Mix.

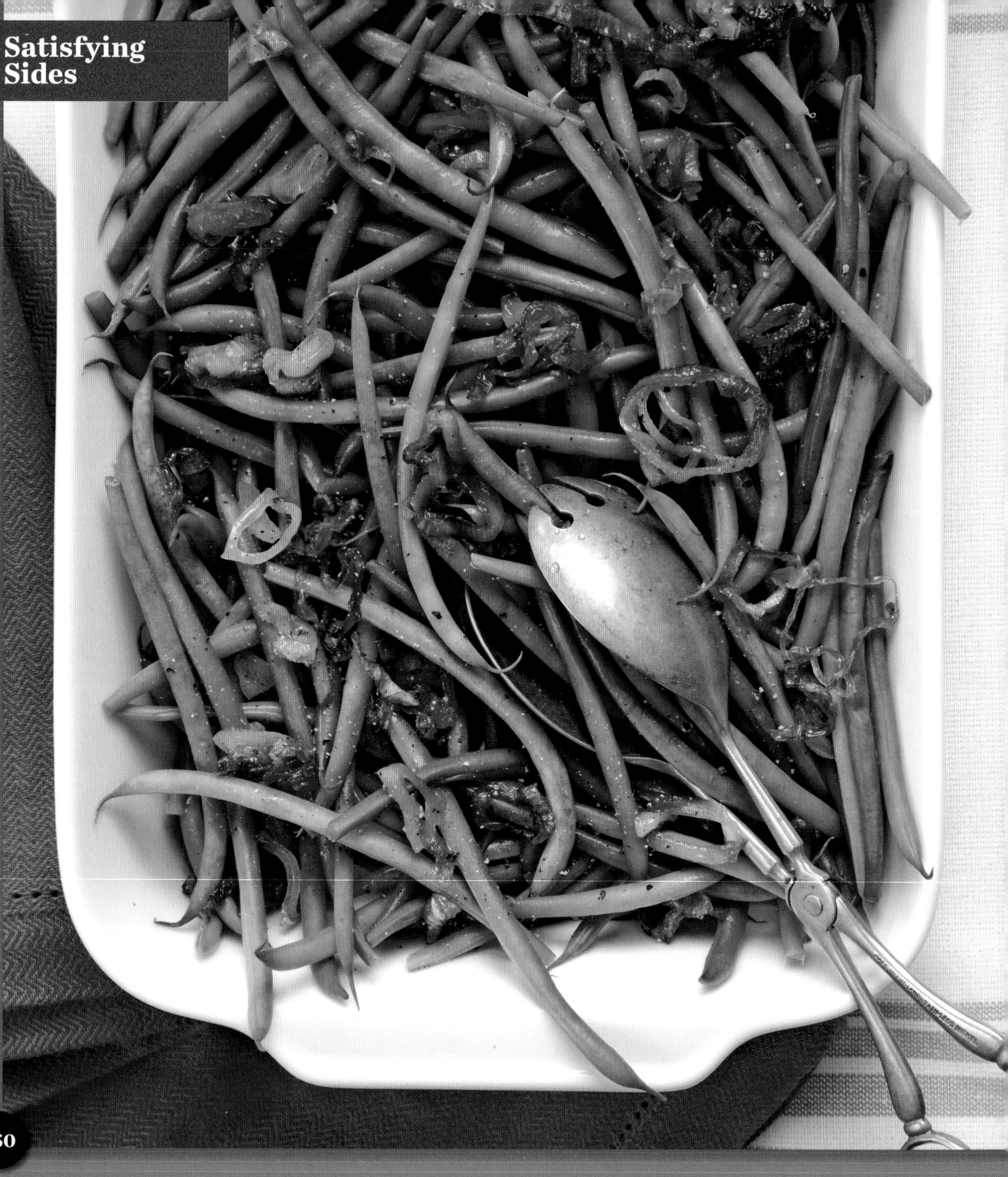

# Green Beans with Caramelized Shallots

*Crisp-tender green beans are given a lift of sweet, smoky flavor with the addition of caramelized shallots.*

**Makes:** 8 to 10 servings    **Hands-on Time:** 30 min.    **Total Time:** 30 min.

- 2 lb. haricots verts (tiny green beans), trimmed
- 3 Tbsp. butter
- 1 Tbsp. light brown sugar
- 1 Tbsp. olive oil
- 1 lb. shallots, peeled, halved lengthwise, and thinly sliced
- 2 Tbsp. red wine vinegar
- Salt and freshly ground pepper to taste

**1.** Cook green beans in boiling salted water to cover 3 to 4 minutes or until crisp-tender; drain. Plunge beans into ice water to stop the cooking process; drain.

**2.** Melt butter and brown sugar with olive oil in a large skillet over medium-high heat; add shallots, and sauté 2 minutes. Reduce heat to medium-low, add vinegar, and sauté 10 minutes or until shallots are golden brown and tender.

**3.** Increase heat to medium-high; add green beans, and sauté 5 minutes or until thoroughly heated. Season with salt and freshly ground pepper to taste.

## NORM'S NOTE
### Cool Green Beans

Cooking green beans until crisp-tender and quickly plunging them into an ice-water bath is a process known as blanching. The icy dip is key, preserving the texture and color of the beans by instantly stopping the cooking process. Be sure to drain the beans well and pat dry with paper towels to remove excess water.

### Make Black-eyed Pea Salad

1. Bring water to a rolling boil before adding the peas. Reduce the heat to low, and simmer for about 20 minutes to get peas al dente.

2. Whisking together the dressing in a 2-cup liquid measuring cup saves you a bowl to wash and makes pouring the dressing into the salad easier.

3. Stir prepared dressing into cooked peas, bell pepper, and onion. Cover and let chill in refrigerator 8 hours to soak up the dressing.

# Lucky Black-eyed Pea Salad

*Peppery watercress stands in for traditional greens in this New Year's Day-appropriate salad. Luckily, January is peak season for fresh Chilean peaches— ripen them at room temperature in a brown paper bag until fragrant and juicy.*

**Makes:** 6 servings    **Hands-on Time:** 10 min.    **Total Time:** 9 hr., 10 min.

1 (16-oz.) package frozen black-eyed peas
¼ cup chopped fresh cilantro
¼ cup red pepper jelly
¼ cup red wine vinegar
2 Tbsp. olive oil
1 jalapeño pepper, seeded and minced
¾ tsp. salt
¼ tsp. freshly ground pepper
1 cup diced red bell pepper
⅓ cup diced red onion
2 large fresh peaches, peeled and diced
2 cups torn watercress

**1.** Prepare peas according to package directions, simmering only until al dente; drain and let cool 1 hour.

**2.** Whisk together cilantro and next 6 ingredients in a large bowl. Add cooked black-eyed peas, bell pepper, and onion, tossing to coat; cover and chill 8 hours. Stir peaches and watercress into pea mixture just before serving.

STEP 1

STEP 2

STEP 3

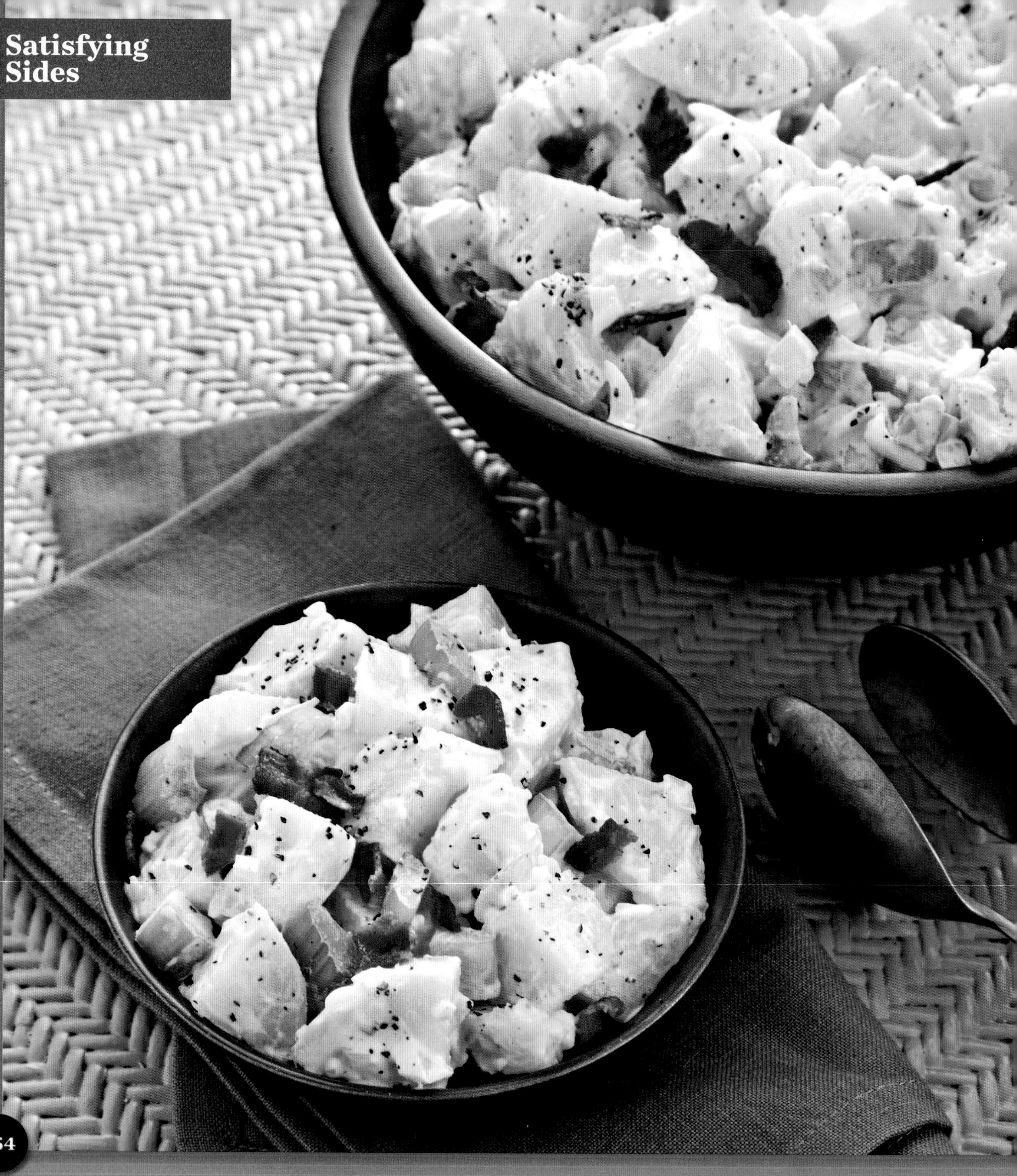

# Picnic Potato Salad

*Add a sprinkling of cooked and crumbled bacon just before serving to put this salad over the top.*

**Makes:** 8 servings
**Hands-on Time:** 20 min.
**Total Time:** 1 hr., 15 min.

- 4 **lb. Yukon gold potatoes**
- 3 **hard-cooked eggs, peeled and grated**
- 1 **cup mayonnaise**
- ½ **cup diced celery**
- ½ **cup sour cream**
- ⅓ **cup finely chopped sweet onion**
- ¼ **cup sweet pickle relish**
- 1 **Tbsp. spicy brown mustard**
- 1 **tsp. salt**
- ¾ **tsp. freshly ground pepper**

**1.** Cook potatoes in boiling water to cover 40 minutes or until tender; drain and cool 15 minutes. Peel potatoes, and cut into 1-inch cubes.

**2.** Combine potatoes and eggs.

**3.** Stir together mayonnaise and next 7 ingredients; gently stir into potato mixture. Serve immediately, or cover and chill 12 hours.

# Church-Style Lemon Roasted Potatoes

**Makes:** 6 to 8 servings
**Hands-on Time:** 28 min.
**Total Time:** 1 hr., 8 min.

- 3 **Tbsp. olive oil**
- 1½ **Tbsp. butter**
- 3 **lb. small Yukon gold potatoes, peeled and cut into ½-inch chunks**
- ¼ **cup lemon juice**
- 4 **tsp. chopped fresh thyme**
- ¾ **tsp. salt**
- ½ **tsp. pepper**

**1.** Preheat oven to 400°. Cook olive oil and butter in a skillet over medium heat, stirring constantly, 3 to 4 minutes or until butter begins to turn golden brown. Remove butter mixture from heat, and add potatoes, tossing gently to coat.

**2.** Spread potatoes in a single layer in a 15- x 10-inch jelly-roll pan.

**3.** Bake at 400° for 40 to 45 minutes or until potatoes are golden brown and tender, stirring twice. Transfer potatoes to a large serving bowl, and toss with lemon juice, chopped fresh thyme, salt, and pepper until well coated. Serve potatoes immediately.

Mashed potatoes pair perfectly with many Southern fried favorites—chicken, steak, and pork chops, to name a few. A trick to creating fluffy mashed potatoes is drying after boiling. To do this, drain water from cooked potatoes, and return the potatoes to a Dutch oven. Place over medium heat, and cook, stirring constantly, 3 to 5 minutes or until the potatoes are dry and crumbly on the outside. Mash the spuds with a large fork or potato masher, and gently stir in milks, butter, and seasonings just until blended.

# Browned-Butter Mashed Potatoes

*Browned butter adds a heavenly toasted nut taste and aroma to traditional mashed potatoes.*

**Makes:** 6 to 8 servings    **Hands-on Time:** 35 min.    **Total Time:** 50 min.

¾  **cup butter**
4  **lb. Yukon gold potatoes, peeled and cut into 2-inch pieces**
1  **Tbsp. salt, divided**
¾  **cup buttermilk**
½  **cup milk**
¼  **tsp. pepper**
   **Garnishes:  chopped fresh parsley, rosemary, thyme**

**1.** Cook butter in a 2-qt. heavy saucepan over medium heat, stirring constantly, 6 to 8 minutes or just until butter begins to turn golden brown. Immediately remove pan from heat, and pour butter into a small bowl. (Butter will continue to darken if left in saucepan.) Remove and reserve 1 to 2 Tbsp. browned butter.

**2.** Bring potatoes, 2 tsp. salt, and water to cover to a boil in a large Dutch oven over medium-high heat; boil 20 minutes or until tender. Drain. Reduce heat to low. Return potatoes to Dutch oven, and cook, stirring occasionally, 3 to 5 minutes or until potatoes are dry.

**3.** Mash potatoes with a potato masher to desired consistency. Stir in remaining browned butter, buttermilk, milk, pepper, and remaining 1 tsp. salt, stirring just until blended.

**4.** Transfer to a serving dish. Drizzle with reserved 1 to 2 Tbsp. browned butter. Garnish, if desired.

**Note:** To make ahead, prepare recipe as directed through Step 3. Place in a lightly greased 2½-qt. ovenproof serving dish; cover and chill up to 2 days. Let stand at room temperature 30 minutes. Bake, uncovered, at 350° for 35 to 40 minutes or until thoroughly heated. Drizzle with reserved browned butter, and garnish, if desired.

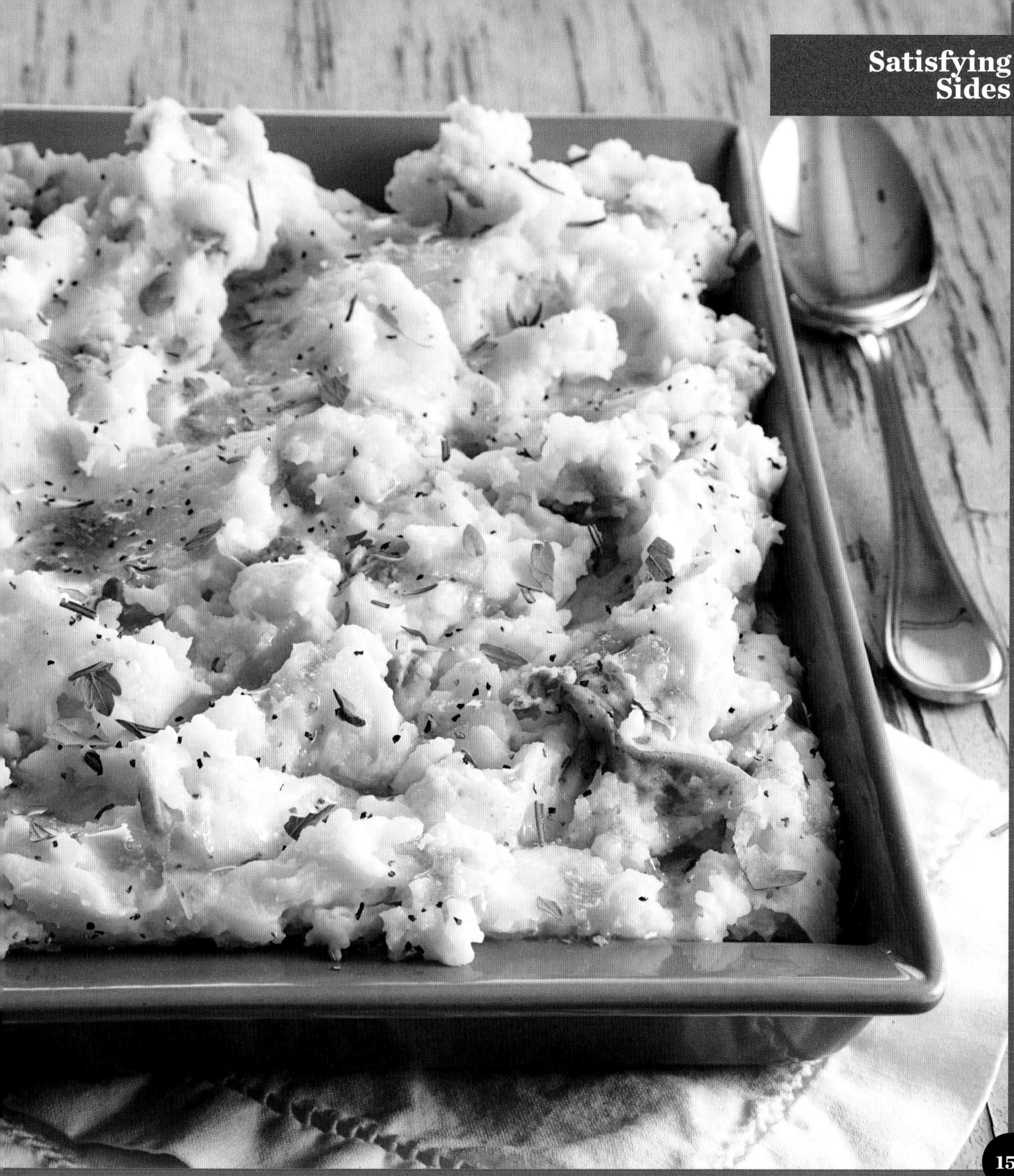

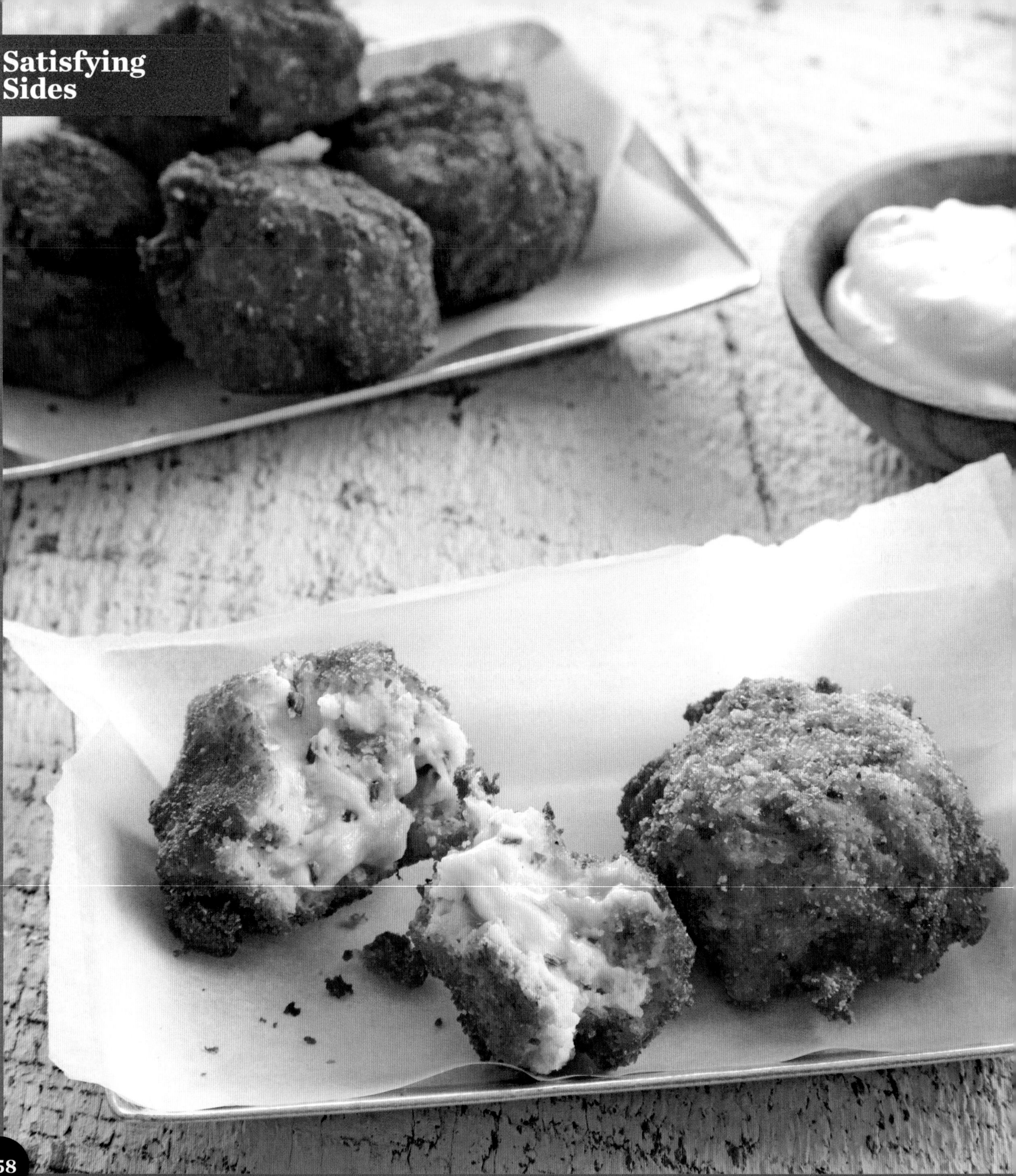

# Fried Potato Bites

**Makes:** 24 servings    **Hands-on Time:** 50 min.    **Total Time:** 50 min.

1  (24-oz.) container refrigerated mashed potatoes
1  cup (4 oz.) shredded sharp Cheddar cheese
4  Tbsp. chopped fresh chives, divided
3  slices bacon, crisply cooked, crumbled
6  large eggs, divided
1¾  cups fine, dry breadcrumbs
    Vegetable oil
1  (16-oz.) container sour cream
2  tsp. dry Ranch dressing mix (from 1-oz. package)

**1.** Mix mashed potatoes, cheese, 2 Tbsp. chives, bacon, and 1 egg with a spoon until blended. Shape mixture into 1-inch balls.

**2.** Place breadcrumbs in a shallow bowl. Beat remaining 5 eggs in another shallow bowl. Coat potato balls with breadcrumbs; dip into beaten eggs. Coat again with breadcrumbs.

**3.** In a deep-fat fryer or heavy saucepan, heat 2 inches oil to 375°. Fry potato balls in hot oil 1 to 1½ minutes or until golden brown. Drain on paper towels.

**4.** Mix sour cream, remaining 2 Tbsp. chives, and dressing mix in a small bowl. Serve potato bites with sauce.

**Serving Tip:** Get all the flavors of a loaded baked potato in one mouthful. These fried mashed potato balls are best served hot while the cheesy center is freshly melted.

## FRY IT SAFELY
### Oil and Water Don't Mix

Be sure to keep any type of water away from the deep fryer or heavy saucepan. Adding a small amount of water can cause the oil to bubble and possibly splatter, causing burns. Make sure that all cooking tools are dry and that there is no water around your cooking area.

# Garlicky "Fried" Vegetables

**Makes:** 6 servings    **Hands-on Time:** 35 min.    **Total Time:** 1 hr., 10 min., including Horseradish Sauce

1  **small green tomato, cut into ¼-inch-thick slices**
⅛  **tsp. salt**
1  **small zucchini, cut into ¼-inch-thick slices**
½  **(8-oz.) container button mushrooms, stems removed**
½  **lb. whole okra**
1  **medium-size red bell pepper, cut into strips**
1  **large garlic clove, minced**
2  **tsp. Creole seasoning**
¼  **cup cornstarch, sifted**
3  **cups panko (Japanese breadcrumbs)**
¼  **tsp. salt**
¼  **tsp. pepper**
6  **egg whites**
   **Vegetable cooking spray**
   **Horseradish Sauce**

**1.** Preheat oven to 400°. Place tomato slices on paper towels; sprinkle with ⅛ tsp. salt, and let stand 5 minutes.

**2.** Place tomatoes, zucchini, and next 4 ingredients in a large bowl. Sprinkle evenly with Creole seasoning and cornstarch; shake to remove excess.

**3.** Combine panko, ¼ tsp. salt, and pepper in a shallow bowl. Whisk 3 egg whites in a small bowl until frothy. Dip half of vegetables in egg whites, draining excess. Dredge vegetables, in batches, in panko mixture. Repeat procedure with remaining egg whites, vegetables, and panko mixture.

**4.** Arrange vegetables on wire racks coated with cooking spray; place racks on aluminum foil-lined pans. (Do not overlap vegetables.)

**5.** Bake at 400° for 30 to 35 minutes or until golden brown. Serve immediately with Horseradish Sauce.

### Horseradish Sauce

**Makes:** ¾ cup
**Hands-on Time:** 5 min.
**Total Time:** 5 min.

¾  **cup sour cream**
2  **Tbsp. buttermilk**
2  **tsp. refrigerated horseradish**
¼  **tsp. salt**
¼  **tsp. pepper**

Stir together all ingredients. Cover and chill until ready to serve.

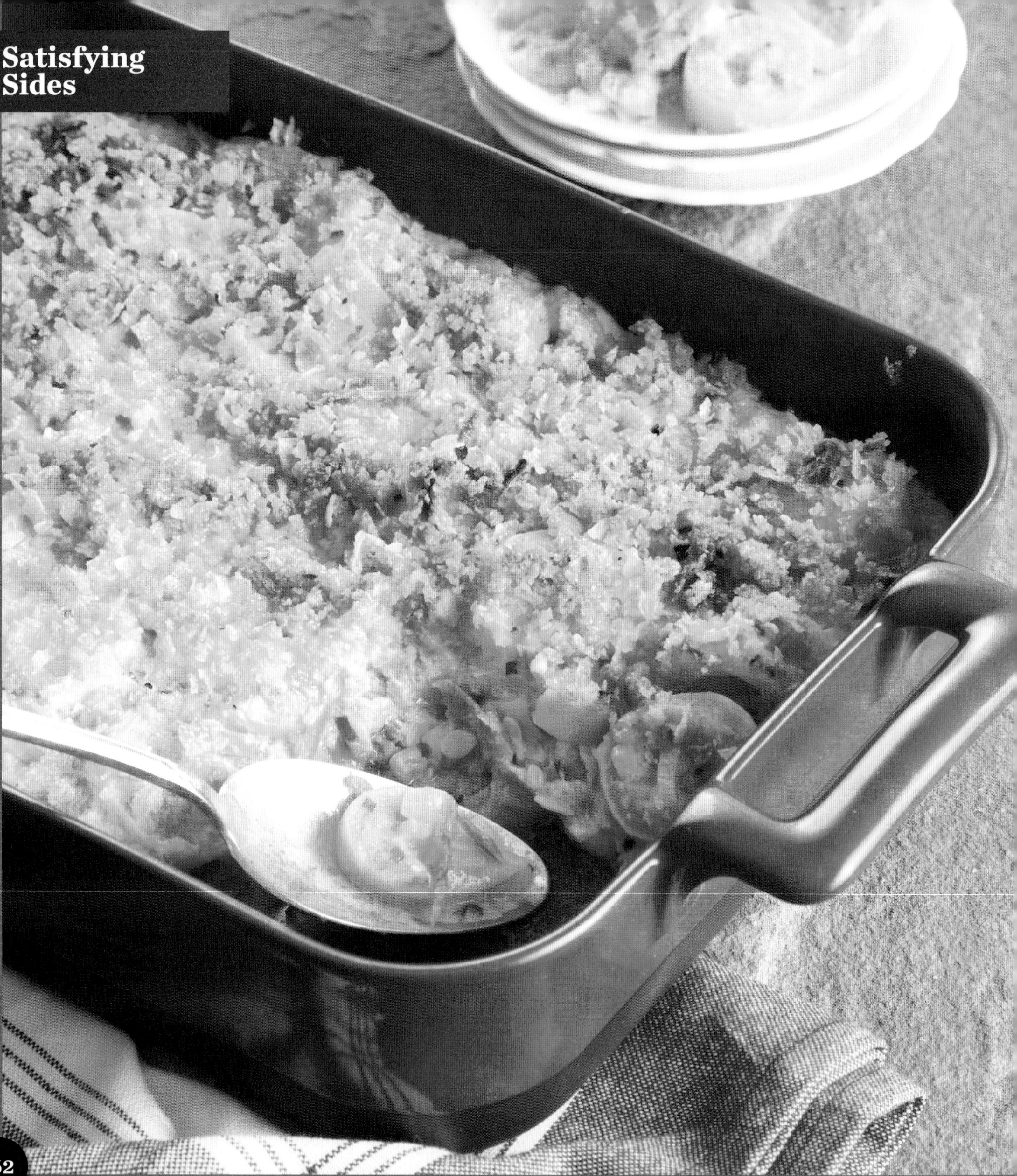

# Squash Casserole

**Makes:** 10 to 12 servings
**Hands-on Time:** 25 min.
**Total Time:** 1 hr., 5 min.

- 3 lb. yellow squash
- ½ cup chopped sweet onion
- 1½ tsp. salt, divided
- 1 cup grated carrots
- 1 (10¾-oz.) can reduced-fat cream of chicken soup
- 1 (8-oz.) container reduced-fat sour cream
- ¼ cup chopped fresh chives
- ½ cup crushed cornflakes cereal
- ½ cup crushed French fried onions
- 2 Tbsp. melted butter
- ¼ tsp. freshly ground pepper

**1.** Preheat oven to 350°. Cut squash into ¼-inch-thick slices; place in a Dutch oven. Add onion, 1 tsp. salt, and water to cover. Bring to a boil over medium-high heat, and cook 5 minutes; drain well, and pat squash dry with paper towels.

**2.** Stir together grated carrots, next 3 ingredients, and remaining ½ tsp. salt in a large bowl; fold in squash mixture. Spoon into a lightly greased 2-qt. baking dish.

**3.** Stir together cornflakes cereal and next 3 ingredients in a small bowl. Sprinkle over squash mixture.

**4.** Bake at 350° for 30 to 35 minutes or until bubbly and golden brown, shielding with aluminum foil after 20 to 25 minutes to prevent excessive browning, if necessary. Let stand 10 minutes before serving.

# Sautéed Garlic Spinach

**Makes:** 4 servings
**Hands-on Time:** 10 min.
**Total Time:** 10 min.

- 1 tsp. olive oil
- 1 garlic clove, pressed
- 1 (10-oz.) bag fresh spinach
  Salt and pepper to taste

Heat olive oil in a nonstick skillet over medium-high heat. Sauté garlic in hot oil 30 seconds. Add fresh spinach to skillet, and cook 2 to 3 minutes or until spinach is wilted. Sprinkle with salt and pepper to taste. Serve spinach with a slotted spoon or tongs.

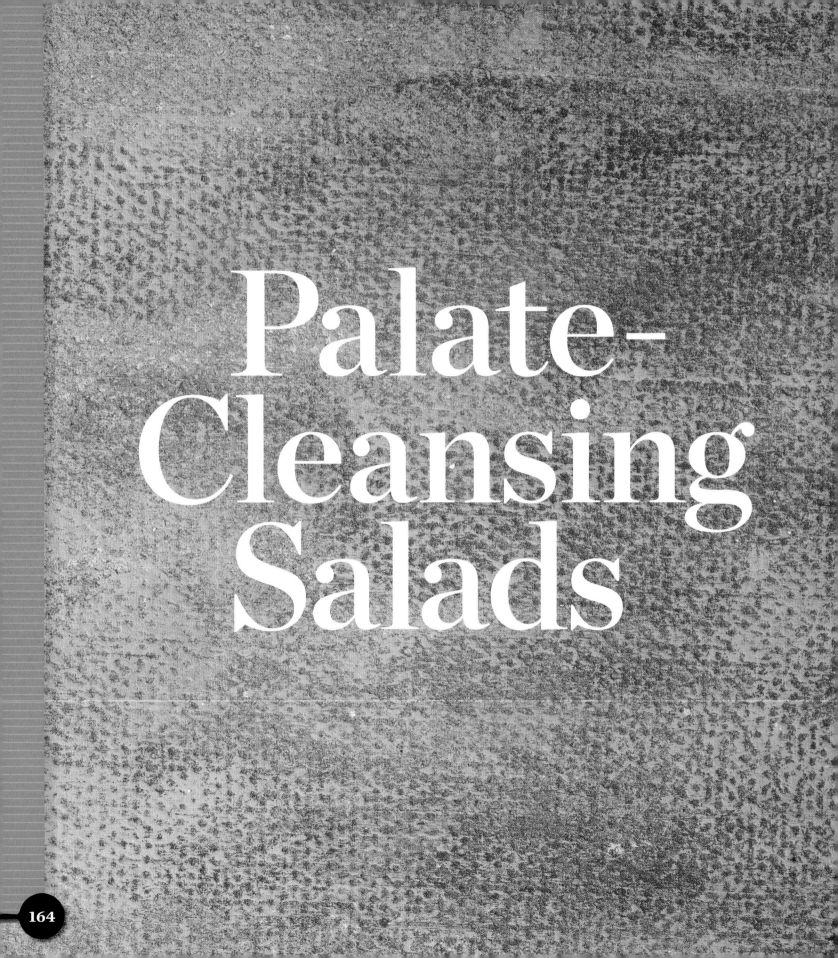

# Palate-Cleansing Salads

Tomato
and
Watermelon
Salad,
*page 167*

Norm selects the freshest tomatoes at a local market to go into his Tomato and Watermelon Salad.

# Tomato and Watermelon Salad

*(pictured on page 165)*

*Combine sweet, juicy watermelon chunks with fresh tomato, onion, and a red wine vinaigrette for a salad that's the essence of summer.*

**Makes:** 4 to 6 servings    **Hands-on Time:** 20 min.    **Total Time:** 2 hr., 35 min.

- 5  cups (¾-inch) seeded watermelon cubes
- 1½ lb. ripe tomatoes, cut into ¾-inch wedges
- 3  tsp. sugar
- ½  tsp. salt
- 1  small red onion, quartered and thinly sliced
- ½  cup red wine vinegar
- ¼  cup extra virgin olive oil
  - Romaine lettuce leaves (optional)
  - Cracked black pepper to taste
  - Garnish: basil leaves

**1.** Combine watermelon and tomatoes in a large bowl; sprinkle with sugar and salt, tossing to coat. Let stand 15 minutes.

**2.** Stir in onion, vinegar, and oil. Cover and chill 2 hours. Serve chilled with lettuce leaves, if desired. Sprinkle with cracked black pepper to taste. Garnish, if desired.

Ripe and juicy vine-ripened tomatoes are one of nature's blessings. Take advantage of the plentiful and diverse varieties of these garden gems while they're in season. Use different shapes, sizes, and colors of tomatoes cut into cubes, wedges, halves, or quarters to mix up the taste and texture of salads. Keep it simple with flavoring and seasonings to accentuate the delicate flavor of the tomato. Spend a Saturday at your local farmers' market, and go wild.

# Melon and Plum Salad

*Try a mix of melons, like cantaloupe, honeydew, or Crenshaw, to change up the taste of this fresh fruit salad.*

**Makes:** 6 servings     **Hands-on Time:** 20 min.
**Total Time:** 30 min., including vinaigrette

- 4 **cups seeded and cubed watermelon**
- 4 **cups honeydew melon balls**
- 3 **red plums, sliced**
- 2 **cups torn watercress**
- 1 **cup crumbled feta cheese**
  **Pepper Jelly Vinaigrette**
  **Salt and pepper to taste**

Gently toss together first 5 ingredients, and place on a serving platter. Drizzle with vinaigrette, and season with salt and pepper to taste.

### Pepper Jelly Vinaigrette

Whisk together ¼ cup rice wine vinegar, ¼ cup hot jalapeño pepper jelly, 1 Tbsp. chopped fresh mint, 1 Tbsp. grated onion, and 1 Tbsp. fresh lime juice. Gradually add ¼ cup canola oil in a slow, steady stream, whisking until smooth. Makes: ¾ cup. Hands-on Time: 10 min.; Total Time: 10 min.

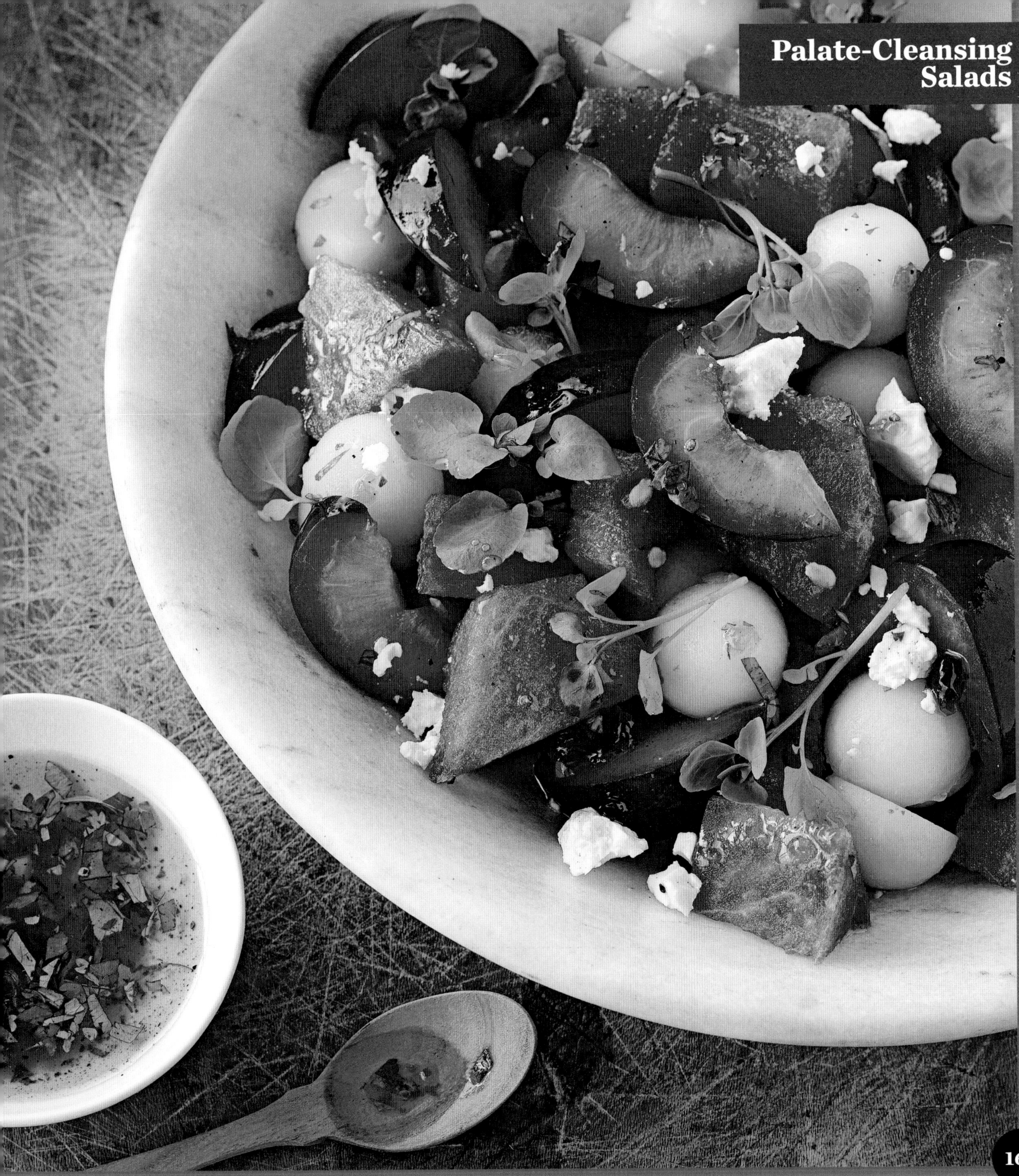

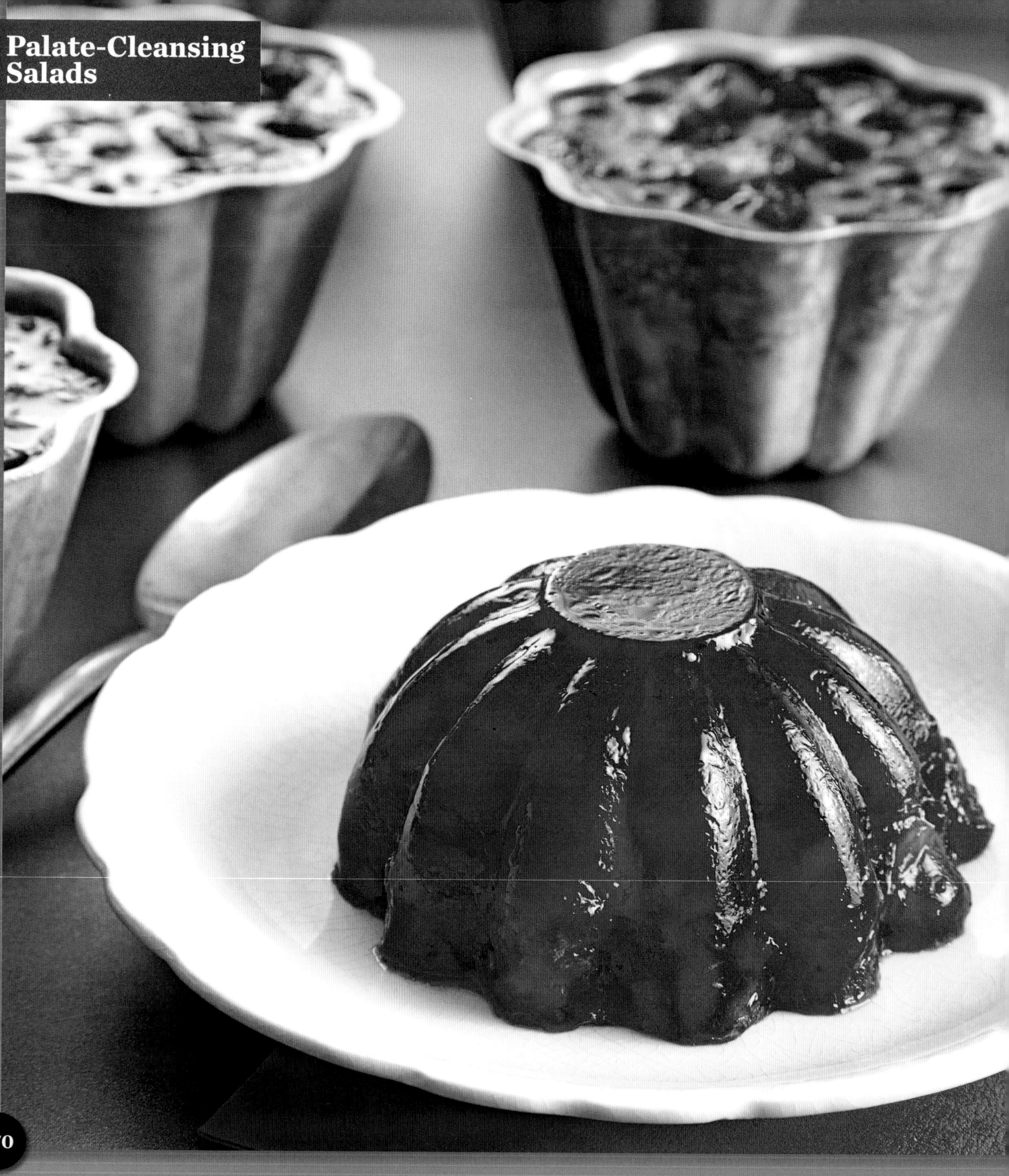

# Cranberry-Strawberry Salad

*This congealed salad is a cool, delicious twist on a retro luncheon staple.*

**Makes:** 12 servings    **Hands-on Time:** 20 min.    **Total Time:** 8 hr., 50 min.

- 1½ cups fresh or frozen cranberries
- 2 cups diced fresh strawberries
- ½ cup sugar
- 2 cups boiling water
- 3 (3-oz.) packages strawberry-flavored gelatin
- 2 cups cranberry juice, chilled
- 1 (8-oz.) can crushed pineapple, undrained
- 1 cup diced celery

**1.** Process cranberries in a food processor 30 seconds or until coarsely chopped, stopping once to scrape down sides.

**2.** Stir together cranberries, strawberries, and sugar in a medium bowl.

**3.** Stir together 2 cups boiling water and gelatin in a large bowl, stirring 2 minutes or until gelatin dissolves. Stir in juice, and chill 30 minutes or until consistency of unbeaten egg white. Stir in cranberry mixture, pineapple, and celery. Spoon mixture into 12 lightly greased (⅔-cup) molds; cover and chill molds 8 hours or until firm.

## NORM'S NOTE
### Fit the Mold

Congealed salads are kind of like the cardigans of the food world, not necessarily high fashion or in vogue, but comfy and classic. I'm proud to say I'm an aficionado of "old school" gelatin-based salads (and cardigans). They are refreshing, they cleanse your palate from greasy or strong flavors, and they can be served as a side salad or dessert.

I love to hit antiques shops and local estate sales, or dig through top cabinets in the Test Kitchen, to unearth some tin relic to use as a mold for a congealed salad. It's kind of like thrift shopping for that unique (ugly) off-green Mr. Rogers-style cardigan that looks great with a pair of dark denim and a crisp white shirt—classic.

## Avocado Fruit Salad

*You can prepare this salad a day ahead, but don't cut up the avocado until just before you serve it.*

**Makes:** 6 cups
**Hands-on Time:** 15 min.
**Total Time:** 1 hr., 15 min.

- 1 (24-oz.) jar refrigerated orange and grapefruit sections, drained, rinsed, and patted dry
- 1 (24-oz.) jar refrigerated tropical mixed fruit in light syrup, drained, rinsed, and patted dry
- 2 cups cubed fresh cantaloupe
- 1 medium-size ripe avocado, halved and cut into chunks
- ¼ cup chopped fresh mint
- 2 Tbsp. lime juice

Toss together all ingredients. Cover and chill 1 hour.

**Note:** We tested with Del Monte SunFresh Citrus Salad and Del Monte SunFresh Tropical Mixed Fruit in Light Syrup with Passion Fruit Juice.

## Bing Cherry Salad

*Try this salad with a dollop of mayonnaise.*

**Makes:** 8 servings
**Hands-on Time:** 12 min.
**Total Time:** 9 hr., 50 min.

- 1 (15-oz.) can Bing cherries (dark, sweet pitted cherries)
- 2 (8-oz.) cans crushed pineapple in juice
- 1 (6-oz.) package cherry-flavored gelatin
- 1 cup cold water
  Mayonnaise (optional)
  Garnish: arugula

**1.** Drain cherries and pineapple, reserving 1½ cups juice in a saucepan. (If necessary, add water to equal 1½ cups.) Bring juice mixture to a boil over medium heat; stir in gelatin, and cook, stirring constantly, 2 minutes or until gelatin dissolves. Remove from heat, and stir in 1 cup cold water. Chill until consistency of unbeaten egg white (about 1½ hours).

**2.** Gently stir in drained cherries and pineapple. Pour mixture into an 8-inch square baking dish or 8 (⅔-cup) molds. Cover and chill 8 hours or until firm. Dollop with mayonnaise, and garnish, if desired.

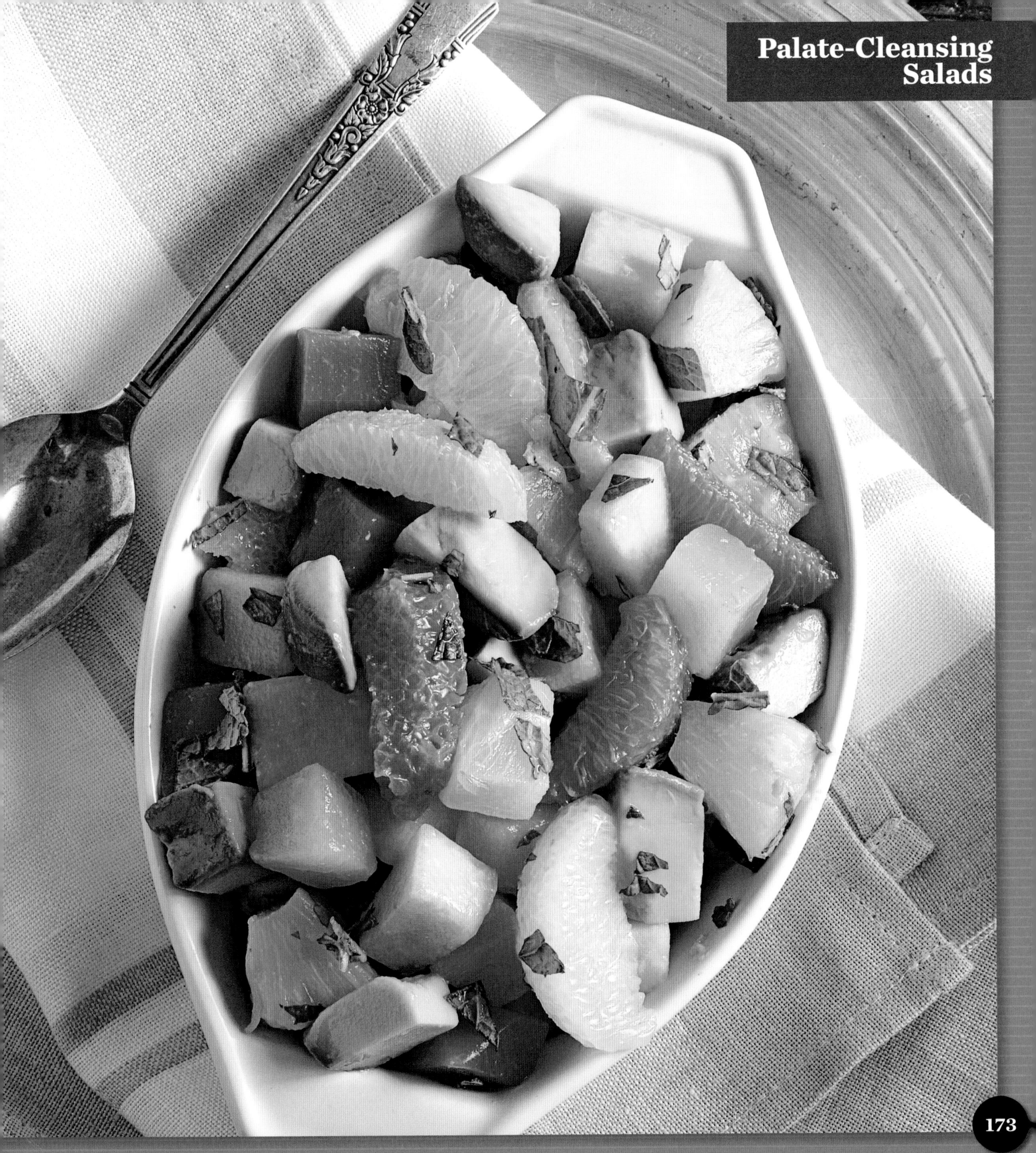

# Palate-Cleansing Salads

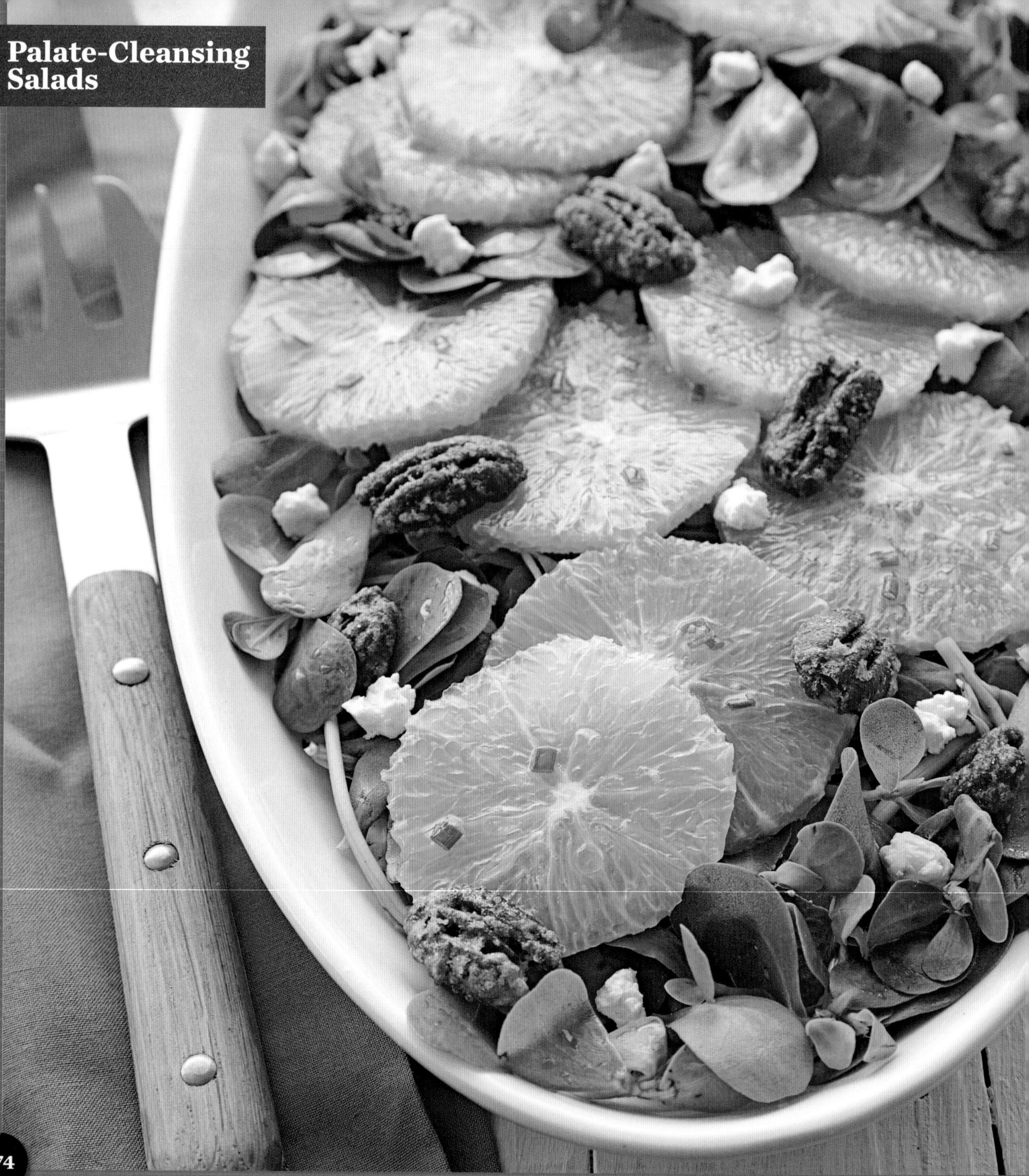

# Spiced Orange Salad with Goat Cheese and Glazed Pecans

*This is a favorite first course for holiday dinner parties. We often substitute Gorgonzola for goat cheese and top the oranges with sliced fresh strawberries.*

**Makes:** 6 servings    **Hands-on Time:** 20 min.    **Total Time:** 20 min.

- 6  large navel oranges
- 6  cups watercress
- ¼  cup canola oil
- ¼  cup rice wine vinegar
- 2  Tbsp. chopped fresh chives
- 1  Tbsp. light brown sugar
- 1  Tbsp. grated fresh ginger
- ¼  tsp. salt
- ½  cup crumbled goat cheese
- 1  (3.5-oz.) package roasted glazed pecan pieces

Peel oranges, and cut into ¼-inch-thick slices. Arrange watercress on a serving platter; top with orange slices. Whisk together canola oil and next 5 ingredients; drizzle over salad. Sprinkle with goat cheese and pecans.

## NORM'S NOTE
### Make Some Orange Appeal

To get beautiful orange slices like those in the photo, use a paring knife to peel the oranges. Remove the stem and navel ends so the orange rests flat on a cutting board. Cut away the peel, starting at the top of the orange and following the curvature of the orange until the knife is touching the cutting board, removing a small amount of the flesh with the peel. Continue until the orange is peeled, and then cut crosswise into ¼-inch slices. Segments can be made by cutting lengthwise along the membranes and allowing the segment to fall away. This technique will work on any citrus fruit.

## Citrus-Walnut Salad

*Refer to Norm's Note on page 175 for insight on how to peel and section the grapefruit.*

**Makes:** 8 servings
**Hands-on Time:** 15 min.
**Total Time:** 30 min., including vinaigrette

- ½ **cup walnut pieces**
- 8 **heads Belgian endive (about 2¼ lb.)**
- ½ **cup firmly packed fresh parsley leaves**
  **Cumin-Dijon Vinaigrette**
- 2 **red grapefruit, peeled and sectioned**

**1.** Preheat oven to 350°. Bake walnuts in a single layer in a shallow pan 6 to 8 minutes or until toasted and fragrant, stirring halfway through.

**2.** Remove and discard outer leaves of endive. Rinse endive with cold water, and pat dry. Cut each endive head diagonally into ¼-inch-thick slices, and place in a serving bowl. Add walnuts, parsley leaves, and desired amount of dressing; toss gently to coat. Top with grapefruit. Serve with any remaining dressing.

### Cumin-Dijon Vinaigrette

Whisk together ½ cup extra virgin olive oil, 3 Tbsp. white wine vinegar, 2 Tbsp. Dijon mustard, and ¼ tsp. each ground cumin, salt, and sugar. Makes: ¾ cup. Hands-on Time: 10 min.; Total Time: 10 min.

## Mango Salad

*Ripe mangoes are the key to making this dish a success. Pick ones that are firm but have gentle give when pressed with your thumb and give off a tropical fragrance.*

**Makes:** 6 to 8 servings
**Hands-on Time:** 25 min.
**Total Time:** 2 hr., 25 min.

- 2 **mangoes, peeled and cut into thin slices**
- 1½ **cups halved, seeded, and sliced English cucumber**
- 1½ **cups halved baby heirloom tomatoes**
- 1½ **cups fresh corn kernels**
- ½ **cup diced red onion**
- ½ **cup chopped fresh basil**
  **Fresh Lime Vinaigrette**
- 4 **cups arugula**

Toss together first 7 ingredients in a large bowl; cover and chill 2 hours. Toss with arugula just before serving.

### Fresh Lime Vinaigrette

Whisk together ¼ cup rice vinegar; 2 Tbsp. sugar; 3 Tbsp. fresh lime juice; 1 garlic clove, minced; and ½ tsp. each salt and freshly ground pepper. Gradually whisk in ½ cup canola oil until blended. Makes: ¾ cup. Hands-on Time: 10 min.; Total Time: 10 min.

# Palate-Cleansing Salads

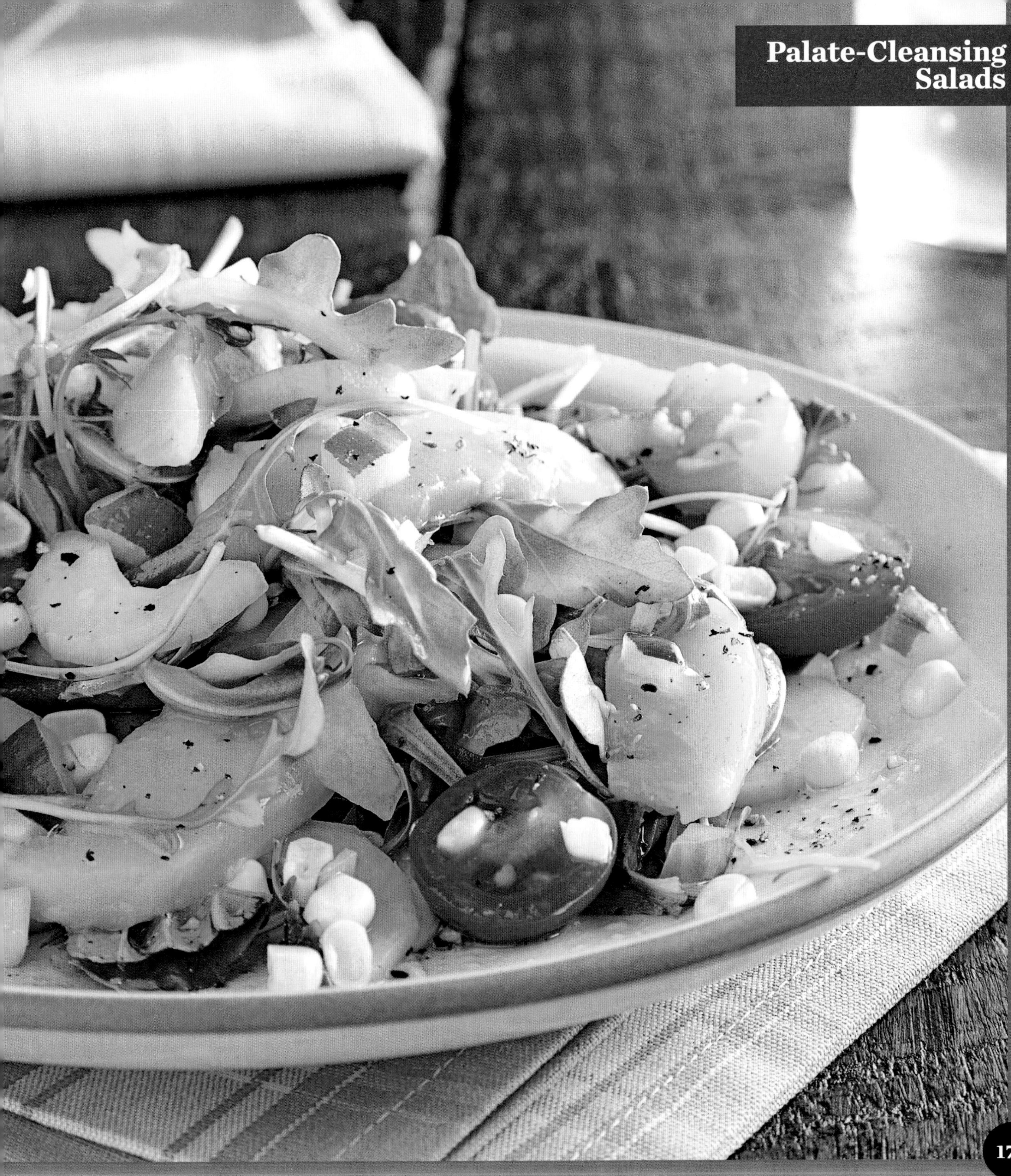

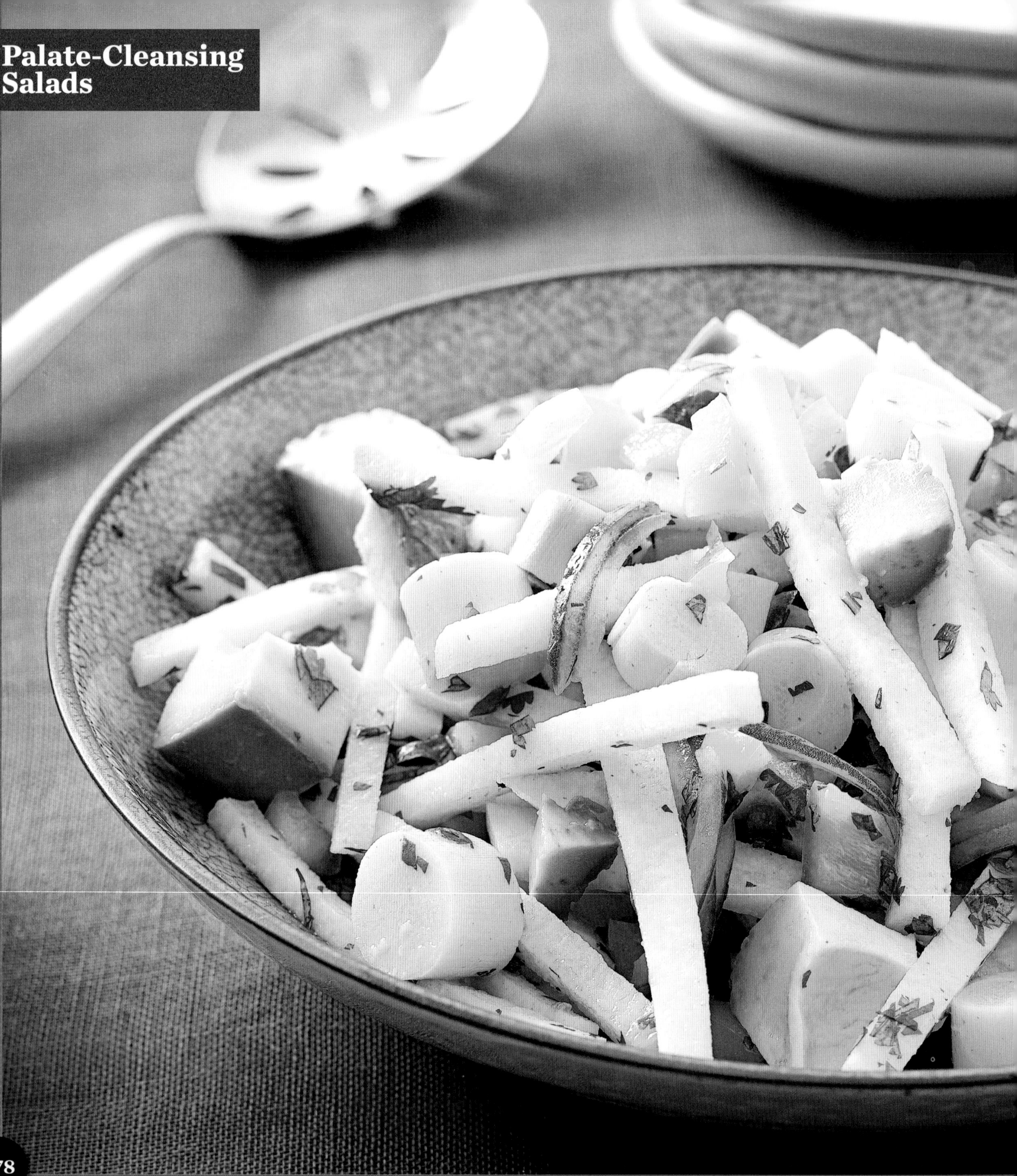

# Hearts of Palm and Jicama Salad

*Pick a jicama that's about the size of a large grapefruit, and use a vegetable peeler to remove the skin.*

**Makes:** 6 to 8 servings
**Hands-on Time:** 20 min.
**Total Time:** 1 hr., 20 min.

- 1 (14.4-oz.) can hearts of palm, drained and rinsed
- ¼ red onion, thinly sliced
- 1 yellow bell pepper, diced
- 1 jicama, peeled and cut into ⅛-inch strips
- 1 jalapeño pepper, seeded and minced
- ¼ cup chopped fresh cilantro
- ¼ cup fresh lime juice
- ¼ cup fresh orange juice
- 2 Tbsp. olive oil
- 1 tsp. salt
- ½ tsp. ground cumin
- 1 avocado, diced

Cut hearts of palm crosswise into ½-inch slices. Stir together hearts of palm and next 10 ingredients in a large bowl. Cover and chill 1 to 8 hours. Stir in avocado just before serving.

# Herbs and Greens Salad

*Lemony olive bread croutons top this lightly dressed salad. Double the dressing, if desired. Prep, bake, and cool the croutons up to three days ahead, and store in an airtight container.*

**Makes:** 6 to 8 servings
**Hands-on Time:** 10 min.
**Total Time:** 30 min.

- ½ tsp. lemon zest
- 4 Tbsp. olive oil, divided
- 3 cups 1-inch olive bread cubes*
- 4 cups torn butter lettuce (about 1 head)
- 2 cups firmly packed fresh baby spinach
- 1 cup torn escarole
- ½ cup loosely packed fresh parsley leaves
- ¼ cup fresh 1-inch chive pieces
- 2 Tbsp. fresh lemon juice
  Salt and pepper to taste

**1.** Preheat oven to 425°. Stir together lemon zest and 1 Tbsp. olive oil in a large bowl. Add bread cubes, and toss to coat. Arrange in a single layer on a baking sheet. Bake 5 minutes or until crisp. Let cool completely (about 15 minutes).

**2.** Meanwhile, combine butter lettuce and next 4 ingredients in a large bowl. Drizzle with lemon juice and remaining 3 Tbsp. olive oil, and toss to coat. Add salt and pepper to taste. Serve immediately with toasted bread cubes.

*Ciabatta, focaccia, or country white bread may be substituted.

# Crispy Sesame Salad Stack

*For a more casual presentation, toss together all the salad ingredients, and serve the Sesame Won Ton Crisps on the side.*

**Makes:** 6 servings   **Hands-on Time:** 15 min.   **Total Time:** 35 min., including won ton crisps and vinaigrette

1 (8-oz.) package mixed salad greens
   Sesame Won Ton Crisps (page 116)
1 (11-oz.) can mandarin orange segments, drained
2 green onions, sliced
6 Tbsp. chopped cashews
   Fresh Orange-Soy Vinaigrette
   Salt and pepper to taste

Layer ½ cup salad greens, 1 Sesame Won Ton Crisp, 3 Tbsp. salad greens, 1 Sesame Won Ton Crisp, and 1 Tbsp. salad greens on a serving plate. Carefully tuck 1 Tbsp. mandarin orange segments into salad greens. Repeat procedure with remaining salad greens, won ton crisps, and orange segments. Sprinkle with green onions and cashews. Drizzle with Fresh Orange-Soy Vinaigrette. Sprinkle with salt and pepper to taste. Serve immediately.

### Fresh Orange-Soy Vinaigrette

*Orange juice replaces much of the oil you would typically find in most salad dressings for a lighter, tangier taste.*

**Makes:** about ½ cup
**Hands-on Time:** 10 min.
**Total Time:** 10 min.

¼ cup rice vinegar
¼ cup orange juice
2 Tbsp. vegetable oil
1 Tbsp. soy sauce
2 Tbsp. dark brown sugar
1 tsp. grated fresh ginger
⅛ tsp. dry mustard
   Salt to taste

Combine ¼ cup rice vinegar and next 6 ingredients in a food processor; pulse 3 to 4 times or until smooth. Season with salt to taste.

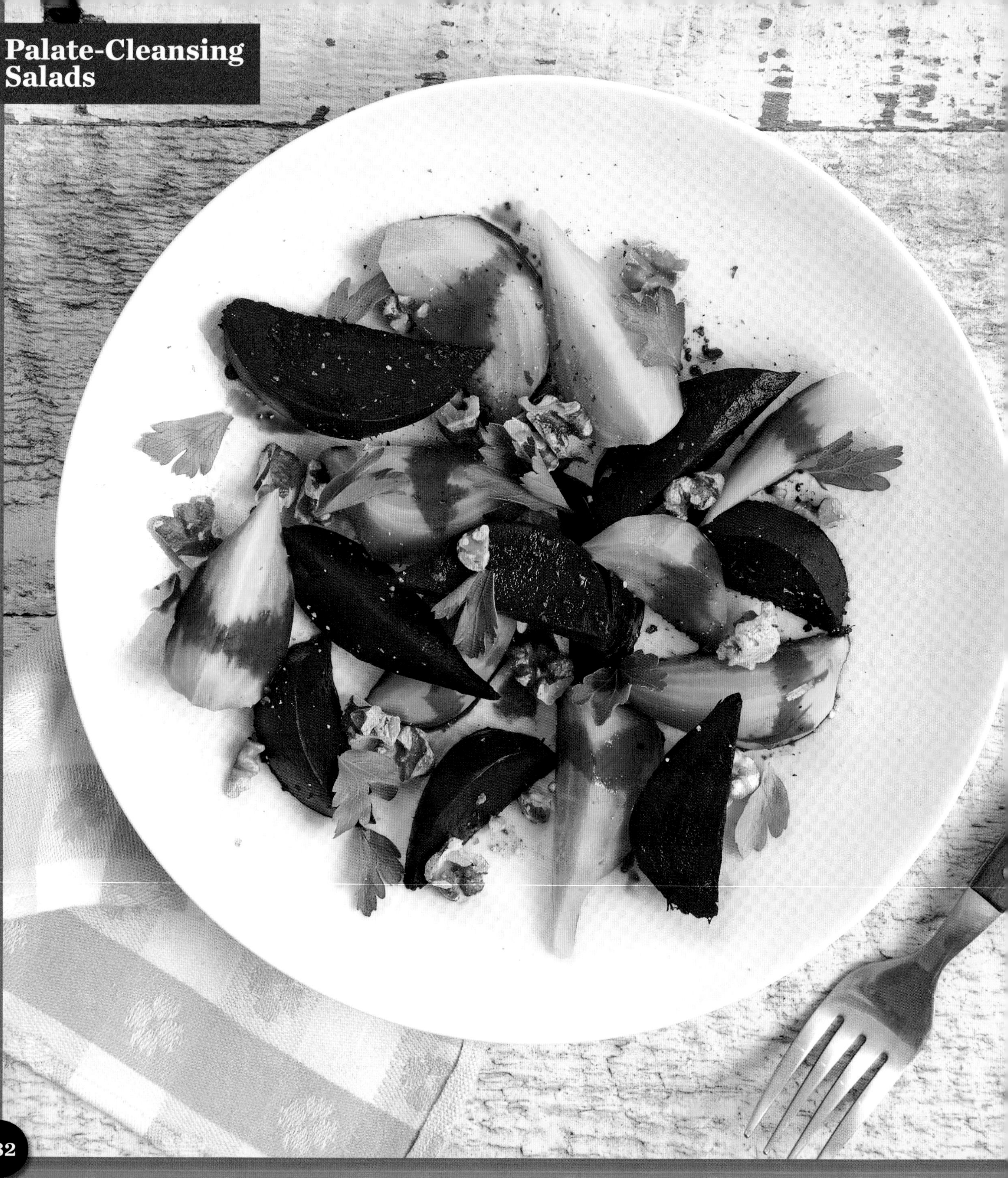

# Simple Beet Salad

*Colorful ingredients and easy preparation deliver delicious dividends. Use a variety of red and yellow beets to add visual appeal.*

**Makes:** 6 to 8 servings    **Hands-on Time:** 20 min.    **Total Time:** 2 hr., 13 min.

- 2  **lb. medium beets**
- ⅓  **cup bottled balsamic vinaigrette**
-    **Salt and pepper to taste**
- ½  **cup chopped walnuts**
-    **Garnish: fresh parsley leaves**

**1.** Preheat oven to 400°. Divide beets between 2 large pieces of heavy-duty aluminum foil; drizzle with balsamic vinaigrette, and sprinkle with salt and pepper to taste. Seal foil, making 2 loose packets.

**2.** Bake at 400° for 45 to 55 minutes until fork-tender.

**3.** Let cool 1 hour in packets, reserving accumulated liquid.

**4.** Bake walnuts at 400° in a single layer in a shallow pan 8 to 10 minutes or until toasted and fragrant, stirring halfway through.

**5.** Peel beets, and cut into slices or wedges. Arrange beets on a serving platter or in a bowl. Drizzle with reserved liquid, and sprinkle with walnuts. Garnish, if desired.

## NORM'S NOTE
### Go for Unbeetable Flavor

Roasting beets is the best way to unlock their sweet caramel-like flavor. I like to roast them using the packet method as described in the recipe, but I'll forgo the packet and roast them with their skins exposed, rubbed in a little olive oil, on a foil-lined jelly-roll pan to contain the mess. Once the beets have cooled, I use a paring knife to scrape off the skins and season them with kosher salt and freshly ground pepper and a squeeze of fresh lemon juice. The end result is well worth stained fingertips.

# Green Beans with Goat Cheese, Tomatoes, and Almonds

*Tender crisp green beans, fresh tomatoes, and a tangy vinaigrette are the simple foundation for a delicious, fresh, and healthy salad.*

**Makes:** 6 to 8 servings     **Hands-on Time:** 21 min.     **Total Time:** 33 min.

- ½  cup sliced almonds
- 2  lb. haricots verts (tiny green beans), trimmed
- 3  Tbsp. sherry vinegar*
- 2  Tbsp. fresh lemon juice
- ¾  tsp. salt
- ½  tsp. pepper
- ⅓  cup olive oil
- 1  pt. cherry tomatoes, halved
- 2  shallots, thinly sliced
- 2  garlic cloves, minced
- ½  (4-oz.) goat cheese log, crumbled

**1.** Preheat oven to 350°. Bake almonds in a single layer in a shallow pan 6 to 8 minutes or until lightly toasted and fragrant, stirring halfway through.

**2.** Cook green beans in boiling salted water to cover 6 to 8 minutes or until crisp-tender; drain. Plunge beans into ice water to stop the cooking process; drain.

**3.** Whisk together vinegar and next 3 ingredients in a large bowl; add olive oil in a slow, steady stream, whisking constantly until blended and smooth. Add cherry tomatoes, shallots, garlic, and green beans; toss to coat.

**4.** Top green bean mixture with crumbled goat cheese and toasted almonds.

*White wine vinegar may be substituted.

# Green Bean Pasta Salad with Lemon-Thyme Vinaigrette

*Casarecce [cah-sah-RECH-ee] pasta looks similar to a scroll with the long sides curled inward toward the center.*

**Makes:** 4 to 6 servings    **Hands-on Time:** 15 min.    **Total Time:** 30 min.

- 12  oz. uncooked casarecce pasta*
- ½  lb. haricots verts (tiny green beans), cut in half lengthwise
- 1  Tbsp. fresh thyme
- 5  tsp. lemon zest, divided
- ¼  cup finely chopped roasted, salted pistachios
- 2  Tbsp. Champagne vinegar
- 1  Tbsp. minced shallots
- 1  garlic clove, minced
- 1  tsp. salt
- ½  tsp. freshly ground pepper
- 5  Tbsp. olive oil
- 1½  cups loosely packed arugula

  Toppings: roasted, salted pistachios; Parmesan cheese

**1.** Cook pasta according to package directions, adding green beans to boiling water during last 2 minutes of cooking time; drain. Rinse pasta mixture with cold running water; drain well.

**2.** Place pasta mixture, thyme, and 3 tsp. lemon zest in a large bowl; toss gently to combine.

**3.** Whisk together pistachios, next 5 ingredients, and remaining 2 tsp. lemon zest in a small bowl. Add oil in a slow, steady stream, whisking constantly until blended. Drizzle over pasta mixture. Add arugula, and toss gently to coat. Serve with desired toppings.

*Penne pasta may be substituted.

## NORM'S NOTE
### Give Haricots Verts a Try

Haricots verts, also known as French green beans, are longer and thinner than traditional varieties of the vegetable. If you can't find them in your area, then you'll want to use the thinnest green beans that you can find. They pair well with pasta and the light lemon-thyme vinaigrette.

Picnics are a seasonal hobby of mine; well, to be honest, they're more like a necessity in the warmer months. I keep a picnic blanket, plastic wineglasses, plates, and flatware, plus a cooler packed in the back of my car for when the mood hits.

One of my favorite picnic sides is Veggie Potato Salad. It's ideal to take on an outing because it's basically a starch and vegetable, making one less thing I have to prepare and carry. My other picnic favorites include Our Best Southern Fried Chicken on page 70, served cold, and sparkling lemonade.

# Veggie Potato Salad

*This "all-in-one" side dish features potato salad with the addition of garden-fresh vegetables such as carrots, celery, radishes, and green beans.*

**Makes:** 10 servings   **Hands-on Time:** 25 min.   **Total Time:** 2 hr., 30 min.

2½  lb.  baby red potatoes, cut into 1-inch cubes
 2  Tbsp. cider vinegar
 1  Tbsp. olive oil
 ½  cup whole buttermilk
 ¼  cup reduced-fat sour cream
 ¼  cup reduced-fat mayonnaise with olive oil
 1  Tbsp. Dijon mustard
 2  carrots, grated
 ½  cup chopped celery
 ½  cup sliced radishes
 ½  cup steamed, cut fresh green beans
 ¼  cup finely chopped fresh parsley
 1  Tbsp. lemon zest
 1  garlic clove, minced
    Sea salt and freshly ground pepper to taste

**1.** Bring potatoes and salted water to cover to a boil in a large saucepan; reduce heat, and simmer 7 to 10 minutes or until tender. Drain. Place potatoes in a large bowl; sprinkle with vinegar and oil, and toss gently. Cool completely (about 1 hour).

**2.** Whisk together buttermilk and next 3 ingredients. Stir in carrots and next 6 ingredients; season with salt and pepper to taste. Spoon buttermilk mixture over potato mixture; toss gently to coat. Cover and chill 1 to 24 hours before serving.

**Note:** We tested with Kraft Reduced-Fat Mayonnaise with Olive Oil.

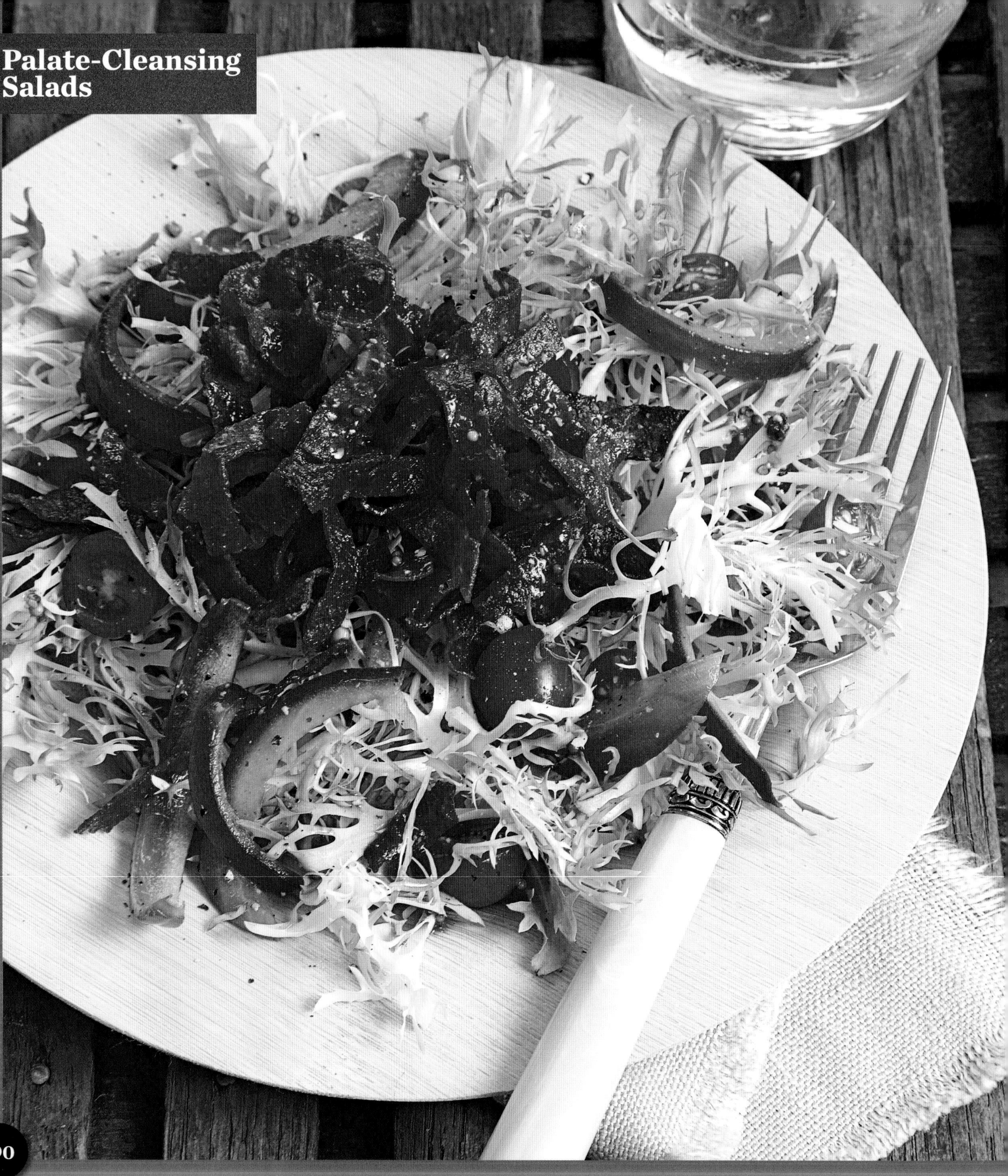

# Warm Frisée Salad with Crispy Kosher Salami

*Frisée is a member of the chicory family often used in mesclun salad mixes. Buy bunches with crisp leaves and no signs of wilting. Use all of the leaves except the core.*

**Makes:** 8 servings    **Hands-on Time:** 33 min.    **Total Time:** 33 min.

- ½  (12-oz.) package kosher beef salami slices
- ¼  cup extra virgin olive oil
- ½  medium-size red onion, sliced
- 1  garlic clove, minced
- ⅓  cup plus 1 Tbsp. sherry vinegar
- 2  tsp. whole grain mustard
- ½  tsp. kosher salt
- ¼  tsp. coarsely ground pepper
- 4  bunches frisée, torn*
- 1  pt. grape tomatoes, halved

**1.** Cut kosher beef salami slices into ¼-inch strips.

**2.** Cook salami strips in hot olive oil in a medium skillet over medium heat 5 to 10 minutes or until crispy. Remove salami with a slotted spoon, reserving remaining oil in skillet. Drain salami pieces on paper towels.

**3.** Sauté onion and garlic in reserved hot oil 2 minutes. Stir in vinegar, mustard, salt, and pepper; cook 1 minute.

**4.** Place frisée and grape tomato halves in a large bowl, and drizzle with vinegar mixture; toss to coat. Sprinkle with crispy salami pieces, and serve immediately.

*2 bunches curly endive may be substituted for frisée.

**Note:** We tested with Hebrew National Kosher Beef Salami.

## NORM'S NOTE
### Discover the Extra-Crispy Salad Secret

To get the crispiest fried salami, let the oil heat up in the pan for a couple of minutes before adding the sliced salami. Letting the oil come to the proper temperature before frying also helps the salami absorb less grease and shortens the cooking time. When draining on paper towels, I often pat with another paper towel to soak up any excess grease.

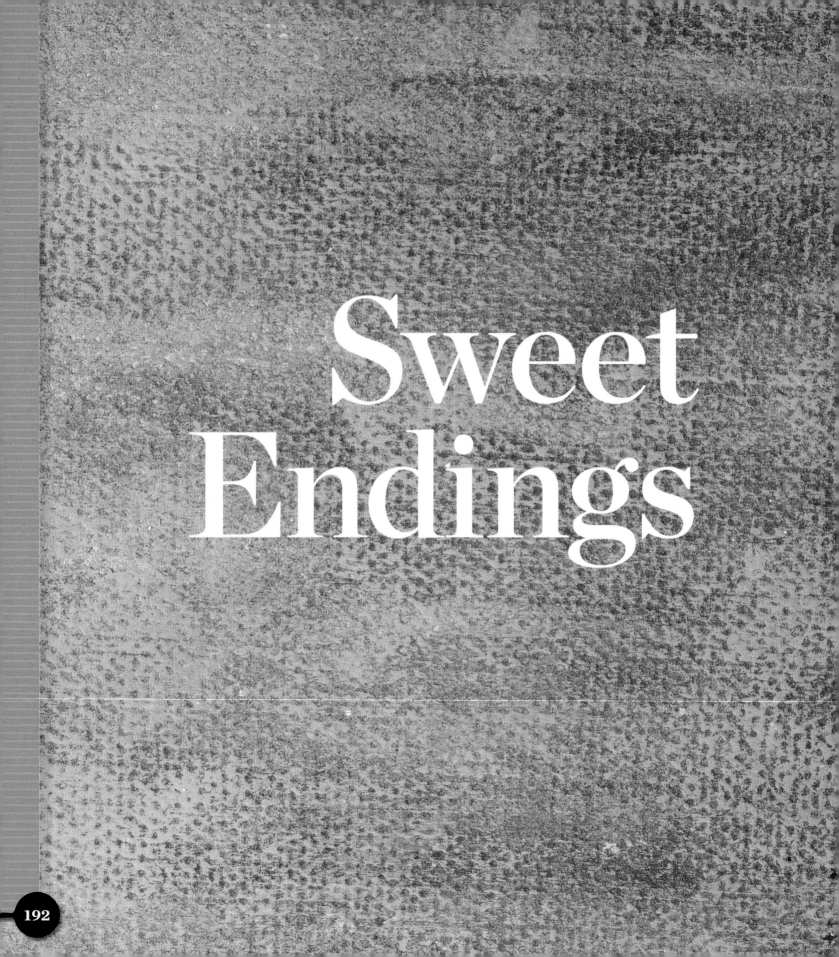

# Sweet Endings

Strawberry-
Rhubarb
Hand Pies,
*page 207*

# New Orleans Beignets

*Puffy, fluffy, delicious beignets can be tumbled in powdered sugar to suit your sweet tooth.*

**Makes:** about 6 dozen    **Hands-on Time:** 43 min.    **Total Time:** 4 hr., 49 min.

- 1   (¼-oz.) envelope active dry yeast
- 1½   cups warm water (105° to 115°), divided
- ½   cup granulated sugar
- 1   cup evaporated milk
- 2   large eggs, lightly beaten
- 1   tsp. salt
- ¼   cup shortening
- 6½   to 7 cups bread flour
-     Vegetable oil
-     Sifted powdered sugar

**1.** Combine yeast, ½ cup warm water, and 1 tsp. granulated sugar in bowl of a heavy-duty stand mixer; let stand 5 minutes. Add milk, eggs, salt, and remaining granulated sugar.

**2.** Microwave remaining 1 cup water until hot (about 115°); stir in shortening until melted. Add to yeast mixture. Beat at low speed, gradually adding 4 cups flour, until smooth. Gradually add remaining 2½ to 3 cups flour, beating until a sticky dough forms. Transfer to a lightly greased bowl; turn to grease top. Cover and chill 4 to 24 hours.

**3.** Turn dough out onto a floured surface; roll to ¼-inch thickness. Cut into 2½-inch squares.

**4.** Pour oil to depth of 2 to 3 inches into a Dutch oven; heat to 360°. Fry dough, in batches, 2 to 3 minutes on each side or until golden brown. Drain on a wire rack. Dust immediately with powdered sugar.

## NORM'S NOTE
### Roll With It

The key to light and fluffy New Orleans-style beignets is rolling the dough to ¼-inch thickness. Any thicker or thinner, and the beignets just don't seem to have the ideal texture after frying. Cutting them into perfect squares helps as well. I use a ruler and a pizza cutter to get the right proportions.

# Jelly Doughnuts (Sufganiyot)

*This traditional Hanukkah treat is deep-fried and injected with a jelly or jam filling.*

**Makes:** 24 doughnuts    **Hands-on Time:** 27 min.    **Total Time:** 3 hr., 2 min.

1  (25-oz.) package frozen bread roll dough, thawed according to package directions
   Vegetable oil
½  cup sugar
1¼  tsp. ground cinnamon
½  to 1 cup seedless raspberry jam*

**1.** Place rolls 2 inches apart on 2 lightly greased baking sheets. Cover and let rise in a warm place (85°), free from drafts, according to package directions.

**2.** Pour oil to depth of 2 inches into a Dutch oven; heat to 350°. Fry rolls, in batches, 1 to 1½ minutes on each side or until fully cooked and golden brown. Drain on a wire rack over paper towels.

**3.** Whisk together sugar and cinnamon in a medium bowl. Add warm doughnuts to sugar mixture, tossing to coat. Let cool completely on wire rack (about 15 minutes).

**4.** Make a small slit in side of each doughnut, using a paring knife. Place jelly in a zip-top plastic freezer bag (do not seal). Snip 1 corner of bag to make a small hole. Pipe jelly into each doughnut.

*Strawberry jelly may be substituted.

**Note:** We tested with Bridgford Easy to Bake Parkerhouse Style Rolls frozen bread dough.

# Oven-Baked Churros

*Easy to make and even easier to eat, these oven-baked goods are great served with strong brewed coffee after dinner. They also go well with a small scoop of ice cream.*

**Makes:** 3 dozen    **Hands-on Time:** 15 min.    **Total Time:** 30 min.

- 1  (17.3-oz.) package frozen puff pastry sheets, thawed
   Parchment paper
- ¼  cup sugar
- 1  tsp. ground cinnamon
- ¼  cup melted butter

**1.** Preheat oven to 450°. Unfold and cut puff pastry sheets in half lengthwise, and cut each half crosswise into 1-inch-wide strips. Place strips on a lightly greased parchment paper-lined baking sheet. Bake 10 minutes or until golden brown.

**2.** Meanwhile, combine sugar and cinnamon. Remove pastry strips from oven, and dip in butter; roll in cinnamon-sugar mixture. Let stand on a wire rack 5 minutes or until dry.

## NORM'S NOTE
### How to Thaw and Cut Puff Pastry

Let the puff pastry thaw overnight in the refrigerator or on the counter for about 30 minutes. It can be a little tricky to handle when it's thawed. I like to lightly dust both sides of the pastry sheets with flour and gently roll with a rolling pin to smooth the folds. This makes cutting and transferring the dough to a baking sheet much easier. If the pastry cracks while you are working with it, you can simply dab a little bit of water on it and press it back together with your fingers.

NORM'S NOTE

**Tea Tricks to Try**

These beignets aren't real strong on tea flavor but the addition does change the texture and appearance. The dough is more tender and silky than traditional beignets and browns to a much deeper tone when fried.

# Sweet Tea Beignets

*These fried dough squares are topped with a sweet, lemony glaze instead of the traditional powdered sugar dusting.*

**Makes:** about 3 dozen    **Hands-on Time:** 30 min.    **Total Time:** 4 hr., 45 min.

2   **family-size tea bags**
1   **(¼-oz.) envelope active dry yeast**
½   **cup sugar**
1   **cup evaporated milk**
2   **large eggs, lightly beaten**
1   **tsp. salt**
¼   **cup shortening**
6½  **to 7 cups bread flour**
    **Vegetable oil**
    **Lemon Glaze**

**1.** Bring 1½ cups water to a boil over medium-high heat. Add tea bags; cover and let steep 10 minutes. Squeeze tea bags to remove excess liquid; discard tea bags. Let cool until lukewarm.

**2.** Combine yeast, ½ cup warm tea, and 1 tsp. sugar in bowl of a heavy-duty electric stand mixer; let stand 5 minutes. Add milk, eggs, salt, and remaining sugar.

**3.** Microwave remaining 1 cup sweet tea until hot (about 115°); stir in shortening until melted. Add to yeast mixture. Beat at low speed, gradually adding

4 cups flour, until smooth. Gradually add remaining 2½ to 3 cups flour, beating until a sticky dough forms. Transfer to a lightly greased bowl; turn to grease top. Cover and chill 4 to 24 hours.

**4.** Turn dough out onto a floured surface; roll to ¼-inch thickness. Cut into 2½-inch squares.

**5.** Pour oil to depth of 2 to 3 inches into a Dutch oven; heat to 360°. Fry dough, in batches, 2 to 3 minutes on each side or until golden brown. Drain on a wire rack over paper towels. Let stand 30 seconds to 1 minute or until cool enough to handle. Dip 1 side in Lemon Glaze, and let drain, glaze side up, on a wire rack 1 to 2 minutes or until glaze is set.

### Lemon Glaze

Stir together 1 cup powdered sugar, 1 Tbsp. milk, ¼ tsp. lemon zest, and 1 to 2 Tbsp. fresh lemon juice in a small bowl until smooth. Makes: about 1 cup. Hands-on Time: 5 min.; Total Time: 5 min.

# Apple Fritters

*These fritters would be great served at breakfast with a drizzle of honey and dipped in creamy yogurt.*

**Makes:** 3 dozen   **Hands-on Time:** 25 min.   **Total Time:** 25 min.

- 3  cups all-purpose flour
- ½  tsp. salt
- 2  tsp. baking powder
- ½  cup sugar
- 1  large egg
- 1  cup milk
- ¼  cup butter, melted
- 2  tsp. orange zest
- ¼  cup fresh orange juice
- 2  cups diced cooking apple
- 1  tsp. vanilla extract
-    Vegetable oil
-    Sifted powdered sugar

**1.** Combine first 4 ingredients; make a well in center of mixture.

**2.** Combine egg, milk, and butter, stirring well; stir in orange zest and next 3 ingredients. Add to flour mixture, stirring just until dry ingredients are moistened.

**3.** Pour oil to depth of 2 inches into a large Dutch oven; heat to 350°. Drop batter by rounded tablespoonfuls into hot oil; fry fritters, in batches, 1½ minutes on each side or until golden brown. Drain fritters well on paper towels, and cool slightly. Sprinkle with sifted powdered sugar.

## NORM'S NOTE
### Use a Little Scoop

Portion the fritters into the oil with a small ice cream scoop to help achieve even sizes. I find it much cleaner as well since you need only one hand to drop the batter into the oil, lessening the chance that raw batter will end up on the counter or floor.

# Deep-Fried Bananas Foster

*The addition of raspberry wheat beer to the batter gives the bananas a
light and airy crust when fried.*

**Makes:** 4 servings    **Hands-on Time:** 25 min.    **Total Time:** 25 min.

1½  **cups all-purpose baking mix**
½  **(12-oz.) bottle raspberry wheat
      beer**
1  **large egg**
¼  **tsp. ground cinnamon**
4  **medium-size ripe bananas
      Vegetable oil**
2  **Tbsp. butter**
¼  **cup firmly packed brown sugar**
1½  **Tbsp. brandy**
1½  **Tbsp. banana liqueur
      Vanilla ice cream
      Garnish: fresh raspberries**

**1.** Whisk together first 4 ingredients in a large bowl. Peel bananas; cut in half lengthwise, then cut in half crosswise.

**2.** Pour oil to depth of 2 inches into a Dutch oven; heat over medium heat to 350°. Dip banana pieces in batter, and fry 30 seconds on each side or until golden brown. Drain on a wire rack over paper towels.

**3.** Heat butter and brown sugar in a large skillet over medium heat, stirring constantly, until bubbly. Remove from heat. Add brandy and banana liqueur. If desired, ignite with a long match or long lighter just above the liquid mixture to light fumes (not liquid itself). Let flames die down. Stir until smooth.

**4.** Assemble bananas in a dish; top with desired amount of ice cream, and spoon sauce over bananas and ice cream. Garnish, if desired.

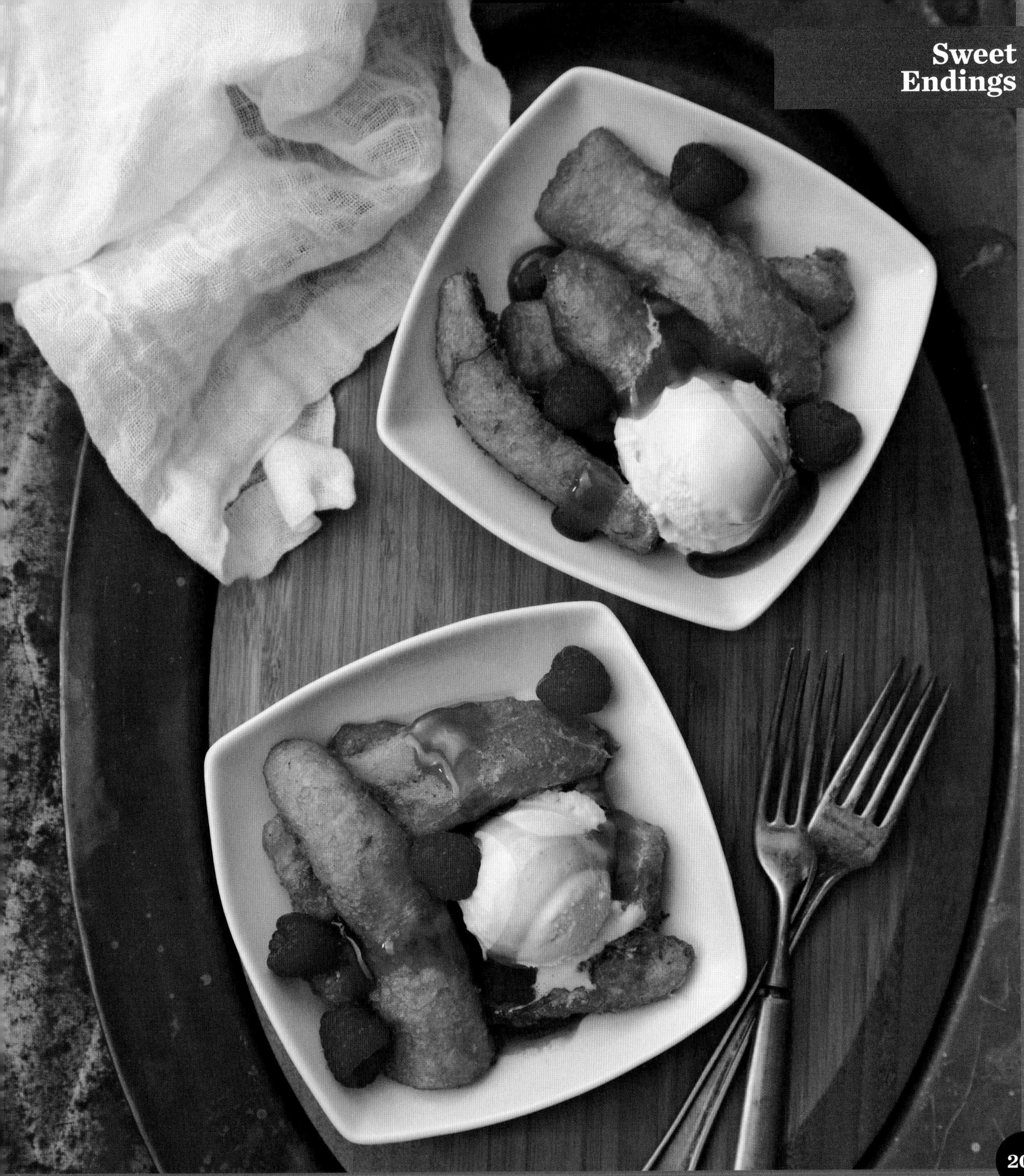

Norm prepares
fresh-from-
the-market
strawberries
for his
Strawberry-
Rhubarb
Hand Pies.

# Strawberry-Rhubarb Hand Pies

*(pictured on page 193)*

*This recipe takes a bit of hands-on time to assemble but the result is well worth your effort. If you can't find fresh rhubarb at your local market, frozen will work. Just be sure that you thaw and pat dry the rhubarb before dicing it.*

**Makes:** 2 dozen    **Hands-on Time:** 1 hr.    **Total Time:** 1 hr., 40 min.

¾ cup finely diced fresh
   strawberries
¾ cup finely diced rhubarb
1 Tbsp. cornstarch
6 Tbsp. sugar, divided
3 tsp. orange zest, divided
2¼ cups all-purpose flour
¼ tsp. salt
½ cup butter, cold
¼ cup shortening, chilled
3 Tbsp. ice water
3 Tbsp. orange juice
   Parchment paper
1 egg yolk, beaten
1 Tbsp. whipping cream
   Sugar

**1.** Combine strawberries, rhubarb, cornstarch, 2 Tbsp. sugar, and 1½ tsp. orange zest in a small bowl.

**2.** Preheat oven to 375°. Combine flour, salt, and remaining ¼ cup sugar in a large bowl. Cut in butter and shortening with a pastry blender until mixture resembles small peas. Stir in remaining 1½ tsp. orange zest. Drizzle with ice water and orange juice. Stir with a fork until combined. (Mixture will be crumbly and dry.) Knead mixture lightly, and shape dough into a disk. Divide dough in half.

**3.** Roll half of dough to ⅛-inch thickness on a heavily floured surface. (Cover remaining dough with plastic wrap.) Cut with a 2¼-inch round cutter, rerolling scraps as needed. Place half of dough rounds 2 inches apart on parchment paper-lined baking sheets. Top with 1 rounded tsp. strawberry mixture. Dampen edges of dough with water, and top with remaining dough rounds, pressing edges to seal. Crimp edges with a fork, and cut a slit in top of each round for steam to escape. Repeat procedure with remaining dough and strawberry mixture.

**4.** Stir together egg yolk and cream; brush pies with egg wash. Sprinkle with sugar. Freeze pies 10 minutes.

**5.** Bake at 375° for 20 to 25 minutes or until lightly browned. Cool 10 minutes. Serve warm or at room temperature. Store in an airtight container up to 2 days.

# Utterly Deadly Southern Pecan Pie

*This ooey-gooey pecan pie is too good to believe. Take the time to savor each delectable piece of this classic pie.*

**Makes:** 8 to 10 servings    **Hands-on Time:** 10 min.    **Total Time:** 4 hr., 10 min.

- ½ (14.1-oz.) package refrigerated piecrusts
- 1 Tbsp. powdered sugar
- 4 large eggs
- 1½ cups firmly packed light brown sugar
- ½ cup butter, melted and cooled to room temperature
- ½ cup granulated sugar
- ½ cup chopped pecans
- 2 Tbsp. all-purpose flour
- 2 Tbsp. milk
- 1½ tsp. bourbon*
- 1½ cups pecan halves

**1.** Preheat oven to 325°. Fit piecrust into a 10-inch cast-iron skillet; sprinkle piecrust with powdered sugar.

**2.** Whisk eggs in a large bowl until foamy; whisk in brown sugar and next 6 ingredients. Pour mixture into piecrust, and top with pecan halves.

**3.** Bake at 325° for 30 minutes; reduce oven temperature to 300°, and bake 30 more minutes. Turn oven off, and let pie stand in oven, with door closed, 3 hours.

*Vanilla extract may be substituted.

### Bourbon Whipped Cream

Combine 1 cup heavy cream, ¼ cup powdered sugar, and 1 to 2 Tbsp. bourbon in bowl of a heavy-duty electric mixer. Beat at medium-high speed until soft peaks form.

# Deep-Fried Pecan Pie

*We froze the pecan pie before frying for easier handling.*

**Makes:** 8 to 10 servings

**Hands-on Time:** 21 min.

**Total Time:** 4 hr., 31 min., including Utterly Deadly Southern Pecan Pie

- Vegetable oil
- Utterly Deadly Southern Pecan Pie, prepared and cooled
- 2 cups buttermilk
- ¼ cup molasses
- 2 large eggs
- 1 cup all-purpose flour
- 2 cups coarsely chopped pork cracklings
- Bourbon Whipped Cream

**1.** Pour oil to depth of 2 inches into a Dutch oven; heat over medium heat to 350°.

**2.** Cut pie into 8 to 10 slices. Whisk together buttermilk and next 2 ingredients in a medium bowl.

**3.** Dredge pecan pie slices in flour, coating on all sides. Dip into buttermilk mixture and dredge in pork cracklings, coating evenly. Fry pie slices, in batches, 1 minute on each side or until golden brown. Drain on a wire rack over paper towels. Top with Bourbon Whipped Cream.

Deep-Fried
Pecan Pie

# Peanut Butter-Banana Icebox Pie

*All of the peanut's best friends—chocolate, bananas, and graham crackers—come out to play in this creamy, dreamy pie. If you're a peanut butter lover, this is the dessert for you.*

**Makes:** 8 servings     **Hands-on Time:** 30 min.     **Total Time:** 9 hr., 10 min.

2  cups cinnamon graham cracker crumbs (about 15 sheets)
½  cup finely chopped honey-roasted peanuts
½  cup butter, melted
1  (4-oz.) semisweet chocolate baking bar, chopped
2  cups whipping cream, divided
1  (8-oz.) package cream cheese, softened
1  cup creamy peanut butter
½  cup firmly packed light brown sugar
2  tsp. vanilla extract
2  large bananas, sliced
   Toppings: sweetened whipped cream, chocolate syrup, chopped honey-roasted peanuts

**1.** Preheat oven to 350°. Stir together first 3 ingredients; firmly press on bottom, up sides, and onto lip of a lightly greased 9-inch pie plate. Bake 10 to 12 minutes or until lightly browned. Remove from oven to a wire rack, and cool completely (about 30 minutes).

**2.** Microwave chocolate and ½ cup whipping cream in a small microwave-safe bowl at MEDIUM (50% power) 1½ minutes or until chocolate is almost melted, stirring at 30-second intervals. Whisk until chocolate melts and mixture is smooth. (Do not overheat.) Spoon chocolate mixture into prepared crust.

**3.** Beat cream cheese, next 2 ingredients, and ¼ cup whipping cream at medium speed with an electric mixer until mixture is light and fluffy.

**4.** Beat vanilla and remaining 1¼ cups whipping cream at high speed until stiff peaks form. Fold one-third of whipped cream mixture into peanut butter mixture to loosen; fold in remaining whipped cream mixture.

**5.** Arrange banana slices over chocolate mixture in crust. Spread peanut butter mixture over bananas. Cover and chill 8 hours. Serve pie with desired toppings.

# Pecan-Peach Cobbler

*Try making this classic recipe when you have more than a few folks visiting; it's always a crowd-pleaser.*

**Makes:** 10 to 12 servings    **Hands-on Time:** 35 min.    **Total Time:** 1 hr., 15 min.

- 12 to 15 fresh peaches, peeled and sliced (about 16 cups)
- ⅓ cup all-purpose flour
- ½ tsp. ground nutmeg
- 3 cups sugar
- ⅔ cup butter
- 1½ tsp. vanilla extract
- 2 (15-oz.) packages refrigerated piecrusts, divided
- ½ cup chopped pecans, toasted, divided
- 5 Tbsp. sugar, divided
  Ice cream

**1.** Preheat oven to 475°. Stir together peaches, flour, nutmeg, and 3 cups sugar in a Dutch oven. Bring to a boil over medium heat; reduce heat to low, and simmer 10 minutes. Remove from heat; stir in butter and vanilla. Spoon half of mixture into a lightly greased 13- x 9-inch baking dish.

**2.** Unroll 2 piecrusts. Sprinkle ¼ cup pecans and 2 Tbsp. sugar over 1 piecrust; top with other piecrust. Roll to a 14- x 10-inch rectangle. Trim sides to fit baking dish. Place pastry over peach mixture in dish.

**3.** Bake at 475° for 20 to 25 minutes or until lightly browned. Unroll remaining 2 piecrusts. Sprinkle 2 Tbsp. sugar and remaining ¼ cup pecans over 1 piecrust; top with remaining piecrust. Roll into a 12-inch circle. Cut into 1-inch strips, using a fluted pastry wheel. Spoon remaining peach mixture over baked pastry. Arrange pastry strips over peach mixture; sprinkle with remaining 1 Tbsp. sugar. Bake 15 to 18 minutes or until lightly browned. Serve warm or cold with ice cream.

# Swoon Pies

**Makes:** 1 dozen   **Hands-on Time:** 45 min.   **Total Time:** 2 hr., 40 min.

1 cup all-purpose flour
½ tsp. baking powder
½ tsp. baking soda
½ tsp. salt
1 cup graham cracker crumbs
½ cup butter, softened
½ cup granulated sugar
½ cup firmly packed light
   brown sugar
1 large egg
1 tsp. vanilla extract
1 (8-oz.) container sour cream
   Parchment paper
   Marshmallow Filling
1 (12-oz.) package semisweet
   chocolate morsels
2 tsp. shortening
   Toppings: chopped roasted
   salted pecans, chopped
   crystallized ginger, sea salt

**1.** Preheat oven to 350°. Sift together flour and next 3 ingredients in a medium bowl; stir in graham cracker crumbs.

**2.** Beat butter and next 2 ingredients at medium speed with a heavy-duty electric stand mixer until fluffy. Add egg and vanilla, beating until blended.

**3.** Add flour mixture to butter mixture alternately with sour cream, beginning and ending with flour mixture. Beat at low speed until blended after each addition, stopping to scrape bowl as needed.

**4.** Drop batter by rounded tablespoonfuls 2 inches apart onto 2 parchment paper-lined baking sheets. Bake, in batches, at 350° for 13 to 15 minutes or until set and bottoms are golden brown. Remove cookies (on parchment paper) to wire racks, and cool completely (about 30 minutes).

**5.** Turn 12 cookies over, bottom sides up. Spread each with 1 heaping Tbsp. Marshmallow Filling. Top with remaining 12 cookies, bottom sides down, and press gently to spread filling to edges. Freeze on a parchment paper-lined baking sheet 30 minutes or until filling is set.

**6.** Pour water to depth of 1 inch into a medium saucepan over medium heat; bring to a boil. Reduce heat, and simmer; place chocolate and shortening in a medium-size heatproof bowl over simmering water. Cook, stirring occasionally, 5 to 6 minutes or until melted. Remove from heat, and let cool 10 minutes.

**7.** Meanwhile, remove cookies from freezer, and let stand 10 minutes.

**8.** Dip half of each cookie sandwich into melted chocolate mixture. Place on parchment paper-lined baking sheet. Sprinkle with desired toppings, and freeze 10 minutes or until chocolate is set.

### Marshmallow Filling

Beat ½ cup butter at medium speed with an electric mixer until creamy; gradually add 1 cup sifted powdered sugar, beating well. Add 1 cup marshmallow crème and ½ tsp. vanilla extract, beating until well blended. Makes: about 1½ cups. Hands-on Time: 5 min.; Total Time: 5 min.

# Peach Melba Shortbread Bars

*Melt-in-your-mouth shortbread and the sweet-tart flavor of raspberry and peach are paired in harmony in this flattened version of a thumbprint cookie.*

**Makes:** 1½ to 2 dozen    **Hands-on Time:** 20 min.    **Total Time:** 2 hr., 20 min.

2  **cups all-purpose flour**
½  **cup granulated sugar**
¼  **tsp. salt**
1  **cup cold butter**
1  **cup peach preserves**
6  **tsp. raspberry preserves**
½  **cup sliced almonds**

**1.** Preheat oven to 350°. Combine first 3 ingredients in a medium bowl. Cut in butter with a pastry blender until crumbly. Reserve 1 cup flour mixture.

**2.** Lightly grease an 11- x 7-inch or 9-inch square pan. Press remaining flour mixture onto bottom of prepared pan.

**3.** Bake at 350° for 25 to 30 minutes or until lightly browned.

**4.** Spread peach preserves over crust in pan. Dollop raspberry preserves by ½ tsp. over peach preserves. Sprinkle reserved 1 cup flour mixture over preserves. Sprinkle with almonds.

**5.** Bake at 350° for 35 to 40 minutes or until golden brown. Let cool 1 hour on a wire rack. Cut into bars.

# Nutter Butter®-Banana Pudding Trifle

*Simplicity is the strength of this recipe. Homemade pudding, fresh bananas, whipped cream, and peanut butter cookies are all it takes to make one of the best banana puddings you can find.*

**Makes:** 8 to 10 servings     **Hands-on Time:** 45 min.     **Total Time:** 3 hr., 15 min.

3   **cups milk**
3   **large eggs**
¾   **cup sugar**
⅓   **cup all-purpose flour**
2   **Tbsp. butter**
2   **tsp. vanilla extract**
5   **medium-size ripe bananas**
1   **(1-lb.) package peanut butter sandwich cookies**
2   **cups sweetened whipped cream**
    **Garnishes: peanut butter sandwich cookies, dried banana chips**

**1.** Whisk together first 4 ingredients in a large saucepan over medium-low heat. Cook, whisking constantly, 15 to 20 minutes or until thickened. Remove from heat; stir in butter and vanilla until butter is melted.

**2.** Fill a large bowl with ice. Place saucepan in ice, and let stand, stirring occasionally, 30 minutes or until mixture is thoroughly chilled.

**3.** Meanwhile, cut bananas into ¼-inch slices. Break cookies into thirds.

**4.** Spoon half of pudding mixture into a 3-qt. bowl or pitcher. Top with bananas and cookies. Spoon remaining pudding mixture over bananas and cookies. Top with sweetened whipped cream. Cover and chill 2 to 24 hours. Garnish, if desired.

**Note:** We tested with Nabisco Nutter Butter® Sandwich Cookies.

# Lemon Curd Pound Cake

*Wait to prepare the Lemon Curd Glaze until the cake comes out of the oven so it will still be warm when spread over the cake.*

**Makes:** 12 servings    **Hands-on Time:** 20 min.    **Total Time:** 2 hr., 45 min.

1   **cup butter, softened**
½   **cup shortening**
3   **cups sugar**
6   **large eggs**
3   **cups all-purpose flour**
½   **tsp. baking powder**
⅛   **tsp. salt**
1   **cup milk**
1   **Tbsp. lemon zest**
1   **tsp. vanilla extract**
1   **tsp. lemon extract**
    **Lemon Curd Glaze**
    **Garnish: lemon zest**

**1.** Preheat oven to 325°. Beat first 2 ingredients at medium speed with a heavy-duty electric stand mixer until creamy. Gradually add sugar, beating at medium speed until light and fluffy. Add eggs, 1 at a time, beating just until yellow disappears.

**2.** Sift together flour and next 2 ingredients; add to butter mixture alternately with milk, beginning and ending with flour mixture. Beat at low speed just until blended after each addition. Stir in lemon zest and next 2 ingredients.

**3.** Pour batter into a greased and floured 10-inch (16-cup) tube pan.

**4.** Bake at 325° for 1 hour and 15 minutes to 1 hour and 30 minutes or until a long wooden pick inserted in center of cake comes out clean. Cool cake in pan on a wire rack 15 minutes.

**5.** Meanwhile, prepare Lemon Curd Glaze. Remove cake from pan to wire rack; gently brush warm glaze over top and sides of cake. Cool completely on wire rack (about 1 hour). Garnish, if desired.

## Lemon Curd Glaze

**Makes:** ¾ cup
**Hands-on Time:** 15 min.
**Total Time:** 15 min.

⅔   **cup sugar**
1½  **Tbsp. butter, melted**
2   **tsp. lemon zest**
2   **Tbsp. fresh lemon juice**
1   **large egg, lightly beaten**

Stir together first 4 ingredients in a small heavy saucepan; add egg, and stir until blended. Cook over low heat, stirring constantly, 10 to 12 minutes or until mixture thickens slightly and begins to bubble around the edges. (Cooked mixture will have a thickness similar to heavy cream.) Use immediately.

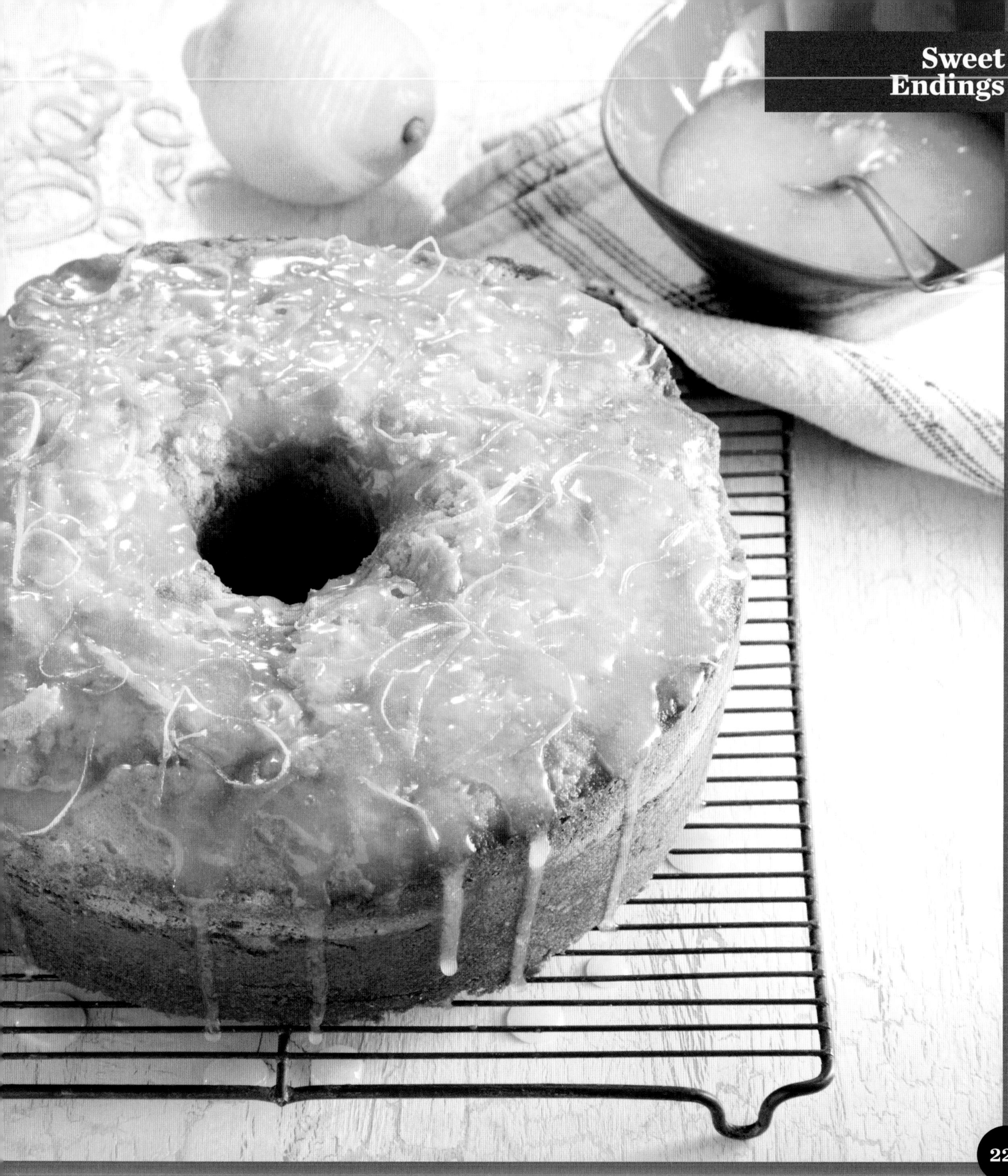

# Chocolate Chip Bundt Cake

*This moist, chocolaty cake is even better after standing for a day. Let it "season" to develop more flavor.*

**Makes:** 12 servings    **Hands-on Time:** 25 min.    **Total Time:** 2 hr., 25 min.

⅔  **cup chopped pecans**
¼  **cup butter, softened**
2  **Tbsp. granulated sugar**
2¾  **cups all-purpose flour**
1  **tsp. baking soda**
1  **tsp. salt**
1  **cup butter, softened**
1  **cup firmly packed dark brown sugar**
½  **cup granulated sugar**
1  **Tbsp. vanilla extract**
4  **large eggs**
1  **cup buttermilk**
1  **(12-oz.) package semisweet chocolate mini-morsels**
  **Powdered Sugar Glaze**

**1.** Preheat oven to 350°. Stir together first 3 ingredients in a small bowl, using a fork. Sprinkle into a greased and floured 12-cup Bundt pan.

**2.** Whisk together flour, baking soda, and salt.

**3.** Beat butter, brown sugar, granulated sugar, and vanilla at medium speed with a heavy-duty electric stand mixer 3 to 5 minutes or until fluffy. Add eggs, 1 at a time, beating just until blended. Add flour mixture alternately with buttermilk, beginning and ending with flour mixture. Beat at low speed just until blended after each addition, stopping to scrape bowl as needed. Beat in chocolate mini-morsels. (Mixture will be thick.) Spoon batter into prepared pan.

**4.** Bake at 350° for 50 to 55 minutes or until a long wooden pick inserted in center comes out clean. Cool in pan on a wire rack 10 minutes; remove from pan to wire rack, and cool completely (about 1 hour). Drizzle with glaze.

### Powdered Sugar Glaze

**Makes:** 1 cup
**Hands-on Time:** 5 min.
**Total Time:** 5 min.

1  **cup powdered sugar**
4  **Tbsp. heavy cream**
½  **tsp. vanilla extract**

Mix together all ingredients to desired consistency.

# Caramel-Pecan Brownies

**Makes:** 4 dozen  **Hands-on Time:** 25 min.  **Total Time:** 2 hr., 30 min.

- 1½ cups coarsely chopped pecans
- 1 (4-oz.) unsweetened chocolate baking bar, chopped
- ¾ cup butter
- 2 cups granulated sugar
- 4 large eggs
- 1 cup all-purpose flour
- 1 cup firmly packed dark brown sugar
- ½ cup milk
- 2 Tbsp. butter
- ¼ tsp. salt
- 1½ cups powdered sugar
- ½ tsp. vanilla extract

**1.** Preheat oven to 350°. Bake pecans in a single layer in a shallow pan 6 to 8 minutes or until lightly toasted and fragrant.

**2.** Microwave chocolate and ¾ cup butter in a large microwave-safe bowl at HIGH 1 to 1½ minutes or until melted and smooth, stirring at 30-second intervals. Whisk in sugar and eggs until well blended. Stir in flour. Spread batter into a greased 13- x 9-inch pan.

**3.** Bake at 350° for 25 to 30 minutes or until a wooden pick inserted in center comes out with a few moist crumbs. Let cool 1 hour on a wire rack.

**4.** Combine brown sugar, milk, 2 Tbsp. butter, and salt in a large saucepan; bring to a boil over medium-high heat, stirring occasionally. Reduce heat to medium-low, and simmer, stirring occasionally, 5 minutes or until slightly thickened. Remove from heat. Let stand 5 minutes. Beat in powdered sugar and vanilla at medium speed with an electric mixer until smooth. Pour over brownies, spreading to edges; sprinkle with toasted pecans. Let cool 30 minutes. Cut into squares.

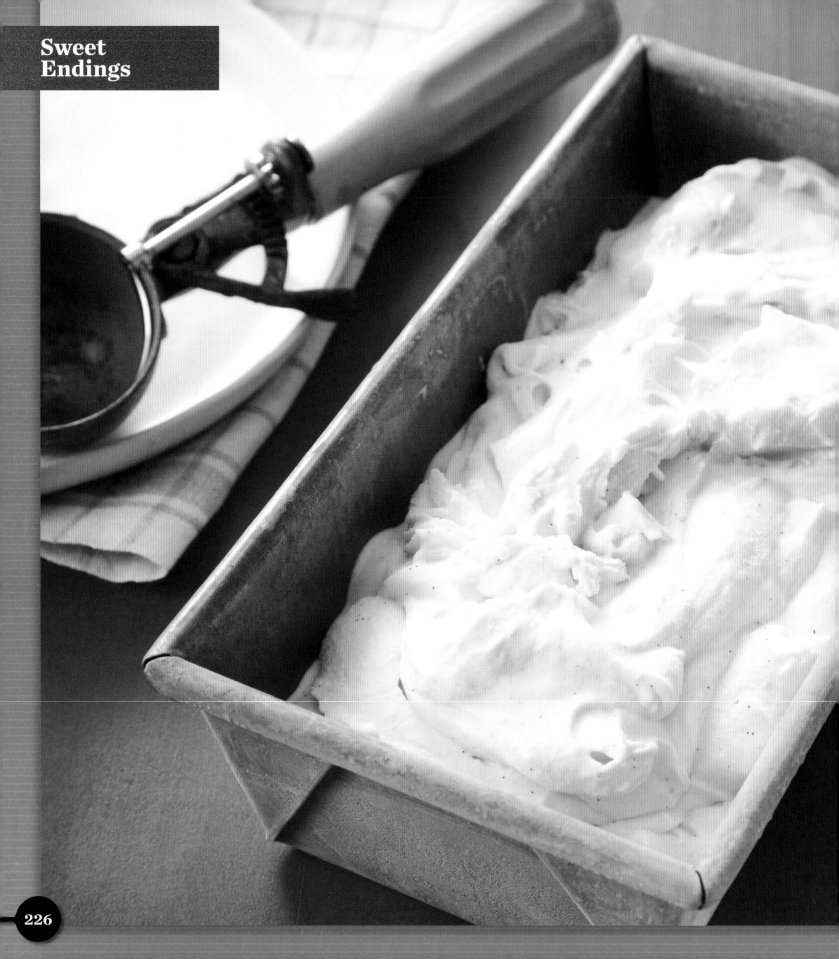

# Vanilla Bean Ice Cream

For firmer ice cream, place a loaf pan in the freezer when you begin freezing the ice cream, then transfer the mixture to the cold loaf pan. Cover with plastic wrap, and freeze overnight to harden.

**Makes:** about 1 qt.    **Hands-on Time:** 20 min.
**Total Time:** 9 hr., 20 min., not including freezing time

- ¾  **cup sugar**
- 2  **Tbsp. cornstarch**
- ⅛  **tsp. salt**
- 2  **cups milk**
- 1  **cup heavy whipping cream**
- 1  **egg yolk**
- 1½  **tsp. vanilla bean paste***

**1.** Whisk together first 3 ingredients in a large heavy saucepan. Gradually whisk in milk and cream. Cook over medium heat, stirring constantly, 10 to 12 minutes or until mixture thickens slightly. Remove from heat.

**2.** Whisk egg yolk until slightly thickened. Gradually whisk about 1 cup hot cream mixture into yolk. Add yolk mixture to remaining hot cream mixture, whisking constantly. Whisk in vanilla bean paste. Cool 1 hour, stirring occasionally.

**3.** Place plastic wrap directly on cream mixture, and chill 8 to 24 hours.

**4.** Pour mixture into freezer container of a 1½-qt. electric ice-cream maker, and freeze according to manufacturer's instructions. (Instructions and times will vary.)

*Vanilla extract may be substituted.

---

**TRY THESE TWISTS!**

**Chocolate-Raspberry Ice Cream:** Before transferring ice cream to a container for further freezing, stir in 4 oz. finely chopped semisweet chocolate, and gently fold in ¼ cup melted seedless raspberry preserves.

**Coconut Cream Pie Ice Cream:** Reduce milk to 1 cup. Stir 1 cup coconut milk into sugar mixture with milk. Before transferring ice cream to a container for further freezing, stir in ¾ cup toasted, sweetened flaked coconut.

---

# Fizzy, Fruity Ice-Cream Floats

Let guests pick their favorite fruit-flavored drink, and watch the fizzy, colorful drinks flow.

> **Fruit-flavored soft drinks, such as grape, lime, or black cherry**
> **Vanilla ice cream**

Let guests pour their favorite fruit-flavored soft drinks over scoops of vanilla ice cream.

# Just for Fun

Beer Batter-
Fried Pickles,
*page 231*

# Deep-Fried Jack and Coke

*I didn't really fry the cocktail, I simply added good ol' Tennessee whiskey to a traditional bourbon ball recipe, deep-fried it, and then drizzled with cola syrup.*

**Makes:** 40 balls
**Hands-on Time:** 34 min.
**Total Time:** 34 min.

- 1 (8-oz.) bottle cola
- 2 Tbsp. granulated sugar
- 2 (12-oz.) packages vanilla wafers, finely crushed, divided
- 1 cup chopped pecans
- ¾ cup powdered sugar
- 2 Tbsp. cocoa powder
- 2½ Tbsp. light corn syrup
- ½ cup Tennessee whiskey
- 1 cup all-purpose flour
- 1 large egg, lightly beaten
  Vegetable oil

**1.** Bring first 2 ingredients to a boil in a small saucepan over medium-high heat, stirring occasionally. Boil 1 minute; reduce heat to low, and simmer 15 minutes, stirring often, until mixture is a syrup-like consistency. Remove from heat.

**2.** Combine 1 package finely crushed vanilla wafers, chopped pecans, and next 2 ingredients in a large bowl. Stir well.

**3.** Combine corn syrup and whiskey, stirring well. Pour bourbon mixture over wafer mixture; stir until blended. Shape into 1-inch balls.

**4.** Roll balls in flour until lightly coated. Dip in egg, and gently press into remaining package of finely crushed vanilla wafers.

**5.** Pour oil to depth of 2 inches into a Dutch oven; heat to 350°. Fry balls, in batches, 30 seconds to 1 minute on each side or until golden brown. Drain on a wire rack over paper towels. Drizzle with cola syrup.

# Beer Batter-Fried Pickles

*(pictured on page 229)*

*My buddy Jason refers to fried pickles as "the ultimate game-day food," and I couldn't agree with him more. These crunchy morsels are great for Saturday or Sunday football get-togethers.*

**Makes:** 8 to 10 servings
**Hands-on Time:** 35 min.
**Total Time:** 45 min., including sauce

- 1 (16-oz.) jar dill pickle sandwich slices, drained
- 1 (16-oz.) jar dill pickle chips, drained
- 1 large egg
- 1 (12-oz.) can beer
- 1 Tbsp. baking powder
- 1 tsp. seasoned salt
- 1½ cups all-purpose flour
  Vegetable oil
  Spicy Ranch Dipping Sauce

**1.** Pat pickles dry with paper towels.

**2.** Whisk together egg and next 3 ingredients in a large bowl; add 1½ cups flour, and whisk until smooth.

**3.** Pour oil to depth of 1½ inches into a large heavy skillet or Dutch oven; heat over medium-high heat to 375°.

**4.** Dip pickle slices into batter, allowing excess batter to drip off. Fry pickles, in batches, 3 to 4 minutes or until golden. Drain and pat dry on paper towels; serve immediately with Spicy Ranch Dipping Sauce.

**Note:** We tested with Vlasic Kosher Dill Stackers.

### Spicy Ranch Dipping Sauce

**Makes:** 1 cup
**Hands-on Time:** 10 min.
**Total Time:** 10 min.

- ¾ cup buttermilk
- ½ cup mayonnaise
- 2 Tbsp. minced green onions
- 1 garlic clove, minced
- 1 tsp. hot sauce
- ½ tsp. seasoned salt

Whisk together all ingredients. Store in an airtight container in refrigerator up to 2 weeks.

# Norm's French Fries

*This is easily my favorite recipe to deep-fry. Be sure to try the Rosemary-Garlic variation.*

**Makes:** 6 to 8 servings  **Hands-on Time:** 50 min.  **Total Time:** 1 hr., 10 min.

- 4 large baking potatoes
  Vegetable oil
  Kosher salt
  Garnishes: sea salt, fried rosemary leaves, freshly grated Parmesan cheese
  Ketchup

**1.** Peel potatoes, and cut into ½-inch strips (about 3 to 4 inches in length). Soak in cold water 5 minutes; drain. Soak 5 more minutes; drain. Pat potatoes dry with paper towels or clean cloth towels.

**2.** Pour oil to depth of 2 inches into a Dutch oven; heat over medium heat to 250°. Cook potatoes, in batches, 8 to 10 minutes or just until tender. Remove from oil, and drain on a wire rack over paper towels. Let cool to room temperature (about 20 minutes).

**3.** Increase heat to medium-high, and bring oil to 325°; cook potatoes again, in batches, 2 to 3 minutes, stirring often, or until crisp and golden brown. Drain on a wire rack. Transfer to a jelly-roll pan; sprinkle immediately with kosher salt to taste. Gently shake pan to coat fries evenly with salt. Garnish, if desired. Serve with ketchup.

**Rosemary-Garlic Fries:** Add 3 crushed garlic cloves and 2 rosemary sprigs to oil in Step 2. Remove and discard garlic and rosemary when potatoes are tender. Proceed with recipe as directed.

# Deep-Fried Barbecue Plate

*I took a plate of smoked chicken, coleslaw, and white barbecue sauce, wrapped it up, and deep-fried it.*

**Makes:** 8 servings
**Hands-on Time:** 40 min.
**Total Time:** 45 min., including barbecue sauce

- 1 lb. smoked chicken
- 3 cups coleslaw mix
- ½ cup White Barbecue Sauce
- 16 egg roll wrappers
- 1 large egg, lightly beaten
  Vegetable oil
  Hot sauce

**1.** Spoon about 1 rounded Tbsp. smoked chicken, 2 Tbsp. coleslaw mix, and 1 heaping teaspoon White Barbecue Sauce into center of each egg roll wrapper. Fold 1 corner over filling. Fold both adjacent corners over filling. Stir together egg and 1 Tbsp. water; brush remaining corner with egg mixture. Continue rolling until closed; press edges of brushed corner to seal.

**2.** Pour oil to depth of 2 inches into a Dutch oven; heat over medium heat to 350°. Fry rolls, in batches, 1 to 2 minutes or until golden brown. Drain on a wire rack over paper towels. Serve with hot sauce.

### White Barbecue Sauce

**Makes:** 1¾ cups
**Hands-on Time:** 5 min.
**Total Time:** 5 min.

- 1½ cups mayonnaise
- ⅓ cup white vinegar
- 1 tsp. pepper
- ½ tsp. salt
- ½ tsp. sugar
- 1 garlic clove, pressed

Stir together all ingredients.

# Deep-Fried Pimiento Cheese Sandwich

**Makes:** 8 sandwiches
**Hands-on Time:** 20 min.
**Total Time:** 20 min.

  Creamy Pimiento Cheese
- 16 slices sandwich bread
- 1 cup milk
- 1 large egg
- 2 cups crushed spicy cheese crackers
  Vegetable oil
  Hot sauce

**1.** Spread about ⅓ cup Creamy Pimiento Cheese on each of 8 bread slices; top with remaining 8 bread slices. Trim crusts from sandwiches, and cut into quarters.

**2.** Whisk together milk and egg in a 9-inch pie plate. Dip sandwich quarters into milk mixture, and dredge in crushed spicy cheese crackers.

**3.** Pour oil to depth of 2 inches into a Dutch oven; heat to 350°. Fry sandwiches, in batches, 1 to 2 minutes on each side or until a light "rust" color. Drain on a wire rack over paper towels. Serve with hot sauce.

### Creamy Pimiento Cheese

**Makes:** 1¾ cups
**Hands-on Time:** 10 min.
**Total Time:** 10 min.

- 1 (10-oz.) block sharp Cheddar cheese, shredded
- ½ cup mayonnaise
- 1 (4-oz.) jar diced pimiento, drained
- 1 tsp. grated onion
- 1 tsp. Dijon mustard
- ¼ tsp. ground red pepper
  Dash of Worcestershire sauce
  Salt and pepper to taste

Beat shredded cheese, mayonnaise, pimiento, grated onion, Dijon mustard, ground red pepper, and Worcestershire sauce at medium speed with a heavy-duty electric stand mixer 1 minute or until creamy. Season with salt and pepper to taste.

This question led me down the path to my current frying adventures on Deep Fried Fridays on SouthernLiving.com. Although the question seemed to suggest an unnecessary contribution to the culinary world, my food-science mind was abuzz as to how to find a way to use deep-frying to make an already indulgent Southern dessert even more sinful.

My goal was to avoid a greasy State Fair-esque batter-fried mess and create a dessert that would enhance the awesomeness of a MoonPie. I settled on a batter-dipped treat that was wrapped in crunchy panko (Japanese breadcrumbs) to protect the delicate chocolate-flavored coating from melting away in the hot oil, and a quick frying time that was just enough to get the coating crisp and slightly warm the marshmallow center. It was just my luck that I got it right on the first try, and I felt a bit of excitement and a bit of guilt biting into a giant fried snack cake. The project was all in good fun, and these creations were made to satisfy curiosity, not to act as a complete dietary disaster.

# Deep-Fried MoonPies

*This is the recipe that started my quirky obsession with all things deep-fried. These are not intended to be eaten as a single serving, but in small, bite-size wedges. A whole fried MoonPie is a little too much fun, if you know what I mean. The only thing you'll miss is an RC Cola.*

**Makes:** 8 servings    **Hands-on Time:** 10 min.    **Total Time:** 10 min.

- 1½ **cups all-purpose flour**
- 1 **cup milk**
- 2 **large eggs**
- 1 **Tbsp. sugar**
- ⅛ **tsp. salt**
- 4 **MoonPies**
- 2 **cups panko (Japanese breadcrumbs)**
- **Vegetable oil**

**1.** Whisk together first 5 ingredients in a medium bowl. Dip MoonPies in batter until coated; dredge in panko.

**2.** Pour oil to depth of 2 inches into a Dutch oven; heat over medium heat to 350°. Fry MoonPies, in batches, 20 to 30 seconds on each side or until golden brown. Drain on a wire rack over paper towels. Cut into quarters to serve.

# Deep-Fried Candy Corn

*You can enjoy these Halloween treats year-round. I often find them sold in the grocer's candy section next to the "church peppermints," orange slices, and circus peanuts.*

**Makes:** 2½ dozen    **Hands-on Time:** 25 min.    **Total Time:** 25 min.

　2　cups all-purpose baking mix
　1　large egg
　½　to ¾ cup buttermilk
　¾　cup candy corn, coarsely chopped
　½　cup cornflakes cereal
　　　Vegetable oil
　　　Powdered sugar

**1.** Stir together baking mix and next 2 ingredients in a large bowl until combined. Stir in candy corn and cornflakes.

**2.** Pour oil to depth of 2 inches into a Dutch oven; heat over medium heat to 350°. Drop batter by rounded tablespoonfuls into hot oil; fry, in batches, 30 seconds to 1 minute on each side or until done. Drain on a wire rack over paper towels. Sprinkle with powdered sugar.

## NORM'S NOTE
### Don't Reuse the Oil

When frying these ghoulishly delicious fritters, the candy corn begins to melt, oozing out of the fritter and settling to the bottom of the pot. Don't be alarmed; it's normal. But the oil is not reusable after all of the batches are cooked. So once it cools, discard it.

**Mix These Favorite Flavors**

This sweet treat is topped with the South's (and possibly America's) favorite food: bacon. The perfect fried bacon will vary from person to person. Some of us like it slightly crunchy yet still tacky, some like it extra crispy, and some even like it slightly chewy. Personally, I like my bacon cooked just until it's lightly crisp and the edges are curled. Start with a large cast-iron skillet, and place it over medium heat. Next, layer 5 to 6 strips in the skillet, and let it cook for about two Nancy Wilson songs and one Frank Sinatra song (that's about 10 minutes), flipping the bacon over about every chorus (that's about a minute or so). When the bacon reaches optimal crispness, remove and drain on paper towels to soak up the excess grease, and enjoy.

# Bacon-Peanut Truffles

*These taste like the chocolate-peanut butter candy sold in bright orange wrappers, but way better. Why? Because bacon makes things better.*

**Makes:** about 2 dozen    **Hands-on Time:** 30 min.    **Total Time:** 4 hr.

 2  **Tbsp. dark brown sugar**
 ¼  **tsp. salt**
 ¾  **cup honey-roasted peanuts**
 8  **thick bacon slices, cooked and divided**
 ⅓  **cup creamy peanut butter**
    **Parchment paper**
 6  **oz. bittersweet chocolate, chopped**

**1.** Process first 3 ingredients and 6 bacon slices in a food processor 20 to 30 seconds or until finely ground. Stir together bacon mixture and peanut butter in a small bowl until smooth. Cover and chill 2 hours.

**2.** Shape rounded teaspoonfuls of bacon mixture into ¾-inch balls. Place on a parchment paper-lined baking sheet; chill 1 hour.

**3.** Chop remaining 2 bacon slices. Microwave chocolate in a microwave-safe bowl at HIGH 1 to 1½ minutes or until melted and smooth, stirring at 30-second intervals. Dip chilled bacon balls into chocolate. Place on a parchment paper-lined baking sheet. Immediately sprinkle tops with chopped bacon. Chill 30 minutes before serving. Store in an airtight container in refrigerator up to 2 weeks.

# Sensational
# Sauces

From left to right, top to bottom: Rémoulade Sauce, *page 245*; Uncle Ellis' Cornmeal Gravy, *page 250*; Green Tomato Salsa, *page 249*; Redeye Gravy, *page 250*; Strawberry Salsa, *page 249*; Cool Ranch Sauce, *page 245*; Tangy Garlic Tartar Sauce, *page 245*; Mike's Cocktail Sauce, *page 250*

Clockwise
from top, left:
Tangy Garlic
Tartar Sauce; Cool
Ranch Sauce;
Rémoulade Sauce

## Tangy Garlic Tartar Sauce

*Use this flavorful sauce on all of your favorite fried seafood dishes.*

**Makes:** about 2¼ cups
**Hands-on Time:** 10 min.
**Total Time:** 2 hr., 10 min.

- 2 cups mayonnaise*
- 1 (3.5-oz.) jar capers, drained
- 3 garlic cloves, pressed
- ¼ cup Dijon mustard

Combine all ingredients in a blender; process until smooth, stopping to scrape down sides as needed. Cover and chill 2 hours before serving. Store in an airtight container in refrigerator up to 3 days.

*Light mayonnaise may be substituted.

## Cool Ranch Sauce

*Serve this sauce as a dip for wings or as a salad dressing.*

**Makes:** 1¼ cups
**Hands-on Time:** 10 min.
**Total Time:** 10 min.

- ½ cup mayonnaise
- ½ cup sour cream
- ¼ cup buttermilk
- 1 Tbsp. chopped fresh chives
- ¼ tsp. lemon zest
- 2 tsp. lemon juice
- 1 garlic clove, minced
   Salt and pepper to taste

Whisk together all ingredients until smooth.

## Rémoulade Sauce

*This zesty sauce isn't just for dipping. You can also use it as you would mayonnaise.*

**Makes:** 1¼ cups
**Hands-on Time:** 5 min.
**Total Time:** 5 min.

- 1 cup mayonnaise
- ¼ cup sliced green onions
- 2 Tbsp. Creole mustard
- 1 Tbsp. chopped fresh parsley
- 1 Tbsp. minced fresh garlic
- 1 tsp. horseradish

Stir together all ingredients; cover and chill until ready to serve.

# Spicy Buffalo Sauce

*Try a drizzle of it on a piece of fried catfish instead of traditional hot sauce.*

**Makes:** 1¼ cups
**Hands-on Time:** 15 min.
**Total Time:** 15 min.

- 1 (8-oz.) can tomato sauce
- 1 (5-oz.) bottle hot sauce
- 1 tsp. Worcestershire sauce
- ½ tsp. salt
- ½ tsp. sugar
- ¼ tsp. pepper

Cook all ingredients in a saucepan over medium heat 8 to 10 minutes or until slightly thickened.

**Note:** We tested with Cholula Original Hot Sauce.

# Peach-Pepper Preserves

*Sweet, spicy, and Southern. Peach-Pepper Preserves could go on just about anything.*

**Makes:** about 3 cups
**Hands-on Time:** 10 min.
**Total Time:** 2 hr., 26 min.

- 4½ cups peeled and diced peaches (about 2½ lb.)
- 1 jalapeño pepper, minced
- ½ red bell pepper, finely chopped
- 1½ cups sugar
- 3 Tbsp. fresh lime juice
- 1 (1.75-oz.) package powdered fruit pectin

**1.** Stir together all ingredients in a 4-qt. microwave-safe glass bowl.

**2.** Microwave at HIGH 8 minutes. (Mixture will boil.) Stir mixture, and microwave at HIGH 8 to 10 minutes or until thickened. (It should be the viscosity of pancake syrup. The mixture will thicken to soft-set preserves after it cools and chills.) Cool mixture completely (about 2 hours). Serve immediately, or cover and chill preserves in an airtight container until ready to serve. Store in refrigerator up to 3 weeks.

# Mustard-Peach Preserves

*These fast preserves pair perfectly with a fried chicken biscuit or fried chicken of any variety.*

**Makes:** 1¾ cups
**Hands-on Time:** 15 min.
**Total Time:** 1 hr., 15 min.

- 1 Tbsp. olive oil
- ½ medium-size sweet onion, finely chopped
- 1 cup peach preserves
- ¾ cup chopped dried peaches
- ¼ cup coarse-grained Dijon mustard
- ¼ tsp. salt
- ¼ tsp. pepper

Heat oil in a large nonstick skillet over medium heat. Add onion, and cook, stirring often, 5 to 6 minutes or until onion is golden brown. Remove from heat, and stir in preserves and remaining ingredients. Cover and chill 1 hour or up to 1 week.

Clockwise
from top, left:
Spicy Buffalo
Sauce; Peach-
Pepper Preserves;
Mustard-Peach
Preserves

Left to right:
Green Tomato
Salsa; Strawberry
Salsa

# Green Tomato Salsa

*The tangy-sweet taste of this quick, colorful salsa pairs perfectly with grilled chicken, pork, or crisp-fried catfish.*

**Makes:** about 4 cups
**Hands-on Time:** 10 min.
**Total Time:** 1 hr., 10 min.

- 2 large green tomatoes, diced
- 1 large fresh peach, diced
- 3 green onions, sliced
- ¼ cup olive oil
- 1 Tbsp. minced fresh cilantro
- 2 Tbsp. white wine vinegar
- 1 Tbsp. honey
- ½ tsp. salt
- ¼ tsp. ground red pepper

Stir together tomatoes, peach, green onions, olive oil, cilantro, vinegar, honey, salt, and ground red pepper. Cover and chill 1 hour before serving.

# Strawberry Salsa

*Serve this fruity delight over tacos, fried pork chops, or fried shrimp, or eat it as is with tortilla chips.*

**Makes:** about 2½ cups
**Hands-on Time:** 15 min.
**Total Time:** 1 hr., 15 min.

- ½ cup red pepper jelly
- ⅓ cup chopped fresh chives
- ⅓ cup chopped fresh cilantro
- 1 Tbsp. lime zest
- ¼ cup fresh lime juice
- ¼ tsp. dried crushed red pepper
- 2 cups chopped fresh strawberries
- ⅓ cup sweetened dried cranberries
- 1 small avocado, diced

Whisk together red pepper jelly, chives, cilantro, lime zest, fresh lime juice, and dried crushed red pepper in a medium bowl. Stir in strawberries and sweetened dried cranberries; cover and chill 1 hour. Stir in diced avocado just before serving. Serve with grilled or pan-fried meats, poultry, or seafood.

## NORM'S NOTE
### Salsa Secret

Chilling your salsa for an hour before serving allows all the flavors to mingle a little better. Be sure to cover the salsa tightly. I like to make salsa the day before to let it chill overnight for best flavor.

# Redeye Gravy

*Redeye Gravy replaces milk gravy on top of Chicken-Fried Steak (page 65). Redeye Gravy is also great served over hot biscuits.*

**Makes:** about 4 cups
**Hands-on Time:** 45 min.
**Total Time:** 45 min.

- ¼ cup butter
- 1½ thick smoked bacon slices, diced
- ½ cup chopped smoked ham
- 1 small onion, diced
- 2 garlic cloves, minced
- 2 tsp. finely chopped fresh sage
- 2 Tbsp. all-purpose flour
- 1 cup milk
- 1 cup beef broth
- ¾ cup brewed coffee
- 1 Tbsp. chopped fresh chives
- 2 tsp. cracked pepper

**1.** Melt butter in a large saucepan over medium heat; add bacon, and cook, stirring occasionally, 5 to 7 minutes or until done. Add ham and next 3 ingredients; sauté 3 to 4 minutes or until onion is translucent. Reduce heat to medium-low. Add flour. Cook, stirring constantly, 3 to 5 minutes or until golden brown.

**2.** Slowly whisk in milk and next 2 ingredients; bring to a boil over high heat, stirring occasionally. Reduce heat to low. Simmer, stirring often, 14 to 18 minutes or until thickened. Remove from heat. Stir in chives and pepper.

# Mike's Cocktail Sauce

**Makes:** about 2 cups
**Hands-on Time:** 10 min.
**Total Time:** 40 min.

- 1½ cups ketchup
- 5 Tbsp. fresh lemon juice
- 2½ Tbsp. extra-hot horseradish
- 1 Tbsp. Worcestershire sauce
- ½ tsp. pepper
- ¼ tsp. salt
- ¼ tsp. hot sauce

Stir together all ingredients until blended. Cover and chill 30 minutes before serving. Store leftovers in an airtight container in refrigerator up to 5 days.

**Note:** We tested with Tabasco hot sauce.

# Uncle Ellis' Cornmeal Gravy

*With the uniquely smoky and nutty flavor of toasted cornmeal, this creamy gravy has a slight grit to it, but is a wonderful addition to chicken- fried anything.*

**Makes:** about 1⅔ cups
**Hands-on Time:** 20 min.
**Total Time:** 20 min.

- ½ cup plain red or white cornmeal
- ½ tsp. salt
- ½ tsp. pepper
- 1 tsp. bacon drippings
- 1 cup buttermilk
- 1 cup hot water

Cook cornmeal in a heavy skillet over medium-high heat, stirring constantly, 4 to 5 minutes or until golden brown. Stir in salt, pepper, and drippings. Stir together buttermilk and hot water; gradually whisk into cornmeal mixture. Bring to a boil, whisking constantly. Reduce heat. Cook, whisking constantly, until thickened. Whisk in additional buttermilk for desired consistency.

Clockwise from top, left: Redeye Gravy, Mike's Cocktail Sauce, Uncle Ellis' Cornmeal Gravy

# Metric Equivalents

*The information in the following charts is provided to help cooks outside the United States successfully use the recipes in this book. All equivalents are approximate.*

### EQUIVALENTS FOR DIFFERENT TYPES OF INGREDIENTS

| Standard Cup | Fine Powder (ex. flour) | Grain (ex. rice) | Granular (ex. sugar) | Liquid Solids (ex. butter) | Liquid (ex. milk) |
|---|---|---|---|---|---|
| 1 | 140 g | 150 g | 190 g | 200 g | 240 ml |
| ¾ | 105 g | 113 g | 143 g | 150 g | 180 ml |
| ⅔ | 93 g | 100 g | 125 g | 133 g | 160 ml |
| ½ | 70 g | 75 g | 95 g | 100 g | 120 ml |
| ⅓ | 47 g | 50 g | 63 g | 67 g | 80 ml |
| ¼ | 35 g | 38 g | 48 g | 50 g | 60 ml |
| ⅛ | 18 g | 19 g | 24 g | 25 g | 30 ml |

### LIQUID INGREDIENTS BY VOLUME

| | | | | | | | | | | |
|---|---|---|---|---|---|---|---|---|---|---|
| ¼ tsp | = | | | | | | | 1 ml | | |
| ½ tsp | = | | | | | | | 2 ml | | |
| 1 tsp | = | | | | | | | 5 ml | | |
| 3 tsp | = | 1 Tbsp | = | | | ½ fl oz | = | 15 ml | | |
| | | 2 Tbsp | = | ⅛ cup | = | 1 fl oz | = | 30 ml | | |
| | | 4 Tbsp | = | ¼ cup | = | 2 fl oz | = | 60 ml | | |
| | | 5⅓ Tbsp | = | ⅓ cup | = | 3 fl oz | = | 80 ml | | |
| | | 8 Tbsp | = | ½ cup | = | 4 fl oz | = | 120 ml | | |
| | | 10⅔ Tbsp | = | ⅔ cup | = | 5 fl oz | = | 160 ml | | |
| | | 12 Tbsp | = | ¾ cup | = | 6 fl oz | = | 180 ml | | |
| | | 16 Tbsp | = | 1 cup | = | 8 fl oz | = | 240 ml | | |
| | | 1 pt | = | 2 cups | = | 16 fl oz | = | 480 ml | | |
| | | 1 qt | = | 4 cups | = | 32 fl oz | = | 960 ml | | |
| | | | | | | 33 fl oz | = | 1000 ml | = | 1 l |

### DRY INGREDIENTS BY WEIGHT

*(To convert ounces to grams, multiply the number of ounces by 30.)*

| | | | | |
|---|---|---|---|---|
| 1 oz | = | 1/16 lb | = | 30 g |
| 4 oz | = | ¼ lb | = | 120 g |
| 8 oz | = | ½ lb | = | 240 g |
| 12 oz | = | ¾ lb | = | 360 g |
| 16 oz | = | 1 lb | = | 480 g |

### LENGTH

*(To convert inches to centimeters, multiply the number of inches by 2.5.)*

| | | | | | |
|---|---|---|---|---|---|
| 1 in | = | | | | 2.5 cm |
| 6 in | = | ½ ft | = | | 15 cm |
| 12 in | = | 1 ft | = | | 30 cm |
| 36 in | = | 3 ft | = | 1 yd = | 90 cm |
| 40 in | = | | | | 100 cm = 1 m |

### COOKING/OVEN TEMPERATURES

| | Fahrenheit | Celsius | Gas Mark |
|---|---|---|---|
| Freeze Water | 32° F | 0° C | |
| Room Temperature | 68° F | 20° C | |
| Boil Water | 212° F | 100° C | |
| Bake | 325° F | 160° C | 3 |
| | 350° F | 180° C | 4 |
| | 375° F | 190° C | 5 |
| | 400° F | 200° C | 6 |
| | 425° F | 220° C | 7 |
| | 450° F | 230° C | 8 |
| Broil | | | Grill |

# Index